NUCLEAR ARMS
IN THE THIRD WORLD

ERNEST W. LEFEVER

NUCLEAR ARMS
IN THE THIRD WORLD

U.S. Policy Dilemma

THE BROOKINGS INSTITUTION
Washington, D.C.

Copyright © 1979 by
THE BROOKINGS INSTITUTION
1775 Massachusetts Avenue, N.W., Washington, D.C. 20036

Library of Congress Cataloging in Publication Data:

Lefever, Ernest W
  Nuclear arms in the Third World.
  Includes index.
    1. Atomic weapons.   2. Underdeveloped areas—
Atomic power.   3. Underdeveloped areas—Military
policy.   4. Military assistance, American.
5. United States—Foreign relations.   I. Title.
UF767.L369   358'.39'091724   78-24810
ISBN 0-8157-5202-4
ISBN 0-8157-5201-6 pbk.

9 8 7 6 5 4 3 2 1

THE BROOKINGS INSTITUTION is an independent organization devoted to nonpartisan research, education, and publication in economics, government, foreign policy, and the social sciences generally. Its principal purposes are to aid in the development of sound public policies and to promote public understanding of issues of national importance.

The Institution was founded on December 8, 1927, to merge the activities of the Institute for Government Research, founded in 1916, the Institute of Economics, founded in 1922, and the Robert Brookings Graduate School of Economics and Government, founded in 1924.

The Board of Trustees is responsible for the general administration of the Institution, while the immediate direction of the policies, program, and staff is vested in the President, assisted by an advisory committee of the officers and staff. The by-laws of the Institution state: "It is the function of the Trustees to make possible the conduct of scientific research, and publication, under the most favorable conditions, and to safeguard the independence of the research staff in the pursuit of their studies and in the publication of the results of such studies. It is not a part of their function to determine, control, or influence the conduct of particular investigations or the conclusions reached."

The President bears final responsibility for the decision to publish a manuscript as a Brookings book. In reaching his judgment on the competence, accuracy, and objectivity of each study, the President is advised by the director of the appropriate research program and weighs the views of a panel of expert outside readers who report to him in confidence on the quality of the work. Publication of a work signifies that it is deemed a competent treatment worthy of public consideration but does not imply endorsement of conclusions or recommendations.

The Institution maintains its position of neutrality on issues of public policy in order to safeguard the intellectual freedom of the staff. Hence interpretations or conclusions in Brookings publications should be understood to be solely those of the authors and should not be attributed to the Institution, to its trustees, officers, or other staff members, or to the organizations that support its research.

For

MARGARET, DAVID, AND BRYCE

Foreword

THE CAPACITY to make nuclear arms is implicit in the technology for nuclear power generation, but the will to make them is rooted in compelling political and security motives. Canada, West Germany, and Japan have not developed nuclear arms though they clearly have the technological competence to do so, whereas at least a dozen Third World governments with access to civilian nuclear technology are weighing the decision to produce nuclear weapons. This study assesses the foreign policy, security position, and domestic politics of several Third World countries with the strongest incentives to develop nuclear arms: South Korea, Taiwan, Egypt, Pakistan, and Iran.

The study is concerned with the short-range and long-range effects of any new Third World nuclear force on regional stability and on the strategic balance between the United States and the Soviet Union. The author considers how the U.S. government, alone or in concert with others, should move to deter, delay, or make more difficult the building of new nuclear forces. He then judges the relative merits of measures such as the nonproliferation treaty, the International Atomic Energy Agency's safeguards system, supplier governments' controls on the export of nuclear facilities, materials, and technology, and nuclear-free zones. He also recommends U.S. policies both to counter the nuclear incentives of countries that feel threatened by hostile powers and to mitigate the destabilizing effects of new nuclear forces.

The study covers relevant events through March 1978. Since then dramatic developments have affected two of the countries examined—Taiwan and Iran. The United States has recognized the People's Republic of China and will terminate its security ties with Taiwan by the end of 1979. The current turbulence in Iran makes it impossible to predict what kind of government will emerge or what foreign policies it will pursue. Having reviewed the sections dealing with these countries, the author maintains that his central argument and conclusions remain valid.

Ernest W. Lefever began his study while he was a senior fellow in the Foreign Policy Studies program at the Brookings Institution. He is now director of the Ethics and Public Policy Center and a professorial lecturer in the Department of Government, both of Georgetown University. His previous Brookings books are *Crisis in the Congo: A United Nations Force in Action* (1965) and *Spear and Scepter: Army, Police, and Politics in Tropical Africa* (1970). His research for this study included numerous interviews with U.S. officials. He wishes especially to acknowledge the contributions of John C. Campbell, Warren H. Donnelly, Philip J. Farley, Amos A. Jordan, Paul H. Nitze, George H. Quester, Riordan Roett, Charles Van Doren, Seymour Weiss, Howard Wriggins, Joseph A. Yager, and William Yeomans. He is grateful for the helpful criticism of Henry Owen, director of the Foreign Policy Studies program at Brookings at the time this study was written, and for the diligent research support of Alan A. Foley. He thanks Caroletta Tresvant, Brenda Claggett, and Judith Hydes for typing the manuscript. Alice M. Carroll edited the manuscript and Diana Regenthal prepared the index.

The views expressed in this study are the author's and should not be ascribed to those he consulted or to the officers, trustees, or other staff members of the Brookings Institution.

BRUCE K. MACLAURY
President

January 1979
Washington, D.C.

Contents

NUCLEAR ARMS
IN THE THIRD WORLD

CHAPTER ONE

The Problem: Technology and Politics

We must not use the difficulty of the nuclear proliferation problem as an excuse to justify timidity . . . in standing up for the goal of world peace.

JIMMY CARTER, 1976[1]

THE UNDERGROUND explosion of a fifteen-kiloton nuclear device at Rajasthan in 1974 made India the sixth country to conduct such a successful test and aroused international apprehension over the risks and problems of rapidly spreading nuclear technology, especially in the Third World. Disclosure in 1976 of a U.S. Central Intelligence Agency estimate that Israel had ten or twenty nuclear weapons "available for use"[2] fueled interest in the potential danger of regional nuclear conflict. The portent of both events, however, was clouded in ambiguity. India's explosion may turn out to have less significance than Israel's nuclear development without an explosion.

The Rajasthan test did not propel India into the exclusive nuclear club whose members also hold the five permanent seats on the United Nations Security Council, but it did set India aside from all nonnuclear weapons states. Undoubtedly it had some impact on the calculations of those governments that will have the technical capacity to develop nuclear arms within the next decade or two. Israel's purported nuclear arsenal would make that tiny country, located in a crucible of conflict, the first since China to acquire a militarily significant force. Though the rumor of its existence was greeted with silence, in sharp contrast to the outpouring of criticism that followed the Indian test, the dramatic, if

1. "Remarks on Nuclear Policy," speech before San Diego City Club, September 25, 1976.
2. David Binder, *New York Times*, March 16, 1976. A CIA document released two years later confirmed the story; see *New York Times*, January 27, 1978.

ambiguous, possibility of Israeli nuclear arms cannot have been ignored by the threshold nuclear states in the Middle East and beyond.

This study is addressed to the problems bearing on U.S. interests that arise from the acquisition of nuclear arms by Third World countries. The potential for acquisition has increased with the significant spread of nuclear technology and materials since the abrupt rise in world oil prices in 1973. Between 1974 and 1975, for instance, the number of reactors operating, being built, on order, or planned in thirty-eight countries other than the United States rose from 348 to 426. The U.S. Energy Research and Development Administration estimated that by 1980 these reactors could produce forty thousand pounds of plutonium a year, enough fissionable material for more than two thousand Hiroshima-sized bombs.[3] It estimated also that by 1990 there will be enough plutonium generated yearly in the less developed countries to produce three thousand small bombs.

U.S. Interest in Nuclear Control

A principal goal of American foreign policy is peace, the absence of strategic and regional military conflict. The United States pursues policies designed to strengthen interstate stability both in the strategic theater of the Northern Hemisphere and among the nonindustrial states of Asia, Africa, and Latin America. Stability in the latter, Third World states is seen as serving U.S. interests, not only in averting war but in creating a climate for constructive economic and political development and in encouraging mutually beneficial relations between the United States and other countries.

As the first nuclear power and the only one to use atomic weapons in war, the United States since the bombing of Hiroshima and Nagasaki has sought to avoid nuclear war and to deter the spread of nuclear weapons. The United States briefly assisted Great Britain after it had established its small nuclear force but has steadfastly pursued policies designed to deter other states, including allies, from acquiring a nuclear capability. These policies are based on the fundamental, but not universally accepted assumption that the risks of nuclear war increase as the number of nuclear states increases. In early 1976 Secretary of State

3. Editorial, *New York Times,* May 14, 1975.

Henry A. Kissinger, in pledging U.S. support for other countries in development of nuclear energy for civilian purposes, emphasized that if additional states acquire nuclear weapons, global stability would be endangered and regional conflicts would run the risk of leading to nuclear war, with potentially catastrophic consequences not only for the nations involved but for all major powers.

We view the peaceful settlement of regional conflicts and a more stable world order as crucial U.S. objectives. Yet a world of many nuclear powers would result in heightened political tensions and increased instabilities flowing from fears that nuclear weapons might be used, whether deliberately or through miscalculation.[4]

Since 1945 the United States has become the most active nuclear power in seeking ways to deter and delay the acquisition of nuclear arms by other states, and since the 1960s the Soviet Union has been a partner in the enterprise. The U.S. concern has been expressed largely in terms of legal instruments and physical safeguards designed to prevent the diversion of nuclear technology and fuels to weapons uses. These efforts moved into high gear in the mid-1950s as knowledge of nuclear technology began to spread.

Beginning with the stillborn Baruch plan of 1946, designed to control nuclear development through internationalization, the United States has sought the twin objectives of exploiting the atom for civilian ends and limiting its military use to as few states as possible. Until the early 1950s, the "promotion of peaceful uses" was "relegated to a distinctly secondary position, while full attention was given to preventing the spread of nuclear weapons technology."[5] After passage of the Atomic Energy Act of 1954, which called on the government to make available to other countries the peaceful benefits of nuclear energy, the U.S. Atomic Energy Commission (AEC) assisted American industry in exporting nuclear technology. More than fifty American-made research reactors were constructed abroad during the next two decades, all under safeguards to prevent weapons application.

The U.S. interest in sharing nuclear technology and insistence on safeguards led to the establishment in 1957 of the International Atomic Energy Agency. This UN agency, with headquarters in Vienna, pro-

4. *Export Reorganization Act of 1976*, Hearings before the Senate Committee on Government Operations, 94 Cong. 2 sess. (Government Printing Office, 1976), p. 767.

5. Fred C. Iklé, director of U.S. Arms Control and Disarmament Agency, "The Role of Congress in Containing the Spread of Nuclear Weapons," speech before Duke University Law Forum, September 18, 1974.

motes the civilian uses of nuclear energy and works to prevent the use of nuclear technology or fuels for arms production. (One hundred and ten countries, only about fifty of them with nuclear facilities, belonged to the IAEA in 1978.) Virtually all nuclear facilities in states that have no nuclear arms are governed by IAEA safeguard agreements calling for on-site inspection of nuclear records, facilities, and processes by IAEA representatives. Most of the agreements are trilateral, among the IAEA, the recipient, and the supplier. (Some nuclear installations in Egypt, Israel, India, Spain, and South Africa are not under IAEA inspection.)

The only means the IAEA has of enforcing its standards is by reporting alleged infractions to the UN Security Council. Since 1970, however, the Treaty on the Non-Proliferation of Nuclear Weapons has strengthened the IAEA safeguard system.[6] The United States and the Soviet Union have vigorously supported the nonproliferation treaty (one hundred and three states were parties to the treaty in 1978 and another eleven, including Egypt, had signed but not ratified it; India, Pakistan, Israel, Brazil, and Argentina, Third World states with a reasonably well-developed nuclear technology, have not signed the treaty). The treaty obligates all parties to refrain from facilitating the acquisition of nuclear explosives. The restriction applies to peaceful devices as well as bombs—as the U.S. government has repeatedly insisted, the two are based on technologies that are indistinguishable. Nonnuclear weapons parties to the treaty are obligated to submit their nuclear facilities to IAEA safeguards. And nuclear weapons parties are required to extend civil nuclear assistance, including the benefits of nuclear explosions, to other parties. These transfers of technology and materials are to be strictly controlled to prevent weapons application.[7]

In its bilateral programs of technical nuclear assistance to friendly governments as well as in its work with the IAEA, the U.S. government has pushed for increasingly stringent safeguards to monitor the distribution of plutonium, uranium, and other materials that could be made into weapons-grade fuels. Neither these efforts by the United States nor those of other advanced nuclear countries to prevent the weapons application of nuclear assistance or materials can be wholly effective, as India has demonstrated (there were, however, no IAEA safeguards and only limited bilateral ones on India's nuclear facilities). The nuclear

6. 21 U.S.T. 483.

7. U.S. Arms Control and Disarmament Agency, *Arms Control and Disarmament Agreements* (GPO, 1977), pp. 77–91.

genie has been released and the spread of nuclear technology and fuels is irreversible. The formal system of safeguards to forestall weapons development is not foolproof and lacks enforceable sanctions. Moreover, the system is not inclusive because the People's Republic of China and France as well as several key nonnuclear weapons states have neither signed nor ratified the nonproliferation treaty.

The IAEA has no effective legal or other sanctions against members that violate its safeguard arrangements.[8] The nonproliferation treaty is a more effective vehicle for IAEA safeguards, but any party to the treaty may withdraw on three months' notice, if it is confronted by what it regards as a threat to its vital interests. Obviously, the multilateral legal structure cannot prevent a determined and technically qualified state from going nuclear. Recognizing this, the United States has undertaken to prevent nuclear arms technology from being developed by non-nuclear weapons states. On a number of occasions it has used its influence with both exporter and importer in an attempt to prevent the transfer of weapons technology. And in 1975, through U.S. initiative, a nuclear suppliers group was established; it consisted initially of the United States, the Soviet Union, Great Britain, West Germany, France, Japan, and Canada, but by 1976 included Sweden, Italy, Belgium, the Netherlands, East Germany, Czechoslovakia, Switzerland, and Poland. The suppliers group adopted a set of principles governing nuclear exports to "inhibit the spread of nuclear weapons."[9] Recipients of nuclear materials from the fifteen supplier states must accept IAEA safeguards on these imports and on any similar items produced in the recipient state. They must give formal assurances that nuclear imports will not be used to produce explosives for any purpose and promise not to export any sensitive enrichment or reprocessing technology without securing identical assurances from their recipient. Further, their imports of nuclear materials and facilities must be placed under "effective physical protection" to prevent theft or sabotage.

These direct restraints on nonweapons states are part of a larger system to deter the spread of nuclear arms. One of the earliest such agree-

8. The limits of the IAEA safeguard system are discussed by John Maddox, *Prospects for Nuclear Proliferation*, Adelphi Paper 113 (London: International Institute for Strategic Studies, 1975), pp. 22–26.

9. Fred C. Iklé, quoted by David Binder in *New York Times*, February 24, 1976. The guidelines agreed to were published in 1978; see Don Oberdorfer, *Washington Post*, January 12, 1978; and Richard Burt, *New York Times*, January 16, 1978.

ments was the Treaty of Antarctica, signed in 1959.[10] Another zonal agreement, the 1967 Treaty for the Prohibition of Nuclear Weapons in Latin America, is the first to cover an inhabited region.[11] These treaties, covering areas where there had been no recent conflict, were much more easily arrived at than the agreements that have come out of the struggle to prevent nuclear conflict between the superpowers. Though the non-weapons states that signed the 1963 and 1974 treaties banning nuclear weapons tests probably saw them as measures to restrain the superpowers, these are instruments that cannot be ignored by any state contemplating the development of nuclear arms.[12]

The agreements between the United States and the USSR to insure against their accidental entry into a nuclear war are another indirect protection against the acquisition of nuclear arms. The hot-line agreement of 1963 provides for communication and consultation in the event of a nuclear arms accident or any other nuclear explosion.[13] And the Agreement on the Prevention of Nuclear War signed by President Nixon and General Secretary Brezhnev in 1973 provides that "if relations between countries not parties to this Agreement appear to involve the risk of nuclear war between the United States of America and the Union of Soviet Socialist Republics or between either Party and other countries, the United States and the Soviet Union, acting in accordance with the provisions of this Agreement, shall immediately enter into urgent consultations with each other and make every effort to avert this risk."[14] To make the agreement workable, this provision excludes all "obligations undertaken by either Party towards its allies or other countries in treaties, agreements, or other documents."

Soviet Views on New Nuclear Arms States

The Soviet Union's views on the acquisition of nuclear arms by additional governments are derived from its own calculus of interests and

10. 12 U.S.T. 794.

11. 573 U.N.T.S. 3; known as the Treaty of Tlatelolco.

12. Treaty Banning Nuclear Weapons Tests in the Atmosphere, in Outer Space and Under Water, 14 U.S.T. 1313, known as the limited test-ban treaty; and Treaty on the Limitation of Underground Nuclear Weapon Tests (see *U.S. Department of State Bulletin,* July 29, 1974, pp. 216–17), known as the threshold test-ban treaty.

13. Memorandum of Understanding, 14 U.S.T. 825.

14. 24 U.S.T. 1478, art. 4.

threats.[15] Within the primary strategic arena the same principles operate on the American and Russian sides, but with different specific implications because of the alignment of adversary and allied forces. The Soviet Union naturally opposed the acquisition of nuclear arms by Britain and France, but it has been much more vehemently against acquisition by West Germany. Even though France is a U.S. ally, the United States was not enthusiastic about the French development and provided no direct assistance. And it has consistently opposed nuclear arms for West Germany. As Henry Kissinger said, "Germany cannot have a nuclear capability, because if it did the Russians would go to war."[16]

When the People's Republic of China exploded its first nuclear device in 1964, each of the two superpowers expressed apprehension. The Soviet Union, which provided technical nuclear assistance to China until 1960, has been particularly concerned because the Chinese development means the Soviet Union is confronted by two nuclear powers, one on each flank. For the United States, of course, China and its nuclear power serve as a counterweight to the Soviet Union, though rapprochement between the two communist states would radically alter this situation.

It is difficult to discern any significant difference between the superpowers in their views on the spread of nuclear arms in the Third World. Both have worked for the nonproliferation treaty. Though the United States has been far more active in the export of civil nuclear technology than the Soviet Union, both have insisted on the need for IAEA safeguards. Their muted public responses to the 1974 Indian explosion differed, however, in tone if not in substance. The Russians simply announced that India had conducted a "peaceful explosion" and had "reaffirmed its strong opposition" to nuclear weapons. A spokesman for the U.S. State Department said the event had an "adverse impact . . . on world stability."[17]

Commenting on the 1975 nonproliferation conference in Geneva, *Pravda* (May 6) noted that the nonproliferation treaty system did not yet "include a number of the 'near-nuclear' countries, in particular South Africa and Israel." It condemned the People's Republic of China's opposition to the treaty. India was not mentioned.

15. A valuable discussion of Soviet views is found in Roman Kolkowicz, Matthew P. Gallagher, and Benjamin S. Lambeth, *The Soviet Union and Arms Control: A Superpower Dilemma* (Johns Hopkins Press, 1970), pp. 70–115.

16. David Nevin, "Autocrat in the Action Arena," *Life*, September 5, 1969, p. 56.

17. *New York Times*, May 19, 1974.

French and Chinese Views on Nuclear Weapons

France had its first nuclear explosion in 1960 and the People's Republic of China in 1964, and both have since developed defensive nuclear arsenals which are very small compared to the nuclear might of the two superpowers. The declaratory positions of France and China on the nonproliferation treaty, the spread of nuclear weapons, and nuclear matters generally are quite similar. Both governments have criticized the limited test-ban treaty and the nonproliferation treaty as devices for preserving the nuclear hegemony of the superpowers and relegating other states to second-class status. National prestige and influence, as well as security considerations, are important in their perspectives. France has sold nuclear technology abroad, but China has transferred neither technology nor fissionable materials to other countries.

Consistent with developing its own nuclear deterrent, France has pursued an independent policy, emphasizing self-reliance in national defense and the exploitation of the political and commercial benefits of its nuclear technology. France has exported nuclear reactors to several countries and is seeking to penetrate the enriched-uranium market. In its export of nuclear technology, the French government insists that it "will behave, in its dealings with non-nuclear states, as if France were a party to" the nonproliferation treaty.[18]

French nuclear strategists, perhaps reflecting France's unique experience, have made a significant contribution to thinking about the implications of additional nuclear arms states. Drawing on the work of Pierre Gallois, the "proportional deterrence" school has postulated that nuclear deterrence can operate at levels other than the strategic level between the United States and the Soviet Union.[19] It contends that a state with even a small nuclear force can under appropriate conditions assure its security by its capacity to inflict nuclear damage out of all proportion to the rationally anticipated gains of an aggressor, whether the latter uses conventional or nuclear means. Depending on circumstances, the unacceptable cost of aggression may be the loss of only one city. Hence, an effective deterrent could consist of a handful of nuclear weapons suitably dispersed or protected so as to survive a possible first

18. Maddox, *Prospects for Nuclear Proliferation*, p. 27.
19. See Pierre Gallois, *The Balance of Terror: Strategy for the Nuclear Age* (Houghton Mifflin, 1961), especially pp. 119–22.

strike. Advocates of nuclear arms within threshold states have drawn on this doctrine of proportional deterrence to support their case.[20] They argue that some new deterrent forces could strengthen regional stability.

Chinese public statements on nuclear arms have been highly political and ideological. After condemning Soviet and American nuclear weapons for years, China was confronted with the necessity of justifying its October 1964 explosion. It did so by distinguishing between "capitalist" and "socialist" bombs, insisting that U.S. and Chinese bombs were "fundamentally different in nature." With its new weapons China would continue to pursue "the foreign policy of peace."[21] These statements are consistent with the Chinese comment on the signing of the limited test-ban treaty by the Soviet Union, the United States, and Great Britain in 1963:

> With regard to preventing nuclear proliferation, the Chinese Government has always maintained that the arguments of the U.S. imperialists must not be echoed, but that a class analysis must be made. Whether or not nuclear weapons help peace depends on who possesses them. *It is detrimental to peace if they are in the hands of imperialist countries; it helps peace if they are in the hands of socialist countries.* It must not be said undiscriminatingly that the danger of nuclear war increases along with the increase in the number of nuclear powers.[22]

Consistent with this view and reflecting its support for Third World positions, China for years said that smaller countries had as much right as the superpowers to have nuclear weapons. But since the Indian explosion, which it condemned as "Indian nuclear blackmail" against Pakistan, the Chinese have quietly modified their position. They have told several Western visitors that China "is against nuclear proliferation" but is not prepared to sign the nonproliferation treaty.[23]

Levels of Nuclear Arms Capability

To calculate the dangers of any particular nuclear acquisition, it is essential to identify the level of nuclear arms in question. The actual

20. See Yair Evron, "Israel and the Atom: The Uses and Misuses of Ambiguity, 1957–1967," *Orbis*, vol. 17 (Winter 1974), pp. 1330–33.

21. "Break the Nuclear Monopoly, Eliminate Nuclear Weapons," *Renmin Ribao*, October 24, 1964, translated in *Peking Review*, vol. 7 (October 30, 1964), p. 6.

22. "Statement by the Spokesman of the Chinese Government," August 15, 1963, in *Peking Review*, vol. 6 (August 16, 1963), p. 12. Emphasis added.

23. Harlan Cleveland, *China Diary* (Georgetown University, Center for Strategic and International Studies, 1976), p. 17.

military capability achieved by a Third World government is important both in itself and in relation to the political and security realities of the region. There is a significant difference between one fifteen-kiloton explosion in 1974 by India, which sees China as its chief adversary, and a hypothetical small arsenal of nuclear bombs held by Brazil facing a nuclear or nonnuclear Argentina. The impact of a new or developing nuclear capability by a Third World state on regional stability depends on the present and potential level of that capability, the intention of the government, political and security conditions in the area, and the perceptions of both the acquiring government and its neighbors.

The level of nuclear arms, measured largely by the capacity to project military force, may be indicated by four principal and slightly over-lapping situations, ranging from a total absence of nuclear arms to a capability to affect the strategic calculus between the United States and the Soviet Union. The great majority of the world's states are destined to remain nonweapons states indefinitely. They lack the technology and resources to manufacture nuclear arms in the foreseeable future. Perhaps only thirty of the more technically advanced states, about half of them in Europe, could develop a nuclear force by the year 2000. Most of these thirty possess nuclear research or power reactors and some of them are keeping the nuclear option open by making appropriate research and development decisions.

Threshold State

States at a threshold stage of development are engaged in a wide range of activities designed to put the government in position to carry out a nuclear explosion. India was a threshold state for perhaps four years before the 1974 explosion. At this stage a state is developing nuclear technology, building or otherwise acquiring reactors or separation facilities, and gaining access to uranium or plutonium that is not monitored by any safeguard system.

Token Nuclear Force

A country enters a token nuclear force stage after it has undertaken a nuclear test, and it remains at that stage until it develops a militarily significant nuclear force. With its fission explosion, India entered the token stage and it will remain there until it develops a nuclear force with a credible delivery system relevant to China or Pakistan. A government may conduct a number of explosions for prestige purposes rather than for direct security reasons, but regardless of the motivation, these explosions constitute a token nuclear force and are a factor to be reckoned with in interstate politics. The development of several fission or fusion bombs, with or without test explosions, provides a government with a token force that will not become militarily significant until other governments are convinced it is usable against a plausible military target.

Militarily Significant Force

A government that has a deliverable nuclear force has reached a militarily significant stage. The delivery system must be reliable and able to survive in most cases. For the Israeli government, an arsenal of ten to thirteen nuclear bombs of twenty-kiloton yield and an appropriate means of delivery is a militarily significant force. Israel's force is significant against its nonnuclear neighbors, the lowest level of military significance. The next level of significance is against a nuclear neighbor with approximately the same capability, and above that against a medium nuclear power (for example, China). The highest level of military significance is against one of the two superpowers. India has not yet reached the lowest level, though psychologically and politically it has achieved a significant level as far as Pakistan is concerned. China's force has direct military significance vis-à-vis India or Taiwan. Only the United States and the Soviet Union have militarily significant forces in relation to one another, though British and French nuclear forces, which include submarines, have some deterrent effect on the Soviet Union.

Technology and Nuclear Arms

A government may acquire nuclear arms by getting them from a nuclear state through gift, purchase, or theft, or by manufacturing them, with or without direct external assistance. This study is concerned only with the manufacture of weapons because the other means of getting them appear unlikely. In the three decades of the nuclear era, no nuclear weapon has ever been transferred from one government to another or to any other organization, as far as is publicly known. President Muammar el-Qaddafi of Libya is reported to have tried since 1970 to buy a nuclear bomb from China and other governments. In early 1975 he said: "Tomorrow we will be able to buy an atom bomb and all its parts. The nuclear monopoly is about to be broken."[24] So far, this has been a vain hope.

Any would-be nuclear state must have considerable economic and technical resources and strong political incentives to engage in the long, difficult, and costly effort that will result in a nuclear explosion or a token force. The development of a militarily significant nuclear arsenal, with a credible delivery system, requires a heavy additional expenditure of human and technical resources. India's nuclear achievement was the result of a well-planned and costly effort that started in 1948. In one sense it was the by-product of a large nuclear power effort that was substantially aided by Canada, France, the United States, and the United Kingdom. But India had a significant indigenous nuclear engineering capability, evident in the atomic research reactor that was designed and constructed without foreign help by 1956. The combination of technical advantages and India's strong security and prestige motives suggests that the Indian explosion was not the harbinger of rapid and widespread arms acquisition in other Third World countries.

It is widely assumed that until 1990 plutonium will remain the principal material that Third World governments would use to make weapons. The plutonium route to nuclear arms involves five key steps—securing uranium ore, fabricating fuel elements, operating a nuclear reactor, separating plutonium from spent reactor fuel, and building the explosive device. For complete independence, a country would need the resources for carrying out these five steps, but the process could be expedited by external assistance at one or more stages. And it could be radically shortened if the first four steps—the complete fuel cycle—were bypassed by the purchase of plutonium. By 1985 or shortly thereafter, some Third World government may decide to make nuclear arms with enriched uranium rather than plutonium. The process would thus be simplified into three principal steps—acquisition of uranium, enrichment to weapons grade, and fabrication of the bomb. Whether the plutonium or uranium route were taken, the nuclear force would not be complete without adequate means to deliver the warheads to appropriate targets.

For either the plutonium or the uranium route to bomb fabrication, uranium ore is essential, and few states have a readily available supply. The communist countries aside, only the United States, Canada, Sweden,

24. Thomas O'Toole, *Washington Post*, May 5, 1975.

South Africa, and Australia have major uranium deposits. Significant deposits of uranium ore have been found in Spain, Portugal, France, Gabon, Niger, and the Central African Republic, and small deposits in Argentina, Brazil, Finland, Greenland, India, Italy, Japan, Korea, Mexico, Turkey, Yugoslavia, and Zaire. The United States is the chief exporter of enriched uranium. It employs strict safeguards to insure that this reactor fuel is not diverted to weapons use, yet the U.S. government does not know exactly how much has been supplied to other countries or precisely where it has gone.[25] The U.S. predominance in the uranium market has diminished as other countries have developed new enrichment technologies.[26]

Just as most countries interested in developing nuclear power rely on external suppliers for natural or enriched uranium, they rely on external technology for the design and building of research and power reactors. A nuclear reactor—a "device in which a controlled, self-sustaining fission chain-reaction can be maintained"[27]—can be used for generating electricity and for producing materials that can be refined for weapons use. Uranium is used in nuclear power reactors to generate heat, which is used to make steam to drive turbines. The fissionable isotope U-235 constitutes 0.71 percent of the element. The bulk of natural uranium, 99.27 percent, consists of the U-238 isotope. During the fission process, some of the U-238 atoms absorb neutrons. In this way, U-238 is ultimately transmuted into plutonium, an element not found in nature. Hence, plutonium is a by-product of a nuclear reactor, whether it is fueled by natural uranium or by uranium with an enriched U-235 content of 3 percent to 4 percent.

The increasing availability of plutonium is obvious in the fact that by the end of 1976 nearly 500 nuclear power plants were operating, under construction, or planned outside the United States, and 57 were in operation in the United States, 143 were under construction, and another 22 were in the planning stage.[28] The United States has been the major exporter of reactors in the noncommunist world, but its share of that

25. David Binder, *New York Times*, December 16, 1976.

26. Joseph A. Yager and Eleanor B. Steinberg, *Energy and U.S. Foreign Policy* (Ballinger, 1974), p. 355.

27. International Atomic Energy Agency, Information Circular, INFCIRC/66/ Rev. 2, September 16, 1968, p. 16.

28. Stockholm International Peace Research Institute, *World Armaments and Disarmament: SIPRI Yearbook 1977* (Stockholm: Almqvist and Wiksell; Cambridge: MIT Press, 1977), table 2.1, pp. 38–39.

market is declining. Between 1956 and 1973, U.S. firms accounted for forty-six of the fifty-eight reactors sold on the international market. In 1974–75, however, U.S. firms accounted for thirteen of twenty-four reactors sold.[29] The decline in the U.S. share of the market reflects increased competition in the sale of nuclear reactors but also the growing American concern about the spread of nuclear technology.

By 1980, nuclear power reactors abroad will be capable of producing enough plutonium to make two thousand Hiroshima-sized bombs a year. But before it can be used to make bombs, plutonium must be separated from spent reactor fuel.[30] This separation process takes about one year and bomb fabrication an additional six months. Separation or reprocessing plants are operated only by the five nuclear powers, several advanced Western European countries and Yugoslavia, Argentina, and India (one was under construction in Japan in 1978). One scientist maintains, however, that reprocessing facilities are within the reach of many countries and would cost less than $100,000. He acknowledges that "a commercially competitive nuclear fuel reprocessing plant that produces separated plutonium and uranium that meets the stringent quality control specifications required by the nuclear industry is a highly complex, sophisticated facility, costing at least several hundred million dollars. But a reprocessing facility designed only to extract plutonium for nuclear weapons could be much smaller, simpler, and less expensive."[31] Other specialists do not accept his low cost estimate but do agree with the thrust of his statement.

The enriched uranium route to nuclear arms has a practical advantage over the plutonium route because fabrication of the bomb is technically less complex and demanding. With the spread and diversification of enrichment technology, uranium bombs are becoming more feasible.

29. Tom Alexander, "Our Costly Losing Battle Against Nuclear Proliferation," *Fortune*, December 1975, p. 145. For further information, see *Facts on Nuclear Proliferation: A Handbook*, prepared by the Congressional Research Service for the Senate Committee on Government Operations, 94 Cong. 1 sess. (GPO, 1975), pp. 193–99.

30. See Victor Gilinsky, "The Military Potential of Civil Nuclear Power," in Mason Willrich, ed., *Civil Nuclear Power and International Security* (Praeger, 1971), pp. 15–19.

31. Theodore Taylor, chairman of the board, International Research and Technology Corp., in *Nuclear Proliferation: Future U.S. Foreign Policy Implications*, Hearings before the Subcommittee on International Security and Scientific Affairs of the House Committee on International Relations, 94 Cong. 1 sess. (GPO, 1975), pp. 81, 88.

Until recently only the five nuclear powers undertook the complex process of enriching uranium to weapons quality. In the past several years at least six other countries have developed new enrichment methods— Australia, Italy, Japan, the Netherlands, South Africa, and West Germany. Several commercial enrichment plants are under construction. With experience, as costs are reduced, an enrichment capability will be in reach of a growing number of Third World countries.

After a would-be nuclear arms state obtains a significant amount of plutonium or enriched uranium, it must still confront the very difficult and dangerous task of constructing an effective explosive device. Though popular writers may claim that a handful of skilled scientists and engineers could construct a crude workable bomb in a few weeks, putting together a reliable and moderately sophisticated bomb requires a high degree of scientific and engineering skill. Few Third World countries possess the advanced techniques demanded in chemical and conventional explosive technology, metallurgy, and nuclear reactor physics.

Cost of Nuclear Arms

The spread of nuclear technology and the availability of plutonium and simplified methods to refine it may have brought the cost of weapons development down. The fabrication of nuclear weapons and the development of delivery systems, however, remain complicated and costly undertakings. In most Third World states, building a militarily significant nuclear force would require resources substantially greater than those presently devoted to the entire conventional military establishment. And few of these societies are as advanced in nuclear technology as India, Argentina, and Brazil. Scientists in technical societies "have little feeling for the fundamental difficulties" that a lack of resources imposes on their counterparts in less favored nations.[32]

Even when costs are known to be great, a highly motivated government may be prepared to pay them. Israel, for example, has mined uranium from phosphate found in the Negev Desert at costs considerably higher than commercially obtainable uranium ore. And it may have also paid a high cost politically in acquiring uranium "by clandestine

32. James R. Schlesinger, "Nuclear Spread," *Yale Review*, vol. 57 (Autumn 1967), p. 81.

means."[33] India has acknowledged spending $56 million for atomic research and development between 1969 and 1974;[34] outside experts put the figure at many times that amount.[35] Since much of the research and development for the Indian nuclear test took place within the civil power program, New Delhi's statement that the 1974 explosion cost only an additional $400,000 may approximate the facts.[36]

A UN study published in 1968 estimated the annual operating costs of producing eighty kilograms of weapons-grade plutonium per year (enough for five to ten small fission bombs) were $84 million. That estimate did not include uranium mining and milling costs or the initial cost of the reactor.[37] A nuclear power reactor of the minimum size considered feasible for a country the size of South Korea would have cost at least $400 million in 1974.[38] A weapons fabrication plant in a country technologically capable of producing ten Hiroshima-sized bombs per year would have cost between $8 million and $10 million.[39]

Fuel fabrication and reprocessing technology is within the means of several Third World states. The initial cost of a reprocessing plant capable of producing enough plutonium for a hundred twenty-kiloton bombs over a five-year period would be $40 million to $50 million and the annual operating expenses $4 million to $6 million. A fuel fabrication facility for the same program could cost as much as $20 million to build, and as much again in annual operating costs.[40] Smaller reprocessing and fabrication facilities would be considerably less expensive.

For a country with a nuclear power system including fuel fabrication and reprocessing technology, the incremental costs essential for making bombs—plutonium metals reduction, weapons fabrication and testing—

33. As reported by David Burnham in *New York Times,* January 27, 1978.

34. "India's War on Want," press release, Indian embassy, Washington, D.C., September 6, 1974.

35. Bernard Weinraub, *New York Times,* May 20, 1974.

36. Another report puts the cost of the test at $3 million. See ibid., May 23, 1974.

37. United Nations, *Effects of the Possible Use of Nuclear Weapons and the Security and Economic Implications for States of the Acquisition and Further Development of These Weapons,* UN Doc. A/6858 (1968), p. 56.

38. See "Asia Joins the Race for Atom Power," *Far Eastern Economic Review,* vol. 86 (November 22, 1974), p. 57. See also Yager and Steinberg, *Energy and U.S. Foreign Policy,* p. 332.

39. Andrew Caranfil and others, "Briefing Notes: Nuclear Proliferation After India" (Croton-on-Hudson, N.Y.: Hudson Institute, November 1, 1974), p. 4.

40. International Institute for Strategic Studies, *Strategic Survey* (London: IISS, 1972), p. 73. Figures are 1972 dollars.

are likely to be less than $50 million.[41] The costs do not end with the construction of a bomb or an arsenal of fifteen to fifty small fission bombs. To be militarily significant, the force must be reliable and survivable—in short, credible in the eyes of other governments, especially potential rivals or adversaries. The force must be militarily relevant to plausible targets, thus requiring either an airborne or a missile delivery system. India, for example, would have to develop an airborne system capable of delivering nuclear bombs to key Pakistani targets or a missile system relevant to China. In the former case, the aircraft would have to be based within striking distance of the target, be protected against Pakistan's air defenses, and be relatively invulnerable against a first strike by Pakistan. All of this costs money.

Depending on the quality of the adversary's defenses, an airborne nuclear force to be credible would need two to four planes for each primary target.[42] This margin would allow for both the risks of preemption and anticipated operational losses. These and related realities point to the unlikelihood of such popular notions as the delivery of a single nuclear bomb by a commercial jet or, for that matter, by an American-built F-4 or a Soviet bomber. A one-bomb-one-plane capability has limited deterrent or blackmail value because it has little solid military significance. Credibility must be rooted in forces in being or in realistically anticipated forces. But since governments, like commodity brokers, deal in futures, a token capability may have a disproportionate influence because neighboring governments evaluate present realities in terms of future probabilities.

For technical and cost reasons, virtually all Third World states seeking to develop nuclear arms would rely in the first instance on aircraft for delivery. For some, this would mean the conversion of modern military, or possibly commercial, aircraft to handle nuclear warheads and to penetrate an adversary's defenses. More advanced countries, like India, Israel, South Africa, Brazil, and Argentina, could configure such aircraft domestically or under license from a foreign manufacturer if neither party were bound by the nonproliferation treaty.

Those few governments that had some hope of developing surface-to-surface missiles would face formidable technical and resource problems.

41. Ibid.
42. See Ian Smart, *Future Conditional: The Prospect for Anglo-French Nuclear Co-operation*, Adelphi Paper 78 (London: International Institute for Strategic Studies, 1971), p. 5.

France, for example, spent approximately $5.7 billion between 1965 and 1970 to perfect its missile technology—on average, almost 17 percent of its military budget and slightly less than 1 percent of its GNP.[43] Further, French expenditures for the entire nuclear force, including missiles, fluctuated widely. Annual spending between 1955 and 1959 averaged about $40 million, but it reached $1 billion in 1965, which amounted to 25 percent of France's defense budget and 50 percent of the equipment portion of that budget.[44] The first French nuclear test was in 1960. The first surface-to-surface ballistic missiles became operational in 1970, two years behind schedule.

The technical difficulties of building a missile system caused Great Britain to cancel plans to build a surface-to-surface missile. The first British atomic test was in 1952 and in May 1957 Britain detonated its first hydrogen bomb. In April 1960, after a five-year effort costing $182 million, Britain abandoned development of the Blue Streak missile[45] and opted for the American-designed Skybolt air-to-surface system instead. Similarly, in 1965 the British government canceled plans for an advanced aircraft delivery system (the TSR-2) primarily because it "would have cost twenty times more to develop and ten times more to produce than the Canberra which it was to replace."[46]

In spite of heavy costs, a technically capable and highly motivated modern industrial state with considerable experience in nuclear power and advanced aerospace technology could, according to the 1967 UN study,[47] produce a modest nuclear force (one hundred twenty-kiloton bombs, thirty to fifty bombers, and fifty surface-to-surface missiles with a fifteen-hundred-mile range) over a ten-year period for $1.68 billion. Allowing for 90 percent inflation in the U.S. dollar since 1967 and an additional 20 percent "margin of inexperience" of the Third World states, the cost for 1978 could be as high as $3.5 billion, a formidable expenditure even for the richer countries. A smaller force of ten bombs and appropriate means of delivery would cost perhaps $400 million.

43. Judith H. Young, *The French Strategic Missile Programme*, Adelphi Paper 38 (London: International Institute for Strategic Studies, 1967), pp. 6–7. See also United Nations, *Effects of the Possible Use of Nuclear Weapons*, pp. 26–27.

44. Young, *The French Strategic Missile Programme*, pp. 6–7.

45. The total cost of the system was expected to be between $1.4 billion and $1.68 billion. Andrew J. Pierre, *Nuclear Politics: The British Experience with an Independent Strategic Force 1939–1970* (Oxford University Press, 1972), p. 198.

46. Ibid., p. 319.

47. United Nations, *Effects of the Possible Use of Nuclear Weapons*, p. 25.

Table 1-1. *Military Budget and GNP of Third World Candidates for Nuclear Arms, 1977*

| | | Military budget | |
| | GNP (millions | Millions of | As percentage |
Country	of dollars)	dollars	of GNP
India	73,000	3,100	4.25
Pakistan	13,000	886	6.82
Iran	66,000	10,150	15.38
Israel	12,100	4,271	35.30
Egypt	12,900	4,370	33.80
South Korea	25,000	1,900	7.60
Taiwan	17,100	1,672	9.77
Brazil	111,700	1,967	1.76
Argentina	42,000	778	1.85
Mexico	79,000	613	0.78
South Africa	29,600	1,900	6.42

Sources: U.S. Central Intelligence Agency, *National Basic Intelligence Factbook, July 1977* (Library of Congress, 1977); and, for Egypt, International Institute for Strategic Studies, *The Military Balance: 1977–1978* (London: IISS, 1977), p. 35.

Only a few of the more advanced Third World states could realistically undertake a nuclear arms program that would cost $3.5 billion over a decade. Iran is the only state whose defense budget could easily accommodate such an expenditure (see table 1-1). The annual cost of such a program would be $350 million. The ten-bomb force would mean an annual expenditure of $40 million which is within the reach of a number of highly motivated Third World states. These expenditures, of course, could be substantially reduced if a friendly government provided free or at a reduced cost missiles for a newly acquired nuclear force in a Third World state.

Incentives for Acquiring Nuclear Arms

The incentives that would lead Third World governments to acquire nuclear arms are interrelated—defense, foreign policy, economic, and domestic considerations. National defense is the chief expressed reason for seeking nuclear arms. Many governments feel insecure because of hostile neighbors, recent border clashes, or serious attacks, or because they cannot rely on friends or allies to aid them if conflict should break out. South Korea and Taiwan are classic cases of widely sensed insecurity; each faces an implacable adversary and fears that it may be abandoned by the United States. Under such circumstances, a government may seek to enhance its security by acquiring nuclear arms to deter nuclear or conventional attack. It may also argue that its possession of nuclear arms will advance regional security by restoring or stabilizing the balance of power.

Some governments may seek to strengthen their bargaining position with other governments with the leverage conferred by a nuclear force. A nuclear explosion is a significant accomplishment that can be assumed to lead to the manufacture of several nuclear weapons and then to a militarily significant capability. As in the case of India, the first explosion endows the government with an aura of big-power status, though it takes a great deal more to achieve that position. Sometimes governments seeking to exercise the weapons option may exaggerate their need for nuclear power reactors, emphasizing the technical and economic benefits of a program designed to produce a nuclear explosion, or arguing that nuclear explosions can be useful for mining or excavation. On occasion, the primary motive for a nuclear arms program may be to buttress internal morale or cohesion, though national leaders will seldom admit so candidly. Increased domestic pride and self-esteem are seen as clear and unambiguous benefits of a nuclear explosion, whatever the near-term impact on national security or foreign policy. Indians in all walks of life expressed overwhelming approval of the 1974 explosion, though their massive show of confidence in the government proved to be ephemeral. The people of any country would bask in the glow of the international attention, approving or critical, accorded such an event. Many Indians took pride in being criticized for a formidable achievement that hitherto had been confined to great powers. Even anticommunist overseas Chinese took pride in China's first nuclear explosion.

Assessment of a government's calculation of national interests—its perception of security threats and the need for national cohesion and prestige, as well as its view of foreign policy and economic benefits—yields a kind of incentive index. India certainly had a high motivation to embark on a nuclear program—a sense of national insecurity and little confidence in external protection, combined with a desire to shore up domestic morale and gain international prestige. Its test probably pushed Pakistan's incentive from medium to high, and it may have had a similar effect on Iran.

In addition to these basic political and security incentives, which are seldom discussed publicly by the government concerned, there are in-

Table 1-2. *Incentives and Capabilities of Third World Candidates for Nuclear Arms, 1985 and 2000*

	1985			2000		
Country	Incentive to arm[a]	Airborne system[b]	Missile system[b]	Incentive to arm[a]	Airborne system[b]	Missile system[b]
India	high	probable	improbable	high	probable	uncertain
Pakistan	high	uncertain	improbable	high	probable	uncertain
Iran	medium	probable	improbable	high	probable	probable
Israel	high	probable	probable	high	probable	probable
Egypt	high	probable	probable	high	probable	probable
South Korea	high	probable	uncertain	high	probable	probable
Taiwan	high	probable	probable	high	probable	probable
Brazil	medium	probable	probable	high	probable	probable
Argentina	medium	probable	improbable	high	probable	probable
Mexico	low	uncertain	improbable	medium	probable	uncertain
South Africa	medium	probable	uncertain	uncertain	probable	probable

a. Estimate based on the probable state of national and regional security.
b. Capability to manufacture nuclear arms and a reliable delivery system.

ternal pressures that tend to reinforce early decisions to keep open the nuclear option. One such pressure comes from the scientific and technical community, whose pride, prestige, and morale are dependent on accomplishing a series of objectives culminating in a major achievement. The U.S. hydrogen bomb, Dr. J. Robert Oppenheimer once said, "was so technically sweet, we had to do it."[48] Another factor is the relative absence of countervailing forces. The secrecy surrounding nuclear development seriously limits public debate on the issue. The small circle privy to nuclear decisions tends to be largely composed of technicians and members of the ruling elite. Legislators and lesser politicians are in a poor position to challenge either the incremental decisions or their potential impact on national security, foreign policy, or the allocation of national resources. This point, which is made in a perceptive study of the development of the American atomic bomb,[49] is supported by the events preceding the Indian explosion.

The incentives of Third World candidates to build a nuclear capability are projected in table 1-2. They are based on four, interrelated assumptions about trends in national security and interstate politics until the turn of the century: there will be a continuing loosening of ties

48. Quoted by George F. Will, *Washington Post*, January 25, 1975.
49. Robert C. Batchelder, *The Irreversible Decision, 1939–1950* (Houghton Mifflin, 1962).

between each of the two superpowers and its allies; Third World governments will feel less protected by U.S. or Soviet security ties or guarantees; competition and rivalry among the larger Third World states within a region will continue and probably intensify; and this rivalry will be exacerbated by the acquisition of nuclear capability by one or more additional states. The combination of estimates of the intensity of Third World states' incentive for going nuclear and of their military and financial capabilities deduced from table 1-1 produces nine candidates, in addition to Israel and India, for the acquisition of nuclear arms by manufacture by 1985 or 2000. Though each candidate's incentive is rated high, medium, or low in table 1-2, whether any or all will move toward an airborne or a missile nuclear force will depend on many unpredictable resource and motivation factors. Four nonnuclear governments are seen as having a high incentive to enhance their security, prestige, and regional position by acquiring nuclear arms before 1985. By the year 2000, the number of highly motivated states increases to seven and it could rise to eight, depending on developments in southern Africa.

This study is limited to those states that clearly fall into the high incentive category. India and Israel have already demonstrated that they are highly motivated. South Korea and Taiwan are under siege and the incentives for exercising the nuclear option are high. Pakistan feels increasingly upstaged and threatened by India. Three states whose incentives are moderate now may be highly motivated by 2000—Iran, an oil-rich state on the periphery of the Soviet Union, is seeking to establish hegemony in the Persian Gulf–Arabian Sea region; Argentina and Brazil are historic rivals in South America. Mexico is not included because analysis of its position would add little to the study. South Africa, a unique case, is also excluded; it has a high level of nuclear technology, but its incentive to produce nuclear arms is problematical.

Factors in the Analysis

This analysis combines case studies of the nine Third World countries with an examination of geopolitical factors that bear on the U.S. interest in regional and global stability. The case studies examine the behavior of each government toward nuclear arms, along with the external and internal incentives and disincentives that bear on its decisions. The study assumes that the United States will continue to pursue policies toward the Third World designed to strengthen interstate stability— that is, to lessen the threat of war. War in Asia, Africa, or Latin America carries the risk of involving the superpowers, would consume resources better devoted to civil production, and would tend to create conditions favorable to the rise of extremist governments. Hence, nuclear developments are assessed in the light of the U.S. interest in regional and strategic stability.

Approximately fifteen Third World governments have the technical capability and financial resources to manufacture a token force by 2000. By 1985, only a small number of the more technically advanced of these states could develop a nuclear force of fifty small plutonium bombs supported by an appropriate delivery system, which together would cost about $1.8 billion over a decade. By 2000, approximately ten could develop a modest nuclear force supported by an airborne or missile delivery system. A larger number could produce a smaller and less expensive force and at an earlier date. The nonproliferation treaty and the IAEA safeguard system (and related export controls) cannot prevent a determined and technically capable state from exercising the nuclear option. The decision is primarily a political one based on the government's perception of external danger, its alliance relationships, its foreign policy objectives, and its quest for prestige abroad and support at home. The effect of a new acquisition will vary with the behavior of the new nuclear state, its neighbors, and the great powers. Nuclear acquisition is not a monolithic phenomenon that can be dealt with by a monolithic response.

The last two chapters of the study consider a number of questions confronting the United States: What is the range of probable near-term and long-term effects of nuclear arms acquisition by various Third World states on regional and strategic stability? Are there situations where a new force or a significantly strengthened force would be highly destabilizing, threatening immediate conventional or nuclear war, and other circumstances where acquisition would correct a regional power imbalance and thus contribute to short-range or long-range stability, and even cases where a new acquisition would have little impact on stability? What effects are new or enhanced acquisitions likely to have on strategic stability between the United States and the Soviet Union? What policies should the United States adopt in response to changes in the nuclear position of Third World governments that contribute to regional or strategic stability; to those that have little impact on stability; and to those that have an adverse effect on stability? What are the most effective policies for preventing, deterring, or delaying an acquisition that would upset stability or otherwise threaten U.S. interests? And what are the most effective U.S. measures to mitigate the adverse effects of a Third World state's nuclear acquisition?

CHAPTER TWO

India and Pakistan: Challenge and Response

We are firmly committed only to the peaceful uses of atomic energy.
                    PRIME MINISTER INDIRA GANDHI, 1974

We are not interested in making an atomic explosion.
                    PRESIDENT ZULFIKAR ALI BHUTTO, 1976[1]

IN SPITE of specific and repeated public warnings about India's interest in peaceful nuclear explosions and widespread knowledge of India's advanced nuclear technology, the world reacted to the May 18, 1974, underground blast with a mixture of surprise and indignation. As early as July 25, 1970, the chairman of India's Atomic Energy Commission had announced that India was examining the advantages of an underground nuclear explosion "for peaceful purposes" and "for the economic benefit of the country."[2] Defense Minister Jagjivan Ram had told parliament on May 2, 1972, that India was studying "the technology for carrying out underground nuclear explosions for peaceful purposes" and that research on underground testing had been underway for two years.[3]

The nuclear powers greeted the Indian explosion with muted concern. As a U.S. official noted a year later, the test did not make India "number six in a so-called nuclear club," though it did make India a precursor of "a great many countries to come, maybe ten, twenty."[4] Most observers believe that India is seeking to achieve a dominant power position in South Asia and perhaps beyond, and Indian officials

1. Bernard Weinraub, *New York Times,* May 19, 1974; and Robert Trumbull, *New York Times,* February 26, 1976.
2. Vikram Sarabhai, *New York Times,* July 26, 1970.
3. *New York Times,* May 3, 1972.
4. Fred C. Iklé, *Washington Star,* March 12, 1975.

have made it clear that India will resist attempts at external interference.

Although India does not possess the economic or military credentials of a great power, it has the eleventh largest gross national product in the world and a military establishment whose size is surpassed only by those of the Soviet Union, China, and the United States. Its annual defense budget is $3.1 billion.[5] Its armed forces number over 1.6 million, including border security units and other paramilitary personnel. Equipped mainly by the Soviet Union and Great Britain, India is largely self-sufficient in the design and manufacture of all but the more advanced military hardware. Its modern weapons include about 2,000 tanks, 8 Soviet F-class submarines, 1 aircraft carrier, and 670 combat aircraft.[6]

The Indian government justified its nuclear test on economic development and security grounds, but its early statements emphasized the former. Prime Minister Indira Gandhi found it difficult "to understand the outcry . . . against something we have been doing for 25 years and which is but an off-shoot of this work. Is it the contention that it is all right for the rich to use nuclear energy for destruction, but not for a poor country to find out whether it can be used for construction?"[7] Mrs. Gandhi's assertion that the test was conducted solely for peaceful purposes was consistent with India's declaratory policy which since 1948 had insisted that atomic energy was a panacea for the country's massive economic ills. An Indian commentator noted: "For such a nation, desperately in search of a major scientific breakthrough that could cut the 'vicious circle of poverty' and conquer the apparently insoluble problems confronting its government, it is but legitimate and right to turn to nuclear technology for the country's emancipation."[8] The government consequently has not viewed the high cost as an insurmountable barrier to its nuclear power and explosion program. The expected dividends, including the spin-off for electronics, engineering, metallurgy, and related technologies, are regarded as well worth the investment.[9]

5. U.S. Central Intelligence Agency, *National Basic Intelligence Factbook, July 1977* (Library of Congress, 1977).

6. International Institute for Strategic Studies, *The Military Balance: 1977–1978* (London: IISS, 1977), p. 58.

7. Speech, May 25, 1974, reported in *Indian and Foreign Review*, vol. 11 (June 15, 1974), p. 5.

8. D. R. Mankekar, "Nuclear Test: A Pre-emptive Verdict," *Indian and Foreign Review*, vol. 11 (June 15, 1974), p. 13.

9. K. Subrahmanyam, "Defense Preparations in India and China," *Bulletin of the Atomic Scientists*, vol. 24 (May 1968), p. 33.

Indian spokesmen have been reticent about the security aspects of nuclear development. Several months after the explosion, however, India's UN ambassador, Rikhi Jaipal, stated that Indian officials were well aware that the peaceful nuclear explosions would have a deterrent effect on potential adversaries. India's consistent objections to, and refusal to sign, the nonproliferation treaty reflect its intention to keep open the nuclear arms option. India's security concerns then and now focus on Pakistan and China, each of which places a constraint on Indian political influence in the region. Indian conventional military superiority over Pakistan was convincingly demonstrated in the Bangladesh war of 1971, but relations between the two have shown uneasy improvement since the signing of the Simla agreement on July 3, 1972, which pledged each side to the peaceful resolution of disputes.

The decision to conduct a nuclear explosion was undoubtedly rooted in several basic motives—to press the economic benefits of nuclear energy, to secure and advance India's geopolitical position in Asia, and to bolster India's morale at home and prestige abroad.

India's Technical Foundation

India's nuclear program, begun shortly after the country became independent in 1947, is rooted in strong technical competence. On August 15, 1948, India established an Atomic Energy Commission under the direct supervision of Prime Minister Jawaharlal Nehru. On December 24, 1952, he announced a four-year program to build an Indian research reactor. By 1954, the commission was replaced by the larger Department of Atomic Energy, still under the prime minister. As in most countries, basic nuclear policy decisions were confined to a small circle. This severely limited public debate on the issues, but public opinion, such as it was, was predominantly favorable to the exploitation of the country's nuclear potential.

In the early years, questions about the military application of atomic energy were overshadowed by the problems of economic development. Since India did not confront a nuclear adversary, the focus was on nuclear power. Dr. Homi J. Bhabha, first chairman of the Atomic Energy Commission, believed that "for the full industrialization of the underdeveloped countries and for the continuance of our civilization and its further development, atomic energy is not merely an aid—it is an absolute necessity."[10] India's (and Asia's) first nuclear research reactor began operation in August 1956.[11] This enriched-uranium reactor had a thermal capacity of one megawatt. By 1962, India had built three research reactors, a fuel fabrication plant, a heavy-water plant, and a supporting infrastructure. Some observers suggested that India would be able to produce a nuclear explosion within one or two years.[12] These predictions proved premature, but India did not neglect the political uses and implications of its nuclear potential. Agreements providing for joint nuclear research and exchange with Hungary (1961) and Egypt (1962) can be viewed as an exercise in atomic diplomacy aimed at increasing Indian prestige and indirectly reinforcing India's declaratory policy of nonalignment.

On August 8, 1963, the United States agreed to help build India's first atomic power plant, supply the uranium fuel, and provide a supporting loan of $80 million.[13] The twin reactor, with an output of 380 megawatts, was built near Tarapur in western India. Canada, on November 15, 1963, agreed to help build a second atomic power plant. Unlike the reactors at Tarapur, which were based on a light-water design and required enriched uranium provided under U.S. safeguards, the Canadian plant was to be based on a heavy-water, natural-uranium design. Natural uranium is much easier to obtain than enriched uranium, and the Indians had had experience in working with the Canadian natural-uranium concept. Under an accord of April 28, 1956, the Canadians had helped in the construction of a forty-megawatt CIRUS research reactor; that reactor eighteen years later supplied the plutonium for India's first nuclear test.

India's Relations with China and Russia

Since 1949 India and the People's Republic of China have vied for leadership in Asia and beyond. This competition between Indian "democracy" and Chinese "communism" provided a backdrop for the bor-

---

10. *Keesing's Contemporary Archives,* vol. 10 (August 6–13, 1955), p. 14360.

11. China's first experimental reactor did not become operational until 1958.

12. Leonard Beaton and John Maddox, *The Spread of Nuclear Weapons* (Praeger, 1962), p. 141. For an American view, see "Secretary Rusk's News Conference of October 8," U.S. *Department of State Bulletin,* October 26, 1964, p. 579.

13. Agreement Concerning Civil Uses of Atomic Energy, 14 U.S.T. 1484.

der clashes of 1962. Recognizing China's avowed nuclear ambitions, India signed the test-ban treaty in August 1963 with the hope that its nuclear abstinence would be an example for China.[14] The Chinese, however, denounced the test ban as a "dirty fraud" aimed at preserving the nuclear monopoly of Great Britain, the Soviet Union, and the United States. As early as 1958, China's relations with the Soviet Union had begun to deteriorate. India was concerned about the potential for U.S. or Soviet involvement in the subcontinent, but its primary focus was on the Chinese problem. Sino-Indian hostility erupted with the border clashes of 1962.

China's detonation of an atomic device on October 16, 1964, was accompanied by its proclamation of peaceful intent. India nevertheless saw the Chinese explosion as a threat. Nuclear arms thus became for the first time an issue of public discussion in India. During parliamentary debate on the issue, three options were considered.

Prime Minister Lal Bahadur Shastri opposed the view that India should develop its own nuclear weapons. He argued that atomic arms were extremely costly, they would antagonize Pakistan, and they would provide little security against China unless there were a sizable arsenal supported by a sophisticated delivery system capable of hitting Chinese targets fifteen hundred miles from Indian forward bases.[15] Further, Mr. Shastri said the Chinese threat was only potential since China had exploded only one bomb.[16] The leader of the right-wing Swatantra party advocated abandoning India's nonalignment policy and seeking an explicit nuclear guarantee from the United States. Many Indians, however, felt that an explicit pledge was unnecessary because they assumed that India was the beneficiary of a de facto, if ambiguous, U.S. guarantee stemming from American hostility toward China. This argument may have been reinforced by the fact that the United States had given military and diplomatic support to India during the 1962 border conflict. Further, the nature of the Chinese threat was so uncertain that the abandonment of nonalignment was regarded as too drastic a measure.

14. As early as 1958, China had proclaimed its ambition to become a nuclear weapons power. See *New York Times*, October 17, 1964. By 1959 the Soviet Union was reluctant to continue aid for China's nuclear program and began to withhold assistance. See also Leo Yueh-yun Liu, *China as a Nuclear Power in World Politics* (New York: Taplinger; London: Macmillan, 1972), p. 34.

15. D. Som Dutt, *India and the Bomb*, Adelphi Paper 30 (London: International Institute for Strategic Studies, 1966), p. 6.

16. *Keesing's Contemporary Archives*, vol. 15 (February 6–13, 1965), p. 20567.

(Prime Minister Shastri informally explored the idea of a guarantee from the Soviet Union which on September 2, 1964, in *Pravda,* accused China of "an openly expansionist program with far reaching pretensions."[17] Indira Gandhi, minister of information and broadcasting, was sent to Moscow in November 1964 to exchange views on the Chinese threat.) The policy that the majority National Congress party endorsed, on January 10, 1965, was to keep open the nuclear arms option by continuing "peaceful" nuclear research while exploiting diplomatically American and Soviet hostility toward China.

The Indo-Pakistani war of 1965 led to greater Soviet influence in India. Following local military engagements in the Rann of Kutch during April and May, India and Pakistan resumed hostilities on a broader scale and by early September the fighting involved air, naval, and land forces on both sides. On September 5, Indian forces invaded Pakistan in the Punjab region south of Kashmir. Two days later the United States suspended all military aid to the belligerents.[18] At first, this move had the ostensible effect of hurting Pakistan more than India since the United States was Pakistan's main weapons supplier. The Soviet Union, India's chief supplier, continued to provide military equipment throughout the conflict. The U.S. suspension of arms aid had the effect of encouraging Soviet influence in India which, in turn, induced China to come to the assistance of Pakistan. On September 19, Soviet Premier Aleksei Kosygin offered to mediate between India and Pakistan.[19] Three days later Prime Minister Shastri, after rejecting American, Canadian, and British offers to mediate, accepted the Soviet offer.[20] Pakistani President Mohammad Ayub Khan, perhaps fearing China's friendly embrace and U.S. displeasure, agreed to Soviet mediation in November.[21]

India thus began to rely increasingly on Soviet assistance which the Russians were willing to provide as long as it did not encourage Pakistan to rely more heavily on China. The meeting in Tashkent in January 1966 among India, Pakistan, and the Soviet Union produced an agreement that was hailed as a diplomatic triumph for the Russians. The agreement provided for the cessation of hostilities and the reestablishment of peaceful intercourse between India and Pakistan but did little to recon-

17. *New York Times,* September 2, 1964.
18. Max Frankel, *New York Times,* September 8, 1965.
19. *New York Times* (Paris; international ed.), September 20, 1965.
20. Ibid., September 23, 1965.
21. *New York Times,* November 17, 1965.

cile their basic political differences.[22] Pakistan was further isolated from the United States and suffered a setback to its territorial claims in Kashmir. India's prewar status was restored, but only because of Soviet intervention.

Indira Gandhi became prime minister on January 24, 1966, after Mr. Shastri's sudden death. The recognition of India's growing dependence on the Soviet Union forced her to reassert the policy of nonalignment which meant playing the United States off against the Soviet Union and, to a lesser extent, each of the superpowers against China. China's first hydrogen bomb explosion on July 1, 1967, deepened India's distrust of China and strengthened pressure in parliament for building an Indian bomb. One observer noted that

all the pressures are driving [India] towards a new and distinctly nationalistic foreign policy. Her government's apparent inability to solve India's internal problems has intensified the sense of frustration at certain levels of [the National Congress party] with the immobilism of India's foreign policy and the country's diminished status in the world. The temptation to take a course of action which will not only raise India's prestige, but also divert attention from the country's real problems—both internal and external—is increasing, and the situation may not be far distant when Mrs. Gandhi will have to succumb or be swept aside.[23]

India's Nuclear Intentions

The signing of the nonproliferation treaty by the superpowers on July 2, 1968, forced Mrs. Gandhi to explain India's refusal to join in. She argued that the treaty preserved the monopoly of the nuclear weapons powers and relegated other countries to second-class status. It discriminated against nonnuclear states and denied them the benefits of peaceful nuclear technology. It did nothing, she held, to further the cause of international disarmament or inhibit vertical proliferation by the big nuclear weapons powers, and it was ineffective so long as China and France remained nonparties.[24] Though there is some validity to these

22. Tashkent Declaration, 560 U.N.T.S. 39.
23. Michael Edwardes, "India, Pakistan, and Nuclear Weapons," *International Affairs* (London), vol. 43 (October 1967), p. 658.
24. See K. Subrahmanyam, "Indian Attitudes Toward the NPT," in Stockholm International Peace Research Institute, *Nuclear Proliferation Problems* (Stockholm: Almqvist and Wiksell; Cambridge: MIT Press, 1974), pp. 259–70.

arguments, Mrs. Gandhi's view can be seen in part as a rationalization for keeping open the nuclear option. She wanted to preserve Indian neutrality and independence and to strengthen Indian security in face of the growing Chinese threat. She accelerated nuclear research and by 1970 government spokesmen were openly discussing the probability of conducting underground nuclear tests while denying any military intent.

Had India decided to explode a nuclear device in 1970, the plutonium could have come either from the CIRUS research reactor built in the 1950s with Canadian help, or from the U.S.-assisted Tarapur power plant which began operation in February 1969. The latter was under strict U.S.-Indian safeguards[25] and subsequently was placed under IAEA inspection. The CIRUS reactor was safeguarded by a 1956 Canadian-Indian agreement which stipulated that it was to be used for peaceful research. Article XI of the agreement stated:

It is the intention of both Governments that the fuel elements for the initial fuel charge and for the continuing requirements of the Reactor will be supplied from Canada save to the extent that India provides them from sources within India. Arrangements for the provision of the fuel elements to India from Canada will be agreed upon by the two Governments before the Reactor is ready to operate; if an international agency acceptable to both Governments has come into being or is in prospect at that time, the terms of such agreement will be in keeping with the principles of that agency.[26]

However, when the International Atomic Energy Agency came into operation, "India resolutely resisted the extension of the Agency's controls to the provision by Canada of the (CIRUS) fuel elements. Meanwhile, Article XI gave India all the choices necessary for independent development. . . . The diplomats were left to agonize over the lack of safeguards while the reactor took shape."[27]

The Indo-Canadian accord stated that Canadian fuel should not be processed to make an explosive device, but it did not mention the possibility of using fuel manufactured by India. The Indians began using their own fuel elements in October 1963. In June 1964 they completed construction of a plutonium separation plant specifically designed to process the spent fuel from the CIRUS reactor. In light of these facts,

25. Agreement Concerning Civil Uses of Atomic Energy, 14 U.S.T. 1484.

26. Agreement Regarding a Nuclear Reactor Project, April 28, 1956, quoted in Barrie Morrison and Donald M. Page, "India's Option: The Nuclear Route to Achieve Goal as a World Power," in *International Perspectives* (Canada), July–August 1974, p. 25.

27. Ibid.

Canadian Prime Minister Pierre Elliot Trudeau's visit to India in January 1971 was significant. Mr. Trudeau knew of official Indian statements on peaceful nuclear explosions and that the CIRUS reactor was the most likely source of plutonium, and he personally urged Prime Minister Gandhi to sign the nonproliferation treaty as evidence of her intention to honor the safeguards agreement. She rejected his suggestion and in July 1971 told parliament that India would conduct peaceful nuclear explosions. By the end of 1972, preparations for a nuclear test were completed at the Rajasthan site.[28] The decision to conduct the test must have been taken in late 1970 or early 1971.[29]

Hostilities between India and Pakistan erupted again in December 1971 during the civil war in East Pakistan where India provided military support for the insurgents. The war resulted in the creation of Bangladesh and established Indian military superiority and political hegemony on the subcontinent and thus had an impact on the Indian nuclear debate. India's strategic position was improved by the neutralization of East Pakistan. This had the double effect of releasing military resources for defense against China and increasing the emphasis on high-technology weapons. The Ministry of Defense report for 1971–72 noted that "the weapons systems we have already acquired and developed are sufficiently sophisticated to meet immediate threats; the trend, however, is towards further sophistication, greater complexity, higher costs. . . . Our approach to Defense Production will have to be increasingly technology-oriented rather than product oriented. Special attention will need to be paid to build up capabilities to design and upgrade the variety of systems on which defense effort must be based."[30]

The Bangladesh war also had an impact on India's relations with the great powers. The United States' disapproval of India's military role, demonstrated by the dispatch of a naval task force into the Bay of Bengal, angered the Indians. Their unhappiness was further exacerbated by a growing Sino-American détente. The subcontinent, one

28. M. L. Sondhi, "India and Nuclear China," *Pacific Community* (Tokyo), vol. 4 (January 1973), p. 274.

29. For a similar opinion, see Wayne A. Wilcox, "Indian Security Environments, 1971–1975: China and Pakistan," in Stanley J. Heginbotham, ed., *India and Japan: The Emerging Balance of Power in Asia and Opportunities for Arms Control, 1970–1975*, India Country Reports ACDA/IR-170 (Columbia University, Southern Asian Institute/East Asian Institute, 1971), vol. 3, p. 175.

30. Annual report of the Indian Ministry of Defense, 1971–1972, quoted in Sondhi, "India and Nuclear China," p. 265.

Indian scholar noted, "remains an area where the Chinese and the Americans will continue to supplement each other's efforts to limit Soviet influence as well as Indian power. This is also the area where the convergence of their interests is most apparent and where it is the easiest for them to maintain parallel policies."[31] And another scholar, remarking on "a rare event in the history of the last twenty-two years," noted that "the United States and the People's Republic of China vigorously supported each other and jointly used the 'Uniting for Peace' procedure in the United Nations for putting pressure on India."[32]

With declining U.S. influence in the subcontinent, India became increasingly dependent on the Soviet Union, a relationship that was formalized in the August 9, 1971, treaty of peace, friendship, and cooperation. Though the commitment was not binding, each country pledged to refrain from joining any military alliance directed against the other and to consult in the event of attack on either. Each saw the pact as a political counter to China and the emerging Sino-American détente. India also regarded the treaty as supporting its posture of nonalignment, because it did not clearly imply a Soviet nuclear guarantee for India in the event of a Chinese nuclear attack.[33]

The 1971 war established India as the dominant regional power, but it remained a secondary actor in the larger arena of international politics and was so regarded by the superpowers and China. The most effective way for India to assert its influence and engender wider respect, as one Indian politician pointed out in 1973, was to demonstrate a nuclear capability:

The strongest case for going nuclear now rests not on "domestic political reasons" as some Western commentators were wont to point out, but on the foreign policy consideration that only a nuclear India can extract political, military and economic advantages from the two Super-powers. The essential line of development of Indian thinking is now to downgrade in the policy area the leverage of the Super-powers in the form of withdrawal of economic aid or outright military threats.[34]

The May 1974 test was both an example of Indian scientific prowess and an expression of the belief that advanced technology—in particular,

31. Sisir Gupta, "Sino-U.S. Detente and India," *India Quarterly*, vol. 27 (July–September 1971), p. 183.

32. K. Subrahmanyam, "External Influences and Pressures," *India Quarterly*, vol. 28 (April–June 1972), p. 132.

33. For an Indian analysis, see J. D. Sethi, "Indo-Soviet Treaty and Nonalignment," *India Quarterly*, vol. 27 (October–December 1971), pp. 327–36.

34. Sondhi, "India and Nuclear China," p. 276.

nuclear technology—would provide a large part of the answer to Indian underdevelopment. It was also a symbol of India's bid for equality with the more advanced industrial states.

Reaction to the 1974 Test

The rapid dissipation of the initial domestic enthusiasm following the May test suggests that confidence, optimism, and pride are likely to be short-lived in the face of chronic economic and social ills and that the euphoria occasioned by a nuclear demonstration is difficult to translate into lasting political dividends. India's nuclear capability, nevertheless, became a new factor in international politics. Its advocates asserted that India should be looked on as the first of a new breed of proliferators— nuclear, but nonmilitary "peaceful technology proliferators."[35] Mrs. Gandhi's public statements appeared to support this view.

The official and press reaction from abroad was generally critical, but it varied in tone. Though most comments acknowledged India's declaration of peaceful intent, few accepted it at face value. In the United States the initial reaction was a low-keyed State Department protest "against nuclear proliferation."[36] In October 1974 in New Delhi, Secretary Kissinger said: "We take seriously India's affirmation that it has no intention to develop nuclear weapons."[37] The United States was embarrassed because the explosion had apparently taken it by surprise and, more important, because of prior nuclear assistance to India. Indian officials denied that U.S. materials were used in the test, but neither Congress nor the administration was fully convinced.

The United States took three relatively mild punitive actions against India. On August 14, 1974, an amendment to the International Development Association Act directed the American representative on the IDA

35. Ashok Kapur, "India's Nuclear Presence," *World Today* (London), vol. 30 (November 1974), p. 464. See also S. P. Seth, "India's Atomic Profile," *Pacific Community* (Tokyo), vol. 6 (January 1975), pp. 272–82; and R. V. R. Chandrasekhara Rao, "Proliferation and the Indian Test: A View from India," *Survival* (London), vol. 16 (September–October 1974), pp. 210–13. For a contrasting view which sees the Indian test as being motivated by considerations of realpolitik, see Wing Commander Maharaj K. Chopra, "India's Nuclear Path in the 1970's," *Military Review*, vol. 54 (October 1974), pp. 38–46.

36. *New York Times*, May 19, 1974.

37. *Department of State Bulletin*, November 25, 1974, p. 743.

board "to vote against any loan for the benefit of any country which develops any nuclear explosive device, unless the country is or becomes" a party to the nonproliferation treaty.[38] Immediately after the May 1974 test, the Atomic Energy Commission had suspended all new licenses for the shipment of enriched uranium to India until it could give satisfactory assurances that U.S. fuel had not been used in the explosion and would not be diverted for future explosions.[39] A shipment approved two days before the test was allowed to go forward on June 19, 1974. The suspension was lifted on September 16 of the same year. That December the Senate voted to cut back the proposed $75.6 million bilateral aid figure for India to $50 million.[40] Since then each license application for enriched uranium has been carefully scrutinized by the Nuclear Regulatory Commission and the State Department to assure that no uranium would be reprocessed for military purposes.[41] These measures are also designed to encourage India to accept IAEA safeguards on indigenous nuclear facilities. They have had little practical effect on the Indian nuclear program, though they may have delayed a second nuclear explosion.

Canada was in a more embarrassing and difficult position than the United States because of its larger role in Indian nuclear development. Both the Canadian government and the press insisted that India had violated the terms of the Canadian aid. On May 18, 1974, Mitchell Sharp, secretary of external affairs, said his government saw no distinction between the development of nuclear explosions for so-called peaceful purposes and explosions for military purposes. On May 22, Canada suspended all nuclear aid to India;[42] two years later, it announced it would not resume such assistance because India would not agree to adequate safeguards.[43] Canadian press criticism was directed against both India and the Canadian government. An editorial in the *Toronto Star* was typical: "There was a good deal of hypocrisy in Ottawa's reactions of outrage at news of the Indian explosion, since there was ample warn-

38. 88 Stat. 445.

39. John W. Finney, *New York Times*, September 8, 1974.

40. See *Foreign Assistance Act of 1974*, H. Rept. 93-1471, 93 Cong. 2 sess. (Government Printing Office, 1974), p. 45.

41. In June 1977 the NRC approved the export of 27,000 pounds of uranium to fuel India's Tarapur atomic power station, warning that further shipments would be stopped if India exploded another nuclear device. *Washington Post*, June 30, 1977.

42. "Canada's Position," *International Perspectives* (Canada), July–August 1974, p. 24.

43. *Washington Post*, May 19, 1976.

ing years ago of what might be coming. India's political position—its rivalry with China, a nuclear power, rather than its long quarrel with Pakistan—also indicated that one day the country would develop atomic weapons."[44]

In Moscow, reaction to the explosion was more like that of an ally of India than a sponsor of the nonproliferation treaty. Paraphrasing the statement of India's Department of Atomic Energy, Tass on May 18, 1974, announced that India had conducted "a peaceful explosion" and had "reaffirmed its strong opposition to the use of nuclear explosions for military purposes."[45] The Soviet position was dictated, in part, by the Soviet Union's continuing insistence that "peaceful explosions" have potential benefits in mining and civil excavations. It also reflected its tensions with China. Certainly Indian nuclear ambitions served to divert some Chinese attention from the Sino-Soviet frontier and in the long run could constitute a modest counterpoise to Chinese nuclear strength. In late 1976 the Soviet Union agreed to sell two hundred tons of heavy water to India since Canada had cut off its supply.[46]

Chinese response to the explosion was muted and reflected China's ties with Pakistan. The May 31 *Peking Review* quoted Pakistani Prime Minister Zulfikar Ali Bhutto's statement that Pakistan "will never surrender our rights or claims because of India's nuclear status." Shortly thereafter it carried an announcement that "the Chinese Government and people firmly support Pakistan and other countries in their just struggle to safeguard national independence and state sovereignty and oppose aggression and intervention from outside, including nuclear blackmail and threat."[47]

India's Nuclear Future

Four years after India had exploded its first nuclear device, it was still not clear to outsiders, and probably not to India's government itself,

44. *Toronto Star*, June 3, 1974.

45. See *USSR and Third World*, vol. 4 (April 22–June 9, 1974), p. 199. *Pravda*, August 7, 1974, carried a long article by I. Shchedrov, suggesting that the USSR would continue to provide assistance to India's peaceful nuclear efforts, but making no mention of nuclear explosions.

46. Don Oberdorfer, *Washington Post*, December 8, 1976; and Thomas O'Toole, ibid., December 12, 1976.

47. *Peking Review*, vol. 17 (May 31, 1974), p. 28; and "A Just Demand," *Renmin Ribao*, June 28, 1974, translated in *Peking Review*, vol. 17 (July 5, 1974), p. 26.

precisely what India's future nuclear policies would be. In early 1976, Prime Minister Gandhi said India would not give up nuclear testing and that India was no "less capable of responsibility" than other states that used nuclear technology to "attain and augment their power and dominance."[48] In January 1978, Prime Minister Desai, reiterating India's objection to international inspection of its indigenous nuclear installations, said, "We do not want to have any atomic weapons under any conditions, and do not want even to have explosions of any kind."[49] India is now in a position to limit its nuclear development to energy projects for civil purposes only, to keep open the nuclear weapons option, or to move rapidly to develop nuclear arms. Each possible course of action has its proponents and opponents within the small circle of advisers around the prime minister.

According to official declarations, the 1974 explosion was conducted and future nuclear developments will be undertaken only for generating electricity and for mining and earth-moving projects. Though few observers take these statements at face value, it is possible that the recognition of certain realities will force India to observe its vow of nuclear arms abstinence. The economic costs of translating a fifteen-kiloton explosion into a militarily significant nuclear force with a supporting delivery system, especially missiles able to reach targets in China, are great. As these costs become more widely known, opposition may develop within the military establishment, rooted in the fear that investment in nuclear arms may be made at the expense of conventional strength. Given India's massive domestic needs, it may become increasingly difficult for the government to justify a costly nuclear program.

A precise calculation of the political costs and benefits of the first Indian explosion is not possible. But the negative response from neighboring countries as well as from the governments and press of the United States, Canada, and a score of other states could prompt Indian politicians to conclude that the political cost may outweigh the benefits of increased attention and prestige from abroad and increased political support at home—both wasting assets. Already, Canada's suspension of assistance has hurt India's nuclear power program. The short-lived U.S. suspension of nuclear aid and subsequent delays were little more than a slap on the wrist. But how these two suppliers of nuclear technology and fuel would react to a second "peaceful explosion," or, more important,

48. *Washington Star*, January 15, 1976.
49. William Borders, *New York Times*, January 13, 1978.

to evidence that India had embarked on a bomb-building program is unknown.

For a variety of reasons India may decide to concentrate its resources on portions of the ambitious three-stage nuclear power program its atomic energy agency proposed in 1970. It suggested that India build seven uranium-fueled heavy-water reactors by 1980, several fast-breeder reactors fueled with plutonium produced in the first stage, and other fast-breeder reactors fueled with U-233 obtained from thorium (India's thorium reserves are the largest in the world). A modified program along these lines could be pursued along with a nuclear arms effort, but the latter would slow down the former unless compensatory resources were made available. Some experts believe that India already has an allocation problem and that it would "be foolhardy for the Indian government to divert its scarce plutonium stocks to support a weapons program at the cost of a carefully planned and nurtured nuclear development program."[50]

If India decided to forgo nuclear arms and to confine its effort to civil pursuits, it would have a problem convincing the world of this decision. Its persuasiveness would be enhanced if it were willing to submit all its nuclear facilities and processes to IAEA safeguards and inspections, become a party to the nonproliferation treaty, enter into a nuclear non-aggression treaty with Pakistan or China, and declare its interest in joining other states in the region in creating a nuclear-free zone. India has not indicated a willingness to undertake any of these steps. On the contrary, the government has consistently refused to open certain of its nuclear facilities to IAEA inspection, though several of its installations are under IAEA safeguards. It has denounced the nonproliferation treaty as an instrument of superpower domination. It has virtually torpedoed a nuclear-free zone in South Asia (proposed by Pakistan) by persuading the UN General Assembly's Political and Security Committee to specify that it could be established only with the consent of all directly concerned countries (which means that any of them could veto the plan). In sum, the evidence suggests that India may be contemplating a military application of nuclear energy.

Virtually all indicators suggest it has embarked on a policy of keeping the nuclear arms option open. This course provides for maximum flexibility, the opportunity to shift to civil or to military development at any point with a minimum loss of time or resources. It also embraces

50. Seth, "India's Atomic Profile," p. 277.

a good deal of ambiguity, both necessary and calculated. It is very difficult for a government in India's position to make an almost irreversible
decision on such a vital issue when the cost-benefit calculus is clouded
by indeterminate political and military factors. This uncertainty is mixed
with an intentional ambiguity designed to keep foes and potential foes
off balance. But ambiguity has its limits, for it contains an element of
bluff which is always dangerous. Politically the costs of keeping the
option open are probably less than those of pursuing a convincing policy
of nuclear chastity.

The resource and manpower costs of keeping the nuclear option
open are greater than those of pursuing a purely nonmilitary alternative. Research, development, and some actual construction must go forward. India must stockpile plutonium, conduct further nuclear explosions, and perhaps build a uranium enrichment plant. It must also work
on airborne and missile delivery systems. A missile development program
is under way, though reportedly behind schedule. Expenditures on the
program "would probably have to be increased considerably (approximately ten-fold) if it were to include the development of a strategic
rocket system. Such a system, in other words, is unlikely to be a reality
during the 1980s."[51] India has, however, built a satellite, which the
Soviet Union launched into earth orbit on April 19, 1975, making India
the eleventh country to orbit one. This satellite reportedly cost more
than $6 million and took twenty-six months to produce. Prime Minister
Gandhi hailed the successful launch and orbit of the eight-hundred-
pound craft as "an important event in India's efforts to harness the
benefits of science."[52]

India thus appears to be technically capable of building nuclear arms
and supporting delivery systems. It is unlikely to do so before 1985. The
most compelling barrier to its doing so is sheer cost. It would require a
drastic reallocation of scarce resources and seriously distort existing development efforts. This could be politically disastrous. If the first explosion boosted Indian morale and pride, a full-scale arms program could
have opposite consequences.

The internal turbulence and dissent that caused the government to
move in a sharply authoritarian direction in 1975 were not fully stilled by

51. John Maddox, *Prospects for Nuclear Proliferation*, Adelphi Paper 113 (London: International Institute for Strategic Studies, 1975), p. 17. See also Seth,
"India's Atomic Profile," pp. 275–76.
52. Bernard Weinraub, *New York Times*, April 20, 1975.

the March 1977 national election. Not only does India seem likely to be faced with serious authority and consensus problems for the indefinite future, but its new prime minister, Morarji Desai, has said that his government does "not believe in atomic weapons at all."[53]

On a wholly practical level, India simply may not have enough plutonium to support a major weapons program. According to one scholar, its unsafeguarded plutonium stockpile totals more than four hundred and forty pounds.[54] But another believes it is only about half that amount, enough for ten Hiroshima-sized bombs, and that plutonium is being produced at a rate sufficient to make only one or two bombs a year.[55] Even a crash program utilizing maximum resources could not yield a militarily significant force, with a missile delivery system capable of reaching a dozen Chinese cities, for a decade or more—a period in which China could develop a deterrent counterforce. It would be difficult on military grounds to justify such a force for defense against Pakistan. Hence, the national security arguments for a full-fledged program do not appear compelling.

On the diplomatic front, such a program would be bound to cause friction with friendly states and could provoke serious punitive action by one or more of the major nuclear powers. India's nuclear arms intention would be registered before the world by further tests. Some of its tests might be conducted in the atmosphere in violation of the limited test-ban treaty to which India is a party (India's first test was conducted under ground). To its neighbors a nuclear arms program would signal a determined effort by India to exercise unquestioned hegemony over South Asia and perhaps a wider area. It could provoke the active hostility of China, the country India fears most, and stimulate rival regional powers, notably Iran, to follow India's example. The most immediate and dramatic impact would be on Pakistan which already has suffered the sting of India's military might. Consequently, India is unlikely to embark on a crash program when it can follow the more prudent and less costly path of keeping open the nuclear arms option.

No plausible nuclear force of India should alarm the United States unless it provokes destabilizing behavior by Pakistan or Iran. Keeping the nuclear option open will have a small and indeterminate impact on regional stability. The same can be said for the development of a token

53. *Washington Post,* March 25, 1977.
54. Seth, "India's Atomic Profile," p. 277.
55. Maddox, *Prospects for Nuclear Proliferation,* pp. 15–16.

force. Only a genuine, though necessarily small, deterrent force relevant to China could have a significant effect on superpower interests. It is possible that both the United States and the Soviet Union, though their interests are not identical, could profit from such a development, each looking on the Indian force as a counterpoise to China. This would change if there were a limited or comprehensive Sino-Soviet accommodation before 2000.

The impact of an Indian force on regional stability could go either way. Each step on the nuclear path would presumably strengthen India's hand, but if that hand proved unsteady, overbearing, or reckless, it could provoke nuclear rivalry or war. If India succeeded in achieving temporary hegemony, it probably would not last if forces within and beyond India moved against the government. India's nuclear capability would be limited largely to its immediate neighbors. It would have little effect on the superpower strategic system because neither the United States nor the Soviet Union has a vital interest in the subcontinent, except possibly in the highly unlikely event of Chinese nuclear intervention. In sum, a creeping nuclear capability in India would not pose an alarming threat either to regional peace or to other U.S. interests, unless it provoked a confrontation with Pakistan, Iran, or China, a possibility that does not appear likely.

Pakistan's Response to India's Explosion

Pakistan has been more directly and more adversely affected by India's nuclear test than any other state. Even though it has only a token nuclear capability, India threatens to relegate Pakistan to permanent political inferiority, to deny Pakistan's aspirations in Kashmir and Jammu, and indeed to challenge Pakistan's very existence. The long-range military implications of the test aside, it was an especially severe blow to Pakistan, coming as it did, on the heels of the India-assisted secession of East Pakistan.

In its weakened condition, Pakistan cannot respond effectively to India's nuclear challenge on the nuclear level. Pakistan has only a modest civil nuclear capability. Its small research effort is centered in the Pakistan Institute of Nuclear Science and Technology located at Nilore near Islamabad and the Atomic Energy Center at Lahore. The institute has a 5-megawatt, enriched-uranium reactor built with U.S. cooperation.

It has been in operation, under IAEA safeguards, since 1965. The Lahore center has no reactors and is devoted primarily to medical and agricultural research. Pakistan also has a natural-uranium power reactor in Karachi, built with Canadian assistance and capable of generating 137 megawatts of electricity. It has been in operation since 1971 and is also safeguarded by IAEA. These modest facilities and the scarcity of highly trained manpower and of industrial resources suggest that Pakistan, unless it has substantial assistance, is unlikely to develop even a token nuclear arms force before 1985.

Like India, Pakistan is not a party to the nonproliferation treaty. But unlike India, Pakistan has submitted all of its limited nuclear facilities to IAEA safeguards and has taken some initiatives to curb nuclear arms development in the region. Pakistan disclaims any intention of building nuclear weapons and makes no secret of its anxiety about India. In response to the Indian test, it embarked on a four-pronged strategy designed to enhance its own power relative to the growing military strength of its historic adversary. It began seeking security guarantees from the great powers and bolstering its own conventional military strength, attempted to neutralize India's nuclear arms development, and set out to develop a nuclear arms option of its own. The various elements of this strategy, which are not wholly consistent with one another, display an ambiguity that is characteristic of the nuclear policy of many countries.

Exploiting the immediate and largely negative world reaction to the Indian test, Prime Minister Bhutto on May 19, 1974, called for "a nuclear umbrella of all five Great Powers, or failing that," a nuclear assurance from "at least one of them" as the "irreducible minimum protection" for a state like Pakistan "against nuclear threat or blackmail."[56] He was bidding in particular for help from the United States or China. Actually, under the 1959 U.S. mutual defense agreement, a nuclear attack on Pakistan could be met by a U.S. nuclear response. The agreement provides that in case of aggression against Pakistan, the United States "will take such appropriate action, including the use of armed forces, as may be mutually agreed upon."[57] The "appropriate action" could theoretically be nuclear, though this is highly unlikely. In any event, Mr. Bhutto received nothing new for his efforts.

At the May 21, 1974, meeting of the Central Treaty Organization in

56. *Pakistan Affairs,* vol. 27 (June 1, 1974), pp. 1–2.
57. Agreement of Cooperation, 10 U.S.T. 318.

Washington, Pakistan reaffirmed its ties to CENTO and condemned the Indian test. It has since then sought to strengthen relations with Iran and, to a lesser extent, with Turkey, both of which expressed serious misgivings about India's nuclear policies and made veiled threats to follow suit. Pakistan has gained little help from Turkey, but Iran has provided both military training and hardware.

Pakistan's military establishment was greatly depleted by the Bangladesh war and Prime Minister Bhutto seized on the Indian test to persuade the United States to lift the 1965 embargo against sales of major arms to Pakistan and India. In February 1975, in spite of Indian protestations, the United States agreed to suspend the arms ban and sell defensive weapons to both countries, but for cash only.[58] Pakistan began to purchase components for an air defense system, apparently designed to deter and blunt either a conventional or a nuclear attack from India. It is also purchasing other modern weapons.

Yet another of its efforts to put India on the spot and curb Indian nuclear arms developments is Pakistan's proposal for a nuclear-free zone in South Asia, put forward in the UN General Assembly on August 21, 1974. The proposal had gained the overwhelming numerical approval of the assembly's Political Committee but was nullified by the General Assembly's acceptance of the Indian stipulation that any such zone must have the prior consent of all states in the region.[59] A nuclear-free zone would impose constraints both on the states in the area and on states that export nuclear technology and materials into the area. Prime Minister Bhutto reportedly indicated Pakistan's willingness to accept international safeguards on all its future nuclear imports and facilities, provided that the country's conventional military needs were met.[60] If Iran were included in the zone, it would have to make a similar pledge, which it might do to blunt nuclear arms development in India. But Iran's position would probably also be affected by the nuclear arms situation in Israel.[61]

India's insistence on the consent of all the states of the region before a nuclear-free zone is negotiated implies that it is opposed to the idea. Such a zone would run counter to any hope of nuclear hegemony by

58. *U.S. Department of State Bulletin*, March 17, 1975, pp. 331–32.

59. December 9, 1974; see *Yearbook of the United Nations, 1974*, pp. 19–21. Also see Kathleen Teltsch, *New York Times*, October 29 and November 21, 1974.

60. *New York Times*, February 6, 1975.

61. Rouhollah K. Ramazani, "Emerging Patterns of Regional Relations in Iranian Foreign Policy," *Orbis*, vol. 18 (Winter 1975), pp. 1062–64.

India. It would also serve, however, to exclude the deployment of U.S. and Soviet nuclear arms in the Indian Ocean zone as well as improve the prospects of Chinese support for a nuclear nonaggression treaty. It is thus possible that India will eventually endorse a nuclear-free zone.

Pakistan's modest nuclear research and power program was significantly upgraded after the Indian explosion, indicating that the government wished at the very least to develop the capability for exercising the nuclear arms option sometime in the future. A study by the IAEA in 1975 reported that Pakistan had a great need for more energy and that the country would have to rely increasingly on atomic power. Though Pakistan has only one small power reactor, it has ambitious plans to build twenty-four medium-sized power plants by the end of the century, according to its UN ambassador.[62]

He stated that "fuel fabrication and reprocessing facilities and a heavy-water plant are ancillary to the plan and will be established as the program is put into effect." Earlier in 1976, Pakistan had made a deal with France to purchase a plutonium reprocessing plant and the two governments had signed a trilateral safeguards agreement with the IAEA. The agreement was necessary "since reprocessed fuel—plutonium—can be used to make bombs." The ambassador asserted that "Pakistan does *not* seek a nuclear arms race in South Asia, for such a race would not add to the security of the countries concerned . . . and would demand an enormous and wasteful diversion of resources." He went on to stress that his country had "voluntarily accepted bilateral and international safeguards designed to permit the peaceful use of atomic energy and prevent its use for military purposes," but warned that "Pakistan is not incapable of fabricating a fuel-reprocessing plant." This unusual mixture of ambiguity and candor dramatizes the dilemma not only of Pakistan, but of other countries like South Korea and Taiwan that feel endangered by hostile nuclear neighbors.

Pakistan has taken steps toward the development of a full nuclear fuel cycle. The proposed acquisition of French reprocessing technology was immediately protested by both Canada and the United States. Canada unsuccessfully sought a special pledge from Pakistan not to use the proposed French plant to process spent fuel from the Canadian-supplied reactor at Karachi, fearing this would lead to a repetition of the Indian experience with a Canadian reactor and Canada would again

62. Iqbal Akhund, *New York Times,* April 23, 1976.

be implicated in an unauthorized nuclear explosion.[63] The United States put heavy pressure on both Pakistan and France to rescind the agreement. As of early 1978 the outcome was problematical.[64]

In essence, Pakistan faces the same nuclear choices that confront India—adhering to a strictly civil use of the atom, developing the capability for nuclear arms but not making them, or mounting a major program to match the Indian explosion. Pakistan appears to be pursuing the second option, combining an ambitious power program with the acquisition of facilities for a complete fuel cycle which will enable it to reprocess plutonium essential to a nuclear test. The resources it devotes to the pursuit of a nuclear arms capability will depend on several factors, including India's nuclear program and security developments in the region generally. It is a classic case of challenge by India and response by Pakistan.

Pakistan could have a token nuclear force by 1985, though is not likely to do so much before the year 2000. Its deterrent force would be very small and would probably have less impact on regional and strategic stability than an Indian force. It would doubtless increase nuclear rivalry between the two states, but the nuclear arms would most likely be used as political rather than military weapons. If both India and Pakistan had nuclear forces and became allies—an unlikely event—Iran might decide to build a nuclear counterforce or augment an existing one. Should this happen, war could erupt, or an uneasy regional stability might develop from a mutual deterrence subsystem similar to the strategic system in the Northern Hemisphere. The ultimate effect would depend on the wisdom and policy continuity of the governments involved.

63. Robert Trumbull, *New York Times*, February 26, 1976.
64. *Washington Post*, January 12, 1978; and Richard Burt, *New York Times*, January 16, 1978.

CHAPTER THREE

Iran: Guardian of the Gulf?

The idea of Iran having nuclear weapons is ridiculous. Only a few silly fools believe it. The best guarantee that I do not want nuclear weapons is the program I have launched in conventional weapons. I want to be able to take care of anything by nonnuclear means.

SHAH MOHAMMED REZA PAHLAVI, 1975[1]

IN SEVERAL important respects Iran is attempting to play the role in the Persian Gulf that Great Britain played at the turn of the century. In 1903, Lord Curzon, viceroy of India, told the Arab leaders of the littoral states that "the peace of these waters must be maintained" by British naval might.[2] The dynamic shah of Iran has made it clear that his country has the chief responsibility for maintaining peace and security in the Gulf. Oil-rich Iran is well situated to play the role of guardian. Its expanding economy supports a population of 35 million. In 1976 the gross national product was $66 billion; from 1970 to 1976 real GNP grew at an annual rate of 13.3 percent. The per capita income was $1,900.[3] Using oil revenues, Iran is engaged in a massive effort to develop a modern industrial economy. It is also investing heavily in the modernization of its army, air force, and navy. In 1974 it launched a determined effort to develop a major nuclear power industry capable of generating thirty-four thousand megawatts of electricity by 1995.[4]

Written in early 1978, this chapter reflects assumptions widely held then about the stability of the shah's government. Its replacement by another regime is briefly considered on page 63.

1. Quoted by Joseph Kraft, *Washington Post*, April 27, 1975.
2. Quoted by Eric Pace, *New York Times*, May 7, 1975.
3. U.S. Central Intelligence Agency, *National Basic Intelligence Factbook, July 1977* (Library of Congress, 1977), pp. 93–94.
4. Anne Hessing Cahn, "Determinants of the Nuclear Option: The Case of Iran," in Onkar Marwah and Ann Schulz, eds., *Nuclear Proliferation and the Near-Nuclear Countries* (Ballinger, 1975), p. 190.

With his considerable international prestige and his detachment from the Arab-Israeli conflict, the shah has diligently pursued his objective of dominating the Gulf and perhaps a wider area by mending fences with his Arab neighbors and by decreasing his dependence on the super-powers.[5] He has settled disputes with the two chief Gulf states, Iraq and Saudi Arabia, and even in May 1975 suggested the possibility of forming a Persian Gulf collective security pact with those states and the smaller Gulf states.[6] The shah's peacekeeping strategy is calculated to neutralize Arab extremists who have become increasingly active along the Gulf. Soviet-backed insurgents have been fighting against Oman, a small state that commands the straits of Hormuz through which some twenty-three million barrels of oil a day are estimated to pass. In recent years Iran has sent as many as three thousand soldiers to support Oman's forces.[7] By early 1978 the situation had so improved that Iran's commitment had been reduced to fewer than a thousand men.

The shah's active diplomacy beyond the Gulf has extended to Egypt in the west and to Afghanistan, Pakistan, and India in the east. Iran has provided substantial economic and military assistance to Egypt, and lesser amounts to other governments. Throughout the years, Iran has sold oil and maintained other trade relations with Israel. It remains a rival of India for influence in the Indian Ocean.

Relations with the Superpowers

Both the United States and the Soviet Union are deeply involved in the Middle East and each has an interest in curtailing what it regards as the excessive influence of the other. The United States, and to a far greater extent its chief allies—Japan and the European members of the North Atlantic Treaty Organization (NATO)—are dependent on Arab and Iranian oil. The Soviet Union is the chief arms supplier of Iraq and India, and was Egypt's chief source of arms until 1976. It also provides some political and material aid to terrorist and insurgent groups

5. A useful interpretation of Iran's new "assertive" foreign policy is found in Rouhollah K. Ramazani, "Emerging Patterns of Regional Relations in Iranian Foreign Policy," *Orbis*, vol. 18 (Winter 1975), pp. 1043–69.

6. Eric Pace, *New York Times*, May 11, 1975.

7. See D. L. Price, "Oman: Insurgency and Development," *Conflict Studies* (London), no. 53 (January 1975).

in the fragmented and troubled Gulf states. The United States is the principal arms supplier of Israel, Turkey, Saudi Arabia, and Iran.

Iran shares a fourteen-hundred-mile border with the Soviet Union and in the west is bordered by Soviet-backed Iraq. Since World War II it has had good reason to fear Soviet political intentions and military moves. After the war Soviet troops stationed in northern Iran actively backed communist revolts which established pro-Soviet regimes in Azerbaijan and Kurdistan. They refused to withdraw until 1947 when pressure from the United States and the United Nations forced them out. The puppet regimes promptly collapsed. Today Iran has normal diplomatic and trade relations with the Soviet Union and has purchased some military equipment from Russia but the ever-present threat from the north remains a lively factor in the shah's security plans. In 1976 Iran broke diplomatic relations with Cuba because Premier Fidel Castro had met earlier in Moscow with the leader of Iran's outlawed Tudeh Communist party[8] (this act may have been a symbolic protest against Soviet-Cuban intervention in Angola and the Soviet naval buildup in the Indian Ocean). The shah also began moving closer to China to offset Soviet influence.

Since 1947, the United States has been Iran's chief external supporter and ally. This relationship was formalized in a bilateral agreement of cooperation signed on March 5, 1959, in which the United States and Iran declare their determination "to maintain their collective security and to resist aggression, direct or indirect."[9] The United States "regards as vital to its national interest and to world peace the preservation of the independence and integrity of Iran." "In case of aggression against Iran," the United States "will take such appropriate action, including the use of armed forces, as may be mutually agreed upon and as is envisaged in the Joint Resolution to Promote Peace and Stability in the Middle East, in order to assist the Government of Iran at its request." In the unlikely event of a nuclear attack on Iran from the Soviet Union, "appropriate action" by the United States could include a diplomatic warning, conventional military assistance, a nuclear alert, or a nuclear response. The United States also "reaffirms that it will continue to furnish the Government of Iran such military and economic assistance as may be mutually agreed upon."

Between 1964 and 1973, slightly more than $1.3 billion in U.S. mili-

8. William Branigan, *Washington Post*, April 15, 1976.
9. 327 U.N.T.S. 278–80.

tary assistance was provided to Iran as well as a little over $1 billion in economic aid. Between 1950 and 1972, close to eleven thousand Iranian military personnel had U.S. training, nine thousand of them in the United States. The Iranian armed forces have been virtually built from the ground up on the U.S. military model, though not all of their equipment is of American origin. The military training system and officer schools, like those in the United States, include a high command and joint staff college, a command and general staff college, and a military academy patterned after West Point. Almost all academy graduates assigned to the navy or air force receive advanced training in the United States. The National Defense University, established in 1968, coordinates all the high command and management schools; its purpose is to acquaint ranking officers with world and national security problems, strategic planning, and the military role in economic and industrial development.

Since Iran's oil revenues began increasing in 1969, U.S. military aid has become nominal, and Iran's defense expenditures have greatly increased. In 1969 Iran spent $768.3 million on defense and in 1973, $2.611 billion; by 1977 the military budget had reached $10.15 billion. Between 1963 and 1973 Iran's military expenditures (calculated in constant dollars) increased by an average of 22.7 percent annually compared to annual increases of 25.7 percent for Israel, 10.3 percent for Egypt, 9.0 percent for Iraq, 12.8 percent for Saudi Arabia, 6.7 percent for Pakistan, and 2.2 percent for India. (The Soviet Union's annual increases in defense spending for the period averaged 3.1 percent, and the United States' 1.0 percent.)[10]

In 1974 there was an announced 50 percent increase in Iran's military spending, a substantial portion to purchase advanced military equipment from the United States.[11] In 1972, U.S. military sales totaled $524 million; they increased to $3.9 billion in 1974 and declined to $2.6 billion in 1975. Iran had about $10 billion in U.S. arms and military services under order in 1976, but rising costs or political troubles could disrupt deliveries of the weapons.[12] As of early 1978, there were approximately twelve hundred U.S. military advisers and technicians in Iran.

10. The military spending data are from U.S. Arms Control and Disarmament Agency, *World Military Expenditures and Arms Trade, 1963–1973* (Government Printing Office, 1975); and, for 1977, from CIA, *National Basic Intelligence Factbook, July 1977*, p. 95.

11. U.S. Arms Control and Disarmament Agency, *World Military Expenditures and Arms Transfers, 1966–1975* (GPO, 1976), p. 33.

12. John W. Finney, *New York Times*, February 4, 1976.

Iran's armed forces are among the strongest and best equipped in the Third World and Iran is clearly the dominant military power in the Persian Gulf. Its forces are believed to be capable of large-scale modern military operations, though they have not been tested in war. Iran is estimated to have 1,870 tanks, including 760 British-made Chieftains. It also has about 2,000 armored personnel carriers. In comparison, Iraq has about 1,500 Soviet-made tanks of various models and 1,800 armored fighting vehicles. Iraq has 369 combat aircraft and Iran 341,[13] but Iran has a capacity to "deliver over twice the ordnance tonnage of Iraq and Saudi Arabia combined."[14] By the end of the 1970s Iran's F-4 Phantom fleet, supported by tanker aircraft, will have a maximum operating radius of 700 miles.

Iran's navy with the largest fleet of hovercraft in the world is impressive. With continuing U.S. assistance, it will be capable of playing an increasingly strong role in an expanding sphere of influence. Among the arms Iran has on order from the United States are four large destroyers and three diesel-powered submarines.[15] Its navy patrols the Persian Gulf, the Gulf of Oman, and occasionally deep into the Indian Ocean. It has protected oil tankers as far south as the tenth parallel with air and naval forces, and it has acquired port facility rights in Mauritius. When its new destroyers and submarines are delivered, its operating capacity will extend beyond the Indian Ocean. In sum, Iran soon may be the strongest regional military power in the Persian Gulf, the Middle East, and the Indian Ocean.

In pursuing his aim of decreasing political dependence on the United States, the shah is skillfully using U.S. assistance to chart a more independent course and to develop regional support for Iran's leadership. In May 1975 he said he eventually wants no permanent U.S. military installations in the Persian Gulf. This would mean the elimination of the American naval facility in Bahrain. As part of the eradication of outside forces, he expects Iraq to agree to the removal of all Soviet military bases in the Gulf area.[16]

---

13. International Institute for Strategic Studies, *The Military Balance: 1977–1978* (London: IISS, 1977), pp. 35–36.

14. Dale R. Tahtinen, *Arms in the Persian Gulf* (Washington: American Enterprise Institute for Public Policy Research, 1974), p. 2.

15. John E. Moore, ed., *Jane's Fighting Ships, 1977–78* (London: Macdonald and Jane's Publishers; New York: Franklin Watts, 1977), p. 237.

16. Gavin Young, *Washington Post*, May 3, 1975.

Policy toward Nuclear Development

In his book, *Mission for My Country*, published in 1961, the shah said Iran was dedicated to the peaceful use of the atom. "Our philosophy is well expressed by the CENTO Institute of Nuclear Science, which is devoted entirely to peaceful applications of nuclear energy."[17] Iran is a party to the limited test-ban treaty and it ratified the nonproliferation treaty in 1970.

Shortly after the Indian explosion in May 1974 the French news weekly *Les Informations* reported that the shah, when asked whether Iran would someday have nuclear weapons, had replied, "Without any doubt, and sooner than one would think."[18] The next day the Iranian embassy in Paris denied the statement, saying the press made it "out of whole cloth and without any foundation."[19] In 1975 Iran's delegate to the Geneva Disarmament Conference, Ambassador Manoutchehr Fartash, said that its adherence to the limited test-ban and nonproliferation treaties means that "Iran has renounced the nuclear weapon option."[20] He noted that Iran was greatly interested in the development of nuclear energy, but mindful of the "ominous military implications," his government had by May 1974 concluded with the IAEA the "safeguards agreement required by" the nonproliferation treaty, making "Iran's emergent peaceful nuclear projects" subject to "international control and inspection."

Ambassador Fartash said that Iran's pledge "never to accept or to manufacture nuclear weapons, or other explosive devices" was also made evident by its ratification of the 1971 treaty excluding nuclear weapons from the seabed. He recalled that the shah in 1974, before the UN General Assembly, had renewed his proposal of several years earlier to create "a denuclearized zone in the Middle East" to "prohibit the manufacture, acquisition, testing, stockpiling, and transport of nuclear arms in the region." Such a zone would require "an effective control system" and a pledge from the nuclear powers "never to use or threaten the use of nuclear weapons against" any parties to the treaty. The proposed

17. Mohammed Reza Pahlavi, *Mission for My Country* (London: Hutchinson, 1961), p. 307.
18. Ronald Koven, *Washington Post*, June 24, 1974.
19. Jonathan C. Randal, *Washington Post*, June 25, 1974.
20. Transcript, meeting of the Geneva Disarmament Conference, March 6, 1975.

treaty "would spare the world the dire possibility of a local nuclear war; it would avert the dangerous instability which the acquisition of atomic weapons by one country of the region would generate; and the countries of the zone would avoid the devouring demands made on their economies as a result of a nuclear arms race."

Although Iran has pledged "never to accept or to manufacture nuclear weapons, or other explosive devices," Mr. Fartash said his country wanted "to see progress made on the question of peaceful nuclear explosions," noting that the threshold test-ban treaty signed in Moscow in 1974 does not prohibit such explosions and that it and the nonproliferation treaty "provide for an international agreement on peaceful nuclear explosions." He added: "It is imperative that such peaceful explosions shall take place only under the most stringent international procedures along the lines of those established by the IAEA," and thus "not be detrimental to the aims of a comprehensive test-ban agreement."

In April 1975 the shah restated Iran's opposition to acquiring nuclear arms in categorical terms, but his supporting argument referred only to Iran's relation to the superpowers. "The idea of Iran having nuclear weapons is ridiculous," he said, because we could "never have enough. How many do you think it would take to count against the Russians? Or the United States? How much would they cost? Then we would have to buy all the equipment for launching missiles."[21] He added, "I want to be able to take care of anything by nonnuclear means." Two months before, however, he had said that "if small states began building" nuclear weapons, "then Iran might have to reconsider its policy."[22] In September 1975 the shah said that the real security of his country lay in the "interdependence between Iran and Europe because we can supply so much of their energy and also close relations with the Americans," adding that this was "our nonnuclear deterrent."[23]

The declarations of a government official at an international arms control forum or of a head of state in an interview with a journalist do not always indicate the underlying views, assumptions, and concerns that motivate actual policy decisions. However, it was the shah's public declaration that he would not allow nuclear missiles to be based in Iran that opened the way to the normalization of Iran's relations with the Soviet Union. There is usually some positive relation between public

21. Quoted by Joseph Kraft, *Washington Post*, April 27, 1975.
22. *Der Spiegel* (Hamburg), February 8, 1975.
23. *New York Times*, September 24, 1975.

pronouncements and private decisions, but there are great technical and political differences between permitting U.S. nuclear missiles poised against the Soviet Union to be emplaced on Iranian soil and beginning the development of Iran's capacity to manufacture a small arsenal of nuclear arms sufficient to offset an Indian capability or to serve as a trigger to involve the United States in the event of a Soviet attack. The shah may be purposely or necessarily ambiguous; the possibility that he told *Les Informations* that Iran would someday have nuclear weapons and that he may have meant it cannot be totally dismissed.

Nuclear Facilities and Plans

Compared to India, South Korea, Taiwan, Israel, Argentina, and Brazil, Iran has a nascent industrial economy and virtually no indigenous nuclear capability, though it has been taking vigorous measures to remedy the situation. The country suffers from an acute lack of skilled nuclear scientists and technicians and is heavily dependent on more developed economies—particularly those of the United States, West Germany, and France—for technology, materials, advice, and training. To fulfill the shah's ambitious nuclear goals, it is estimated that by the end of the 1980s Iran will need fifteen thousand highly skilled technicians to operate as many as twenty power reactors. In early 1976 the Iranian Atomic Energy Organization had a staff of some hundred and fifty persons with various levels of training in nuclear physics; all but 10 percent of them were foreigners. The planners in Teheran hope that by the time the complete system is in operation, 60 percent of the reactor personnel can be Iranian.[24]

The technology gap is being bridged not only by importing skilled personnel but by cooperating with nuclear firms in other countries, operating training programs abroad, and conducting on-the-job training, all paid for out of oil profits. Admiral Oscar Armando Quihillalt, who for fifteen years headed Argentina's nuclear program, was hired as a chief consultant to the Iranian Atomic Energy Organization. He was referred to Iran by the IAEA. There is no government-to-government agreement between Iran and Argentina, but as of 1975 more than half of the foreign staff at Iran's Atomic Energy Organization were from

24. George H. Quester, "The Shah and the Bomb" (1975), pp. 1–5; and Cahn, "Determinants of the Nuclear Option," pp. 190–94.

Argentina.[25] Iran also has cooperative arrangements with atomic energy agencies or firms in the United States, West Germany, France, India, Belgium, Canada, and Italy. In 1976 there were some three hundred Iranian technicians in Western Europe and the United States for advanced training, including about twenty-five at the Massachusetts Institute of Technology.

Most of Iran's external assistance has come from the United States which helped establish in 1958 the Teheran University Nuclear Center, whose director and chief reactor engineer were educated in the United States. The center's principal facility, a 5-megawatt pool-type research reactor, was built with U.S. assistance and about 80 percent of its components are American-made. The reactor is safeguarded by a trilateral U.S.-IAEA-Iran agreement which came into force on December 4, 1967, three weeks after the reactor began operating. The reactor is used primarily to produce isotopes and promote research in nuclear physics, electronics, and chemistry. In 1975 it was operated only once or twice a week because of lack of demand and of skilled personnel. The Teheran center also has a 3.5-megavolt Van de Graaff proton accelerator, a cobalt source, a mass spectrometer, and other nuclear equipment.

The Atomic Energy Organization of Iran, replacing the earlier Atomic Energy Commission, was established in 1974. It is responsible directly to the prime minister and is governed by a High Council of Atomic Energy which includes the ministers of water and power, finance, economy, agriculture and natural resources, and science and higher education, as well as the directors of planning and budget and of environmental conservation. With both development and regulatory functions, the organization represents Iran at international conferences and has the authority to determine Iran's role in joint nuclear projects. The shah, of course, makes all the major decisions.

As a member of the International Atomic Energy Agency, Iran by September 1974 had received technical assistance—equipment, fellowships, and advice—valued at slightly over $1 million. Reactor fuel (5.158 kilograms of U-235 and 0.112 kilogram of plutonium) valued at $62,000 was transferred from the United States to Iran through the IAEA. Iran's known indigenous uranium sources are not large enough to supply a nuclear power industry or a nuclear weapons program, but exploration is continuing. Uranium deposits have been found near Yazd and Anarak in east-central Iran, the latter reported to be the richer, though the

25. Quester, "The Shah and the Bomb," p. 7.

quality of the ore has not been announced. Uranium ore has also been reported at five other locations. In 1975 Iran reportedly made an agreement with South Africa to purchase fourteen thousand tons of uranium oxide worth about $700 million and to put up part of the money for a large uranium enrichment plant to be built in South Africa.[26]

In February 1974 Iran launched its effort to develop a substantial nuclear power industry by signing a $1.2 billion trade deal with France to build in Iran five atomic power plants with a total capacity of five thousand megawatts. On June 30, the U.S. Atomic Energy Commission signed contracts to provide Iran uranium-enriching services for two power reactors in the twelve-hundred-megawatt range and tentative contracts to build six power reactors. With the six U.S. reactors, five French, and two West German, Iran has on order or planned thirteen power reactors. Each of the power plants will be capable of producing about four hundred pounds of plutonium a year, which by 1984 would amount to as much as five thousand pounds annually. Half of the plutonium is scheduled for reprocessing outside the country, which means that twenty-five hundred pounds could accumulate in Iran every year. A small bomb can be made with less than twenty pounds of plutonium.

Early in 1976 the shah discussed with West German specialists a possible deal to provide uranium-enrichment and plutonium-reprocessing technology which would eventually give Iran a complete fuel cycle and thus enable it to manufacture nuclear arms without external help.[27] The United States opposes such transfers of technology and it immediately made its views known in Bonn and Teheran. A similar attempt a year earlier to persuade West Germany and Brazil to abandon a comprehensive nuclear assistance agreement had failed.[28] The U.S. pressure on Iran to abandon its plans led to protracted bilateral discussions. They included the concept of Iran's sharing the operational control of any reprocessing facility with at least one industrial country, a measure designed to insure that spent reactor fuel will not be diverted to weapons use. Since Iran is a signatory of the nonproliferation treaty, the facility would be under IAEA safeguards.

The difficulties of technology and the barriers imposed by bilateral or IAEA safeguards notwithstanding, a determined Iran probably could produce by the late 1980s several first-generation nuclear bombs. And

26. Thomas O'Toole, *Washington Post*, October 12, 1975.
27. Craig R. Whitney, *New York Times*, April 18, 1976.
28. See chapter 6.

it could with considerably less cost and trouble develop an airborne delivery system capable of reaching plausible targets in the region. By 1985 the Iranian air force is expected to have over three hundred first-rate combat aircraft, including F-4 and F-14 planes.[29] The F-4 Phantom has an operational radius of approximately four hundred and fifty miles and the F-14 has a similar capability for deep penetration. With in-flight refueling, the F-4 radius can be stretched to seven hundred miles.

Incentives to Develop a Nuclear Force

Given the shah's expansive foreign policy, there are a number of prestige, security, and political incentives for him to exercise the nuclear weapons option. He may have already made some important decisions. But there are, as his public statements attest, constraints as well as incentives in each of the important areas—defense, foreign policy, economic, and domestic considerations—that affect such decisions. For each pressure toward development of nuclear arms there are counterpressures and counterarguments.

Sharing borders with the USSR and Soviet-backed Iraq, Iran is deeply concerned with the defense of its territory. It has land links with Turkey in the west and Pakistan in the east, but neither of these friendly states would be able to provide much help if the Soviet Union engaged in direct or indirect aggression. Iran's conventional military establishment, even if greatly strengthened, could not deter a determined Soviet Union. If Iran perceived a weakening of the U.S. will, expressed in the 1959 agreement, to defend "the independence and integrity of Iran," it is possible that Iran, like France in an earlier period, would seek an independent nuclear deterrent.[30] There is, however, a significant difference between the independent deterrent of the French operating under the U.S. nuclear umbrella and a small independent nuclear force with only an implied guarantee of nuclear protection by the United States. Hence, it is difficult to conclude that a small Iranian nuclear force would have a significant deterrent effect on the Soviet Union. In fact, it might have a provocative effect, depending mainly on relations between the superpowers. The Soviet Union is not likely to attack Iran as long as

29. Barry Wheeler, comp., "World Air Forces 1977," *Flight International* (London), vol. 112 (July 2, 1977), p. 52.
30. 10 U.S.T. 314.

that government is allied with the United States, and the existence of a token Iranian force would make little difference to the Soviet Union one way or the other.

It would appear, therefore, that an Iranian force would have considerably greater impact on Iran's smaller regional neighbors, particularly rivals like India and Saudi Arabia. At some point the shah may decide to go nuclear to reinforce his claim for leadership and hegemony. This, of course, might prompt his neighbors to gang up on him in a defensive alliance, provoke them into going nuclear, or even induce a nuclear India to threaten to use its force.

If the shah really believes that Iran's ultimate security rests on Europe's need for Iranian oil and America's guarantee, his heavy reliance on conventional arms is a plausible course. A crash nuclear weapons program would divert resources from a conventional buildup, though the consequences would be less dire in oil-rich Iran which in 1977 was spending 15.38 percent of its $66 billion GNP on conventional arms than in India which was spending 4.25 percent of its $73 billion GNP (see table 1-1).

If India developed a small nuclear force and Iran followed suit, the resulting mutual deterrence subsystem, similar to the superpowers' strategic system, might enhance the security of both countries. But incipient conflict in the region could be exacerbated rather than tamed by nuclear rivalry between the two.

A small nuclear force would probably have greater consequences for Iran's foreign policy than for its security as such. There is some merit in the view that such a force would increase Iran's stature and undergird its leadership, thus enhancing regional stability under certain conditions, but there are counterarguments. If Iran's principal aim were to establish clear hegemonic influence in the Persian Gulf and the Gulf of Oman by assuring its military superiority over present or nascent rivals, India would be its most plausible rival. Iran's acquisition of nuclear arms would tend to reinforce India's determination to stay ahead. This could lead to a regional nuclear arms race, in which case Iran's nuclear acquisition would be destabilizing and could provoke India into a desperate attack. If, however, Iran established dominance, this could enhance stability until Iran was effectively challenged by another claimant within or outside the region.

If Iran's position in the region can be considered already hegemonic, the new power and prestige conferred by its acquisition of nuclear arms would tend to consolidate that position. Iran would then have the capacity to keep the peace in the region largely on its own terms. This would strengthen regional stability, again until Iran's position was effectively challenged. But if Iran were seeking to expand its influence beyond the Gulf of Oman into the Arabian Sea and the northern Indian Ocean, an Iranian nuclear force would be destabilizing. Its dominance of a region stretching from Kuwait in the west to the southern tip of India, and embracing a large portion of the Arabian peninsula and the horn of Africa, would challenge India's secondary interests in the Indian Ocean. Though India's vital interests would not be threatened, the appearance of a powerful, nuclear-armed Iran could be mitigated only by striking a new regional military balance or by the establishment of hegemony by one of the two powers.

Whether Iran were seeking to establish hegemony in the Gulfs of Oman and Persia, or to consolidate its position there, or to extend its influence far into the Indian Ocean, its acquisition of nuclear arms would introduce a new element of instability. The immediate effect of a consolidating effort would tend to be stabilizing, but as Iran's position strengthened, rivals would move to challenge Iran, thus causing instability.

There is much to the argument that an Iranian force would enhance Iran's international prestige, influence, and bargaining power both within and beyond the region. The extent of this new influence would depend on the level of nuclear force and how it was perceived, especially by neighbors and rivals. A token nuclear capability might have only a temporary effect. But in Iran's case, any nuclear capability would be buttressed by strong conventional military power, a growing economy, and, if the shah's policies persist, an active and assertive foreign policy. Thus, a nuclear force would be a net asset in supporting Iran's external objectives, but it would carry risks. With increased prestige, influence, and power would come increased criticism, fear, and anxiety. As India's nuclear potency has demonstrated, the benefits of prestige may in the long run not be worth the costs of criticism—especially once the impact of rival states' threats to pursue the nuclear route is felt.

It is doubtless argued in Teheran that nuclear arms would advance Iran's claim to big-power status, an objective frequently mentioned by the shah. Yet West Germany and Japan are great powers though neither has a nuclear force. And India, though it has had a nuclear explosion, is not a great power because it lacks the capacity to project its influence beyond its immediate neighbors. Iran's claim to great-power status may already be clearer than India's because of its oil, its capacity to modernize, its greater per capita income ($1,900 as opposed to India's $117 per capita in 1977),[31] its growing military power, and its strategic location. Although India's gross national product was larger than Iran's in 1977, a higher proportion of Iran's was available for industrial expansion, including the training of scientists, engineers, and other professionals. It will take a long time, however, for Iran to match the size and quality of India's impressive scientific establishment.

The argument that an Iranian force would enable Iran to be more independent of the superpowers has some merit, but the degree of dependence on Washington or Moscow is a function of strategic, political, economic, and other nonnuclear factors. In fact, nuclear acquisition by Iran could so disturb relations with the United States that American military or economic cooperation would be withdrawn, thus making Iran either more vulnerable to or dependent on the Soviet Union. The argument that a nuclear force would strengthen Iran's capacity to develop mutually beneficial alliances with neighbors, out of fear or respect, has equally compelling counterarguments—it might sow fear and distrust among neighbors and provoke a counteralliance or it could estrange a more distant ally or patron. In sum, it would appear that the net effect of Iranian nuclear arms on regional stability would be negative. This does not mean that if Iran abstains, it will therefore play a stabilizing role. Iran's impact on stability will depend on its foreign and military policies as a whole, and in certain circumstances the nuclear factor could be only marginal.

The net impact of nuclear arms on Iran's national security and foreign policy goals is uncertain. There would be clear benefits in prestige and influence, but these would be substantially offset by costs in fear, anxiety, and countermeasures by neighbors and rivals, and perhaps by the superpowers.

Iran could argue, as India has, that a nuclear explosion or nuclear arms development would advance the economy by stimulating the growth of research, technology, skilled manpower, and a supporting industrial base, but these economic benefits are available from a civil nuclear power program at less economic cost and less political risk. The contention, mainly advanced by the Soviet Union, that nuclear explosions are useful for major mining or earth-moving projects remains to be

31. CIA, *National Basic Intelligence Factbook, July 1977*, pp. 91, 94.

proved. The U.S. Plowshare program to exploit nuclear explosions for civil projects has not demonstrated that such explosions are economically sound, and obligations imposed by the limited test-ban treaty (as well as environmental considerations) have virtually ended the U.S. program.

Even first-generation nuclear devices are expensive to manufacture, and they have the effect of diverting resources from domestic programs or the conventional military establishment. A militarily significant nuclear force is still more expensive because it requires plausible airborne or missile delivery systems, although if it is developed as a substitute for a major conventional capability, the savings thus realized could partially reduce costs. In sum, the economic arguments are almost totally without merit.

The pressure for greater prestige at home and abroad also affects any government's nuclear arms design. Prestige was clearly a factor in India's case as it would be in Iran's. Enhanced international prestige resulting from a nuclear achievement is reflected, at least temporarily, in increased national morale and cohesion. As an occasion for celebration and self-esteem, it tends to strengthen the central government against internal centrifugal or other opposing forces. The longer range effects may, however, lead to division as important elites or the general population become aware of the costs, risks, and ambiguous benefits. "What's in it for us?" is a perennial political question. The nuclear adventure could be attacked as a deliberate effort by the government to divert attention from pressing and unpleasant domestic problems. Iran may have less need for a problem-diverting spectacular than India, with its seemingly unmanageable and insoluble problems, but all national leaders recognize the value of acclaimed accomplishments.

A nuclear explosion or the development of a nuclear arsenal may shift the internal balance of forces in unpredictable and disturbing ways. The equilibrium among the scientific community, the development-oriented managers, the military, the professional politicians, and various sectors of the government bureaucracy may be upset, giving undue influence or control to new groups. This is a greater danger in a society with an authoritarian structure like Iran's than in a more pluralistic and democratic society. A nuclear-military-industrial complex could emerge that would distort or frustrate the shah's domestic reform and development policies. New instabilities could create a climate conducive to a coup against the monarchy and lead to an extremist, pro-Soviet regime that would serve neither the interests of the Iranian people nor the stability of the region.

Domestic considerations are unlikely to be determinative in Iran's nuclear decisions because the temporary benefits of prestige may be more than offset by the risks of internal dissension and disruption. Nor is any serious leader likely to be convinced to go nuclear by the economic argument. In the Indian case, national security and foreign policy considerations seem to have been the prime factors in the decision to explode a nuclear device. It would appear that the same will be true in Iran—regardless of which way the decision may turn.

Iran's Nuclear Future

Iran faces the same three nuclear options confronting India and Pakistan: developing nuclear energy for civil purposes only, keeping the option of developing nuclear arms open, and developing such arms as soon as possible. Though Iran is significantly less advanced in nuclear technology than several other Third World states, the external assistance it is planning to receive would make possible a nuclear explosion by 1985 or shortly thereafter. Iran has a medium, as distinct from high or low, security and foreign policy incentive for exercising the nuclear option (see table 1-2). The incentive for Pakistan and Egypt, for example, appears to be high; for Argentina and Brazil, medium; and for Mexico, low. Incentives, like constraints, fluctuate of course with changing circumstances. Iran, though it has signed the nonproliferation treaty, has not forsworn all interest in acquiring nuclear arms. It is pursuing a policy similar to India's in the early years—keeping the option open by developing capabilities that could be used to manufacture weapons if that decision were made. Iran probably has not yet decided to manufacture either a token or a militarily significant nuclear force.

Two of the major factors affecting its decision are the government's perceptions of external danger and of opposition to Iran's regional ambitions, both of which are affected by the behavior of Iran's neighbors and the big powers. Though almost anything could happen, the rivalry between the United States and the Soviet Union is likely to continue for the next decade or two, and the United States and its allies will probably make determined efforts to maintain access to Middle Eastern oil at bearable prices.

Keeping its options open has many security and political benefits for Iran. It embraces both necessary and calculated ambiguity and gives Iran the best of both worlds. For an indefinite period Iran can avoid the political risks and costs associated with nuclear power and at the same time be in a position to acquire such power on relatively short notice if it is convinced that its defense and foreign policy interests would be served thereby.

The policy of the United States will be the single most significant external factor in Iran's decision. The decline or perceived decline of American power, influence, or will to support its interests with military force in the Middle East and elsewhere could prompt Iran to go nuclear.

Iran would probably develop a small force designed to deter a Soviet attack and to reinforce its own position of regional leadership. If the present government were replaced by a leftist regime favorable to the Soviet Union, the regional stability that is consistent with U.S. interests would be in jeopardy. If moderate domestic and foreign policy leadership continues until 2000, stability would be the result, unless Iran's nuclear force should provoke countermeasures by the Soviet Union or a new Pakistani-Indian nuclear axis, neither of which is likely. The Soviet Union is likely to respect the integrity of a U.S.-backed Iran whether or not Iran has nuclear arms. There are also potential regional rivalries with Saudi Arabia and Iraq, but Iran appears to be getting on reasonably well with both.

Even if power alignments shifted somewhat (but not to the extent of Iran becoming an ally of the Soviet Union), nuclear acquisition by Iran would not necessarily be catastrophic for the United States or, for that matter, for the Soviet Union. As in the case of India, neither superpower would be likely to make a nuclear response to conflict in the area unless the other moved first. Hence, Iran lacks the capacity to trigger a nuclear confrontation between the superpowers, but a nuclear Iran could provoke serious regional conflict.

CHAPTER FOUR

Israel and Egypt: States in Conflict

Israel has no atomic arms and will not be the first to introduce them into our region.

PRIME MINISTER LEVI ESHKOL, 1966

We shall also [like Israel] find a way of having atomic bombs.

PRESIDENT ANWAR EL-SADAT, 1974[1]

THE FESTERING Arab-Israeli conflict which has erupted into open war four times in recent years continues to be one of the world's most dangerous flash points. Both Israel and its principal adversary, Egypt, are heavily armed, the former mainly by the United States and the latter by the Soviet Union. Israel still occupies most of the Arab territory it took in the 1967 and 1973 wars. The Arab states and the Palestinians continue to insist that Israel should return the conquered land.

The tense Middle East situation has been complicated by a series of reports that Israel has a small arsenal of nuclear weapons. The *New York Times* of March 16, 1976, reported that the U.S. Central Intelligence Agency estimated that Israel had ten to twenty nuclear weapons "available for use." Since the mid-1960s it had been widely assumed that Israel had a small but growing nuclear arms capability, and the *New York Times* report erased much of the ambiguity that had surrounded Israel's nuclear development. Less than a month later, a report in *Time* stated that Israel possessed "a nuclear arsenal of 13 atomic bombs, assembled, stored and ready to be dropped on enemy forces from especially equipped Kfir and Phantom fighters or Jericho missiles."[2] The magazine also reported that the thirteen bombs had been

1. James Feron, *New York Times*, May 19, 1966; and *New York Times*, December 17, 1974.
2. "How Israel Got the Bomb," *Time*, April 12, 1976, p. 39.

"hastily assembled at a secret underground tunnel during a 78-hour period at the start of the 1973 October War." When "the battle on both fronts turned in Israel's favor," the bombs were returned to their "desert arsenals."

The CIA on January 26, 1978, released a memorandum dated September 4, 1974, that disclosed its conclusion that Israel had produced atomic weapons. The conclusion was based on "Israeli acquisition of large quantities of uranium, partly by clandestine means; the ambiguous nature of Israeli efforts in the field of uranium enrichment; and Israel's large investment in a costly missile system designed to accommodate nuclear warheads."[3] The *New York Times*, in reporting the CIA release, recalled that in November 1977 the new U.S. Department of Energy had "made public two previously secret documents that suggested American intelligence agencies believed in 1976 that Israel might have obtained uranium in the mid-1960's from a government-sponsored nuclear facility at Apollo, Pa."[4] These reports, which appear to be substantially correct, indicate that Israel, not India, became the sixth nuclear weapons state.

There is no evidence to indicate that either Egypt or any other Arab country possesses a nuclear weapon, though Egypt is probably capable of building a small airborne nuclear force by 1985. Hence, Egypt and Israel pose a unique situation in the Third World—two hostile states, each heavily armed with conventional weapons, and one having a militarily significant nuclear force. Under these circumstances, it is possible that another Israeli-Arab war would involve nuclear weapons.

The United States seeks to achieve greater stability in the Middle East and to maintain access to oil for its use and that of its allies. To these ends, it pursues policies designed to support Israel, strengthen ties with the Arab states, facilitate a lasting settlement of the Arab-Israeli conflict, and curtail excessive influence by the Soviet Union in the region. As Israel's chief and almost exclusive supporter, the United States has provided massive economic and military assistance. It has also provided substantial military and economic aid to Jordan, substantial military aid to Saudi Arabia, and modest military assistance to Kuwait. And since

3. Memorandum, U.S. Central Intelligence Agency, "Prospects for Further Proliferation of Nuclear Weapons," September 4, 1974, p. 1.

4. See David Burnham, *New York Times*, January 27, 1978. See also Deborah Shapley, *Washington Post*, January 28, 1978; and John J. Fialka, *Washington Star*, January 27 and 28, 1978.

September 1975 it has encouraged Egypt to purchase military goods from U.S. manufacturers.[5]

Through U.S. efforts an interim agreement between Egypt and Israel was negotiated in September 1975. It called for a pullback of Israeli troops from occupied Sinai territory in exchange for permission for non-military Israeli cargoes to pass through the Suez Canal.[6] Shortly thereafter President Sadat visited Washington; at that time President Ford said he was prepared to sell Egypt "nonlethal" military equipment.[7] Six months later Mr. Sadat unilaterally abrogated the Soviet-Egyptian treaty of friendship and cooperation concluded in 1971, which had the effect of cutting off the supply of military hardware from Russia.[8]

For years the Soviet Union has sought to gain influence in the Middle East by supporting the more militant Arab states, principally Egypt, Syria, and Iraq. It backed them in their conflict with Israel and gave diplomatic support to the oil boycott launched after the 1973 war. By supporting the Palestine Liberation Organization and other dissident groups in the Arab world, the Soviet Union has sought to harass Israel and disrupt moderate Arab governments in its effort to establish radical regimes and undermine Western influence. Since 1975 Soviet influence has declined in Egypt as President Sadat has turned increasingly to the United States for diplomatic and military support. In April 1976 Egypt and China signed a military protocol, reportedly to provide Egypt with spare parts for its MIG-17 and MIG-21 planes, types common to both countries.[9]

Israel's Nuclear Policy

Israel, like India, demonstrated an interest in nuclear research and development from the time it became a state in 1948. Almost immediately it initiated exploration for uranium within the country. Its Atomic Energy Commission was established in 1952 under the jurisdiction of the Defense Ministry. In 1966 it was reorganized and placed under the direct control of the prime minister who became its chairman.

Israel's extensive nuclear activities quite naturally have bred anxiety

5. *Washington Post*, September 25, 1975.
6. *U.S. Department of State Bulletin*, September 29, 1975, pp. 466–69.
7. Oswald Johnston, *Washington Post*, September 25, 1975.
8. Henry Tanner, *New York Times*, March 15, 1976.
9. *New York Times*, April 22, 1976.

in a region of tension and conflict. As early as 1965, several Arab governments claimed that Israel had mastered the basic technologies of nuclear arms manufacture and possibly had developed the capability to construct such a weapon.[10] These assertions may have been premature, but they reflected a genuine Arab concern and received some attention and understanding from governments outside the region. It was reported, for example, that the United States in the mid-1960s conveyed assurance to the Egyptian government that Israel's nuclear activities did not involve weapons production.[11]

Israel's few carefully guarded official statements on nuclear matters and its policy of strict secrecy have perpetuated the uncertainty and ambiguity surrounding its activities and intentions. Nuclear developments are shrouded from public view, and nuclear facilities are accessible only to workers, key government officials, and a very few officially approved outsiders under carefully controlled conditions. The sparse nuclear information available to the domestic and foreign press is strictly censored. Occasional cryptic government statements on the nearly forbidden subject add to the mystery. In May 1966, in response to a surge of American curiosity and to reports that Egypt was actively seeking Soviet nuclear assistance, Prime Minister Levi Eshkol asserted that Israel had no atomic arms and made a plea for nuclear arms control in the Middle East.[12] Several Israeli spokesmen affirmed and elaborated this position: "Israel would not be the first to introduce nuclear weapons into the Middle East, but it would not be the second either."[13] In December 1974 Israeli President Ephraim Katzir reiterated an earlier "no first use" pledge, but added that Israel "has the potential" to build nuclear weapons and could do so "within a reasonable period of time."[14] In September 1975 Prime Minister Yitzhak Rabin said Israel was "a nonnuclear country" and repeated that it "will not be the first to introduce nuclear weapons into the area." But Rabin refused to say that Israel had no nuclear arms, though he said that after "an overall settlement" of the Mideast conflict, "we will sign every agreement" related to the nonproliferation treaty.[15]

10. Yair Evron, "The Arab Position in the Nuclear Field: A Study of Policies up to 1967," *Cooperation and Conflict*, vol. 8 (1973), pp. 19–31.

11. Ibid., p. 29.

12. James Feron, *New York Times*, May 19, 1966.

13. Yigal Allon in *Jewish Observer*, December 24, 1964.

14. Victor Cohn, *Washington Post*, December 3, 1974.

15. Transcript, ABC News, "Issues and Answers," September 7, 1975.

Over the years, the Israeli statements have been deliberately ambiguous. The protection provided by ambiguity was virtually removed, however, with the disclosure of the CIA estimates of Israel's nuclear stockpile. Nevertheless, after the CIA's release of its document in 1978, just as after the 1976 report of the CIA estimate, a spokesman in Israel's Washington embassy repeated the old refrain—"Israel will not be the first to introduce nuclear arms in the Middle East."[16] So did Israeli officials in Jerusalem after the *Time* story broke.[17]

Although Israel is a member of the International Atomic Energy Agency, it has refused to sign the nonproliferation treaty, claiming that the treaty does not provide it with adequate security guarantees. It has, however, signed the limited test-ban treaty and has from time to time expressed interest in regional arms control measures, provided that they apply to conventional as well as nuclear arms.[18]

Israel's Nuclear Development

Both France and the United States have contributed to Israel's nuclear development. In 1953 Israel began an extended period of collaboration with France from which both governments reaped significant benefits. Each was determined to gain nuclear independence for political and security reasons. Israel offered France its knowledge of how to produce heavy water and to extract uranium from low-grade ore, both reportedly of considerable help to the French in decreasing their reliance on American technology. In return, France concluded an agreement with Israel providing Israeli scientists with access to basic French nuclear technology and training, quite possibly including detailed information from the results of the early French atomic tests in the Sahara.[19] It is possible that a bomb of French-Israeli design was tested by the French in their

16. *Washington Star*, March 16, 1976; and David Burnham, *New York Times*, January 28, 1978.

17. *New York Times*, April 6, 1976.

18. For a brief summary of Israel's declaratory policy on the nonproliferation treaty and nuclear arms control, see Stockholm International Peace Research Institute, *The Near-Nuclear Countries and the NPT* (Stockholm: Almqvist and Wiksell; New York: Humanities Press, 1972), pp. 27–30.

19. For a discussion of Israeli-French nuclear cooperation, see Fuad Jabber, *Israel and Nuclear Weapons: Present Options and Future Strategies* (London: Chatto and Windus, for International Institute for Strategic Studies, 1971), pp. 20–24.

Sahara facility in the early 1960s, though there is no public evidence of this.

The center of Israel's nuclear activities is the Negev Nuclear Research Center at Dimona. Its twenty-six-megawatt natural-uranium reactor was built under a bilateral agreement with France. Details of the agreement are still kept secret even though collaboration between the two countries was apparently terminated by January 1969 when the French embargoed conventional arms to Israel. Existence of the Dimona facility first became publicly known in December 1960 following American charges that Israel was secretly building an atomic reactor at a site forty miles north of Beersheba. After initially claiming the facility was a textile plant, Israel and France announced that they were engaged in a program of nuclear cooperation that included the construction of a natural-uranium reactor.[20] Israel stated, however, that its nuclear efforts were devoted "exclusively" to peaceful uses.

Formal U.S. nuclear assistance to Israel began in July 1955 with an agreement under which Israel received a U.S. research reactor, fuel for its operation, and training for Israeli scientists at American installations.[21] The five-megawatt reactor, constructed at Nahal Soreq, south of Tel Aviv, is fueled with highly enriched uranium provided by the United States under safeguards. On June 15, 1966, the bilateral safeguards were reinforced by a trilateral agreement that included IAEA safeguards.[22] The Dimona facility remains totally unsafeguarded; it is operated by the Israeli Defense Ministry and has no French-imposed safeguards.[23]

Several American officials and scientists have been permitted to visit the Dimona reactor. The visitors on the guided tours between 1964 and 1966 concluded that the facility was not being used for weapons purposes.[24] But in 1969 a U.S. team reported that it could not guarantee that there was no weapons-related work at Dimona because it was not permitted to move about freely. Likewise, a U.S. congressional inquiry into Israeli and Egyptian nuclear efforts complained of the lack of "any

20. John W. Finney, *New York Times*, December 20, 1960.
21. 6 U.S.T. 2641.
22. 573 U.N.T.S. 3.
23. *U.S. Foreign Policy and the Export of Nuclear Technology to the Middle East*, Hearings before the Subcommittee on International Organizations and Movements and on the Near East and South Asia of the House Committee on Foreign Affairs, 93 Cong. 2 sess. (Government Printing Office, 1974), pp. 144–45.
24. John W. Finney, *New York Times*, March 14, 1965, and June 28, 1966.

detailed knowledge by the United States of the purposes, research, and experiments conducted at the Dimona research facility."[25] In November 1976, thirteen U.S. senators on a nuclear fact-finding tour of the Middle East were barred from the facility.[26]

In addition to the reactor, there are large-scale facilities for separating weapons-grade plutonium from spent fuel at the Soreq Research Establishment at Dimona, and there may be such plants elsewhere. If the reports of Israel's having obtained enriched uranium from the nuclear facility at Apollo, Pennsylvania, are true, the country has the basic materials to construct nuclear weapons by either the plutonium or the enriched-uranium route. Certainly the building of nuclear bombs is well within the capability of Israel's scientists and technicians (a significant number of them gained valuable information and experience by working in the French and U.S. nuclear arms programs).[27] Israel doubtless has both the expertise and the industrial capacity to manufacture warheads for airplane delivery, and probably to make smaller and more sophisticated ones for missiles.

The *Time* report that Israel in 1973 was prepared to deliver thirteen twenty-kiloton warheads by "specially equipped Kfir and Phantom fighters or Jericho missiles" is entirely plausible.[28] Israeli aircraft, such as the Mirage 3 and the A-4 or F-4 Phantoms, can be adapted to carry and drop nuclear bombs.[29] And the Jericho is a short-range surface-to-surface missile that not only is fully capable of carrying a nuclear warhead but is so lacking in accuracy that fitting it with a conventional warhead would make little sense. The Jericho, which was developed in Israel with French cooperation, could reach Cairo, Alexandria, the Suez Canal, Damascus, and Amman from launching sites within the pre-1967 borders of the country. The Aswan Dam could be reached only from a forward base in the Sinai. Several Israeli planes could deliver nuclear bombs to Baghdad. "By any combination of delivery modes," one scholar concludes, "an Israeli strike force armed with even a few atomic bombs

25. *U.S. Foreign Policy*, Hearings, p. vii.

26. *Washington Post*, November 9, 1976.

27. Isadore Perlman, for example, an American nuclear chemist involved in the Manhattan Project, migrated to Israel in the spring of 1973 after serving as associate director of the Lawrence Radiation Laboratory in California. See Todd Friedman, "Israel's Nuclear Option," *Bulletin of the Atomic Scientists*, vol. 30 (September 1974), p. 32.

28. "How Israel Got the Bomb," p. 39.

29. International Institute for Strategic Studies, *Strategic Survey, 1974* (London: IISS, 1975), table 6, p. 38.

of modest yield could threaten damage adequate to deter any rational Arab adversary. No city of the Arab world would be immune."[30]

The United States in 1975, as a reward for Israel's signing the Sinai interim accord, promised to give favorable consideration to selling Israel two nuclear-capable systems—the $8 million F-15 fighter-bomber and the 460-mile Pershing missile which could reach Cairo and the Aswan Dam.[31] Though Israel promised not to fit the Pershing with nuclear warheads, the proposed sale provoked so much controversy in Washington that Israel withdrew its request for the missiles. Congress concurred in providing twenty-five F-15s,[32] which were delivered in early 1977. The Israelis then requested an additional twenty-five. These advanced U.S. systems augmented Israel's already adequate capability to threaten the most plausible Arab targets with nuclear weapons. It seems reasonable therefore to conclude that Israel has a militarily significant force of ten to twenty nuclear bombs and to assume that it has the capacity and intention to increase the size, accuracy, and range of this force.

Egypt's Nuclear Status

Egypt's nuclear technology is far less advanced than that of Israel. The great disparity between the two has had an impact on Egypt's military, diplomatic, and nuclear policies. Its ambiguous response to Israel's nuclear advances is apparent in Egypt's position on the nonproliferation treaty, which it has signed but not ratified. By signing the treaty, Egypt hoped to bring international pressure on Israel to renounce the nuclear option and at the same time to create the impression of its own reasonableness and restraint. Egypt reserved its nuclear option by not ratifying the treaty. It claims the treaty fails to provide adequate security assurances for states threatened by nuclear aggression and that such assurances should include "a pledge by the nuclear Powers to consider the

30. Stephen J. Rosen, "Nuclearization and Stability in the Middle East," in Onkar Marwah and Ann Schulz, eds., *Nuclear Proliferation and the Near-Nuclear Countries* (Ballinger, 1975), p. 164.

31. Drew Middleton, *New York Times*, September 18, 1975; Marilyn Berger, *Washington Post*, September 16 and 18, 1975; and George C. Wilson, *Washington Post*, September 17, 1975.

32. *Washington Star*, September 26, 1975; and Drew Middleton, *New York Times*, January 18, 1976.

threat or use of nuclear weapons against a non-nuclear party to the treaty as sufficient to prevent" their use, or failing that to "retaliate against nuclear aggression as a measure of collective self-defense."[33]

In 1966 Egypt reportedly was offered security guarantees from the Soviet Union against the possibility of a nuclear threat from Israel.[34] Seven years later, during the October 1973 war, Russian surface-to-surface Scud missiles were sent to Egypt, but they remained under Soviet control. Whether nuclear warheads were provided for the missiles is not known, but in this brief collaborative effort the Soviet Union and Egypt employed the tactics of nuclear ambiguity for which Israel is renowned.

In 1974 Egypt responded positively to a U.S. offer to sell American-built power reactors in the six-hundred-megawatt range to Egypt and Israel. The United States made it clear that each reactor would have to be fully safeguarded and implied that all other nuclear facilities in the recipient country would also have to accept strict U.S. safeguards and provide full access to IAEA inspectors. Egypt was quite prepared to open its modest facilities. By its evident willingness to accept the U.S. offer, it scored a political point against Israel. The Israelis declined the offer because they feared that their Dimona facility would have to be opened to IAEA inspection.[35] A year later, the U.S. offer to Egypt was formalized by the initialing of a proposed cooperation agreement on the peaceful uses of atomic energy. The two governments "agreed in principle to conduct a program of cooperation" covering the "design, construction and operation of research and power reactors, desalinization, the beneficial uses of radio-isotopes and radiation sources, the exploration and development of uranium resources, and related health and safety considerations."[36] Egypt would be permitted to buy two reactors and related equipment which would cost an estimated $1.2 billion. They would operate under a trilateral U.S.-IAEA-Egypt safeguards agreement, said to be the most stringent in the world.

The purchase agreement with Egypt was initialed on August 5, 1976.

33. "Statement by the U.A.R. Representative (El Kony) to the First Committee of the General Assembly: Nonproliferation of Nuclear Weapons, May 28, 1968," in U.S. Arms Control and Disarmament Agency, *Documents on Disarmament, 1968* (GPO, 1969), p. 402.

34. Hedrick Smith, *New York Times,* February 4, 1966.

35. John W. Finney, *New York Times,* December 17, 1974; and Marilyn Berger, *Washington Post,* December 14, 1974.

36. *U.S. Department of State Bulletin,* November 25, 1975, p. 732.

The next day an identical pact was initialed with Israel. Two years later, the agreements had not been submitted to Congress for approval. No matter how promptly they might be approved, the U.S. reactors could not become operational before the mid-1980s.

France and West Germany also have shown interest in assisting Egypt. In a joint communiqué in December 1975, France said it was prepared to assist in the construction of nuclear power plants in Egypt.[37] During President Sadat's visit to West Germany in April 1976, he was shown the twelve-hundred-megawatt nuclear power plant at Biblis like those sold to Iran and Brazil.[38]

Egypt's only nuclear reactor is a two-megawatt research facility located at Inchass, about twenty miles from Cairo. Built with Soviet aid, this reactor began operating in 1961. Although the reactor is not subject to IAEA safeguards, "the Soviets have controlled the disposal of irradiated fuel."[39] The plutonium production from the research reactor is estimated only to be large enough for "one low-kiloton bomb every eight years."[40] On several occasions the Soviet Union has offered to sell a nuclear power reactor to Egypt, and once made an extensive feasibility study. A Soviet offer made in December 1974 coincided with the U.S. reactor offer to Egypt and Israel. This Soviet approach may have superseded an earlier pledge to build a one-hundred-and-fifty megawatt nuclear power plant near Alexandria.[41] Both technical and political factors seem to have been involved in the failure of these Soviet offers to materialize. The dearth of Egyptian experts appears to have been secondary to the problems of Soviet influence or control over the facility.

There have been occasional rumors that the Soviet Union or China might provide nuclear weapons to Egypt. In 1965 Egypt reportedly sought to purchase nuclear arms from the Soviet Union, but was refused.[42] In 1967 Egypt again reportedly sought to buy nuclear weapons —this time from China, which admonished Egypt to rely on its own resources.[43]

37. *New York Times*, December 15, 1975.
38. Craig R. Whitney, *New York Times*, April 18, 1976.
39. Lewis A. Frank, "Nasser's Missile Program," *Orbis*, vol. 11 (Fall 1967), p. 748.
40. Ibid.
41. See Leonard Beaton, "Capabilities of Non-Nuclear Powers," in Alastair Buchan, ed., *A World of Nuclear Powers?* (Prentice-Hall, 1966), p. 21.
42. Hedrick Smith, *New York Times*, February 4, 1966.
43. Mohammed Hassanein Heykel, *Al Ahram* (Cairo), November 23, 1973, reported in Raymond H. Anderson, *New York Times*, November 24, 1973.

Egypt does not possess the required technical and industrial infrastructure to manufacture a nuclear weapon in the near term. In a determined effort, it could manufacture a first-generation nuclear bomb by 1985, but only with considerable external assistance. This means that Egypt would have to purchase most of the spent fuel it would need for reprocessing into weapons grade plutonium. It would probably have to import technicians to fabricate the explosive device. If these steps were accomplished, it would have relatively little difficulty in adapting its MIG-21 or MIG-23 aircraft for nuclear missions. Its air capability would be greatly enhanced if it bought only a portion of the fifty F-5E and F-5F fighter-bombers that President Carter proposed selling to Egypt in February 1978.[44] The building of even a few small bombs by 1985 would be very difficult and would be virtually impossible without financial assistance from Saudi Arabia or Kuwait. Neither of these countries is likely to look on the emergence of a nuclear-armed Egypt with equanimity.

Israel's Nuclear Arms Situation

Assuming that Israel has a small nuclear force with both air and missile delivery means that can cover all plausible Arab targets, how is this capability likely to be used? And is the Israeli force likely to be stabilized at its present size and range? There are no public statements or other official evidence of Israeli intentions. The government did show intense interest in 1975 in acquiring the U.S. F-15 and F-16 fighter bombers and Pershing missiles offered by the Ford administration. Though Israel withdrew the request for the Pershings, it appears determined to increase the range and versatility of both its air and missile systems for delivering nuclear arms. This suggests that it is seeking to increase the size of its nuclear arsenal rapidly in order to cover a greater number of potential targets. It is plausible to assume that Israeli technicians are moving ahead to perfect smaller and more sophisticated warheads for missiles and perhaps to improve the accuracy of the missiles, though that would not be necessary if the Israeli deterrent is targeted primarily against cities rather than military installations.

One thing that seems clear is Israel's intention to continue to pursue

44. *Washington Post,* February 15, 1978.

a strategy of calculated ambiguity about its capabilities, intentions, nuclear doctrine, and wartime strategy. Despite the CIA's release of its estimates, the entire subject of Israel's nuclear weapons remains under a cloud of uncertainty, to the considerable advantage of Israel. There has been no official U.S. announcement of a nuclear test, as in the cases of India, China, and the Soviet Union. And Israel repeats its ritualized pledge not to be the first to introduce nuclear weapons into the region.

The geopolitical realities and recent history of the Middle East conflict make it reasonable to assume that Israel's leaders have devised both deterrent and war-fighting doctrines and strategies to govern the employment of its nuclear force. One of the Arab writers who point to the stabilizing effect of an Israeli force predicted that Israel's acquisition of the bomb would produce a "stalemate" followed by an Egyptian bomb that would reinforce the situation in which "neither country would dare attack the other."[45] An Iraqi colonel suggested in 1961 that "Israel's acquisition of atomic weapons will decrease the value of ordinary weapons in the hands of the Arab armies and the importance of their numerical superiority" and thus "serve as a permanent deterrent to the Arabs."[46] Israeli writers have not been so confident; according to Stephen Rosen, "almost the entire literature by Israelis . . . is broadly hostile to the strategic and political consequences of the open introduction of nuclear deterrence capabilities by one or both sides."[47] But most of the commentators assume that the Arabs would have the bomb, which would make concentrated Israeli population centers highly vulnerable. For some years, however, Israel will have a nuclear monopoly in the region. The principal function of nuclear weapons, to be sure, is to deter, not to fight wars. In any event, Israeli prime ministers and other top leaders have apparently rejected the antinuclear advice of the early 1960s, such as that of Nahum Goldmann, president of the World Zionist Organization, who saw "no advantage whatsoever nor any moral or security justification for the manufacture of atomic bombs."[48]

The deterrent value of Israel's force has doubtless been enhanced by the *Time* report of its nuclear mobilization during the 1973 war. Any

45. Ahmad Samih Khalidi, "An Appraisal of the Arab-Israeli Military Balance," *Middle East Forum*, vol. 42 (1966), p. 55.

46. Hussan Mustafa, quoted in Rosen, "Nuclearization and Stability in the Middle East," p. 162.

47. Ibid., p. 163.

48. Quoted in ibid.

prudent adversary must calculate that Israel might very well be prepared to use the weapons in extreme circumstances. The belief that Israel might use its weapons could, of course, prompt Egypt to take nuclear countermeasures.

Since the effectiveness of deterrence depends on a genuine war-fighting capability—particularly the capacity to deliver an unacceptable blow after being struck first by a nuclear or massive conventional attack —Israel's nuclear weapons would be targeted against Arab urban centers and installations like the Suez Canal and the Aswan Dam; major military targets would be secondary objectives, to be attacked if sufficient warheads were available. Because of Israel's small territory, the probable short time span of any war, and the limited number of warheads available, it is unlikely that Israeli planners contemplate any tactical deployment of nuclear ordnance. It is possible, however, that they are considering nuclear-tipped tactical weapons to blunt a massive tank invasion, though the advent of precision-guided conventional arms makes this less probable.

With a delivery system capable of reaching all major Egyptian, Syrian, and Jordanian cities, as well as Aswan and Suez, what targets are likely to come under fire? Most observers believe that Israel would not use its nuclear arms to launch a war, even a preemptive war, but that it would use them against countervalue targets if the continued existence of Israel were thrown into question. A high U.S. State Department official suggested in 1975 that the Israelis would use nuclear weapons only if their armed forces were no longer able to operate or their major population centers were being destroyed. The view that Israel would not hesitate to destroy Arab cities to prevent the ultimate catastrophe, the holocaust, is supported by *Time*'s account of its behavior in the 1973 war:

The Egyptians had repulsed the first Israeli counterattacks along the Suez Canal, causing heavy casualties, and Israeli forces on the Golan Heights were retreating in the face of a massive Syrian tank assault. At 10 p.m. on Oct. 8, the Israeli Commander on the northern front, Major General Yitzhak Hoffi, told his superior: "I am not sure that we can hold out much longer." After midnight, Defense Minister Moshe Dayan solemnly warned Premier Golda Meir: "This is the end of the third temple." Mrs. Meir thereupon gave Dayan permission to activate Israel's Doomsday weapons. As each bomb was assembled, it was rushed off to waiting air force units. Before any triggers were set, however, the battle on both fronts turned in Israel's favor. The 13 bombs were sent [back] to their desert arsenals.[49]

49. "How Israel Got the Bomb," p. 39.

The effect of such an attitude toward nuclear arms must be included in any consideration of the impact of Israel's nuclear force on its Arab neighbors and on U.S. interests in the Middle East.

Egypt's Nuclear Incentives

Caught up in an unresolved conflict with a nuclear adversary, Egypt has greater security and political incentives for developing a nuclear deterrent than most Third World states. South Korea and Taiwan are in somewhat similar circumstances. Egypt's primary motivation for acquiring a nuclear deterrent is to counter Israel's nuclear force. For a decade it may have been inhibited from undertaking such drastic military action as a massive bombing of cities, for fear of nuclear retaliation. Now that Israel's nuclear status seems less ambiguous, Egypt's fear has scarcely lessened. Egypt's problem is serious because its modest nuclear program is barely capable of producing even a few first-generation bombs by 1985, and then only with extraordinary and highly unlikely external assistance.

With declining Soviet military support and increasing U.S. military assistance, Egypt would be ill advised to place any confidence in the Soviet Union's ambiguous nuclear deterrent. The Soviet nuclear weapons that are thought to have been introduced briefly into Egypt during the 1973 war were probably a carefully controlled Soviet venture designed to deter a nuclear response by Israel to Egypt's attack across the canal. Egypt could not realistically expect a nuclear guarantee on the part of the United States unless there should be substantial movement toward a comprehensive peace settlement in the Middle East.

Without assured protection from either superpower, Egypt faces a nuclear Israel. A nuclear program of its own is tempting, but it is not without risks. Any determined effort to build nuclear arms would tend to alienate the United States, and it would almost certainly prompt Israel to accelerate its nuclear efforts. Moreover, even the knowledge that Egypt was on the verge of a nuclear explosion would carry the risk of an Israeli threat to use nuclear arms if Egypt persisted in its nuclear military development or if Egypt made a significant conventional military move against Israel. It would be very difficult for Egypt to catch up with Israel and establish a balance of terror that might prove stabilizing.

Any nuclear showdown in the next fifteen years—whether an exchange of threats or actual war—could mean disaster for both sides.

Egypt may also be motivated to seek nuclear arms status to enhance its general diplomatic posture and reinforce its position in the Arab world. By championing the Arab cause and by its modest military (and much greater political) success in the 1973 war, it gained respect among moderate Arab leaders, though it is still assailed by Libya. That position now depends heavily on the outcome of President Sadat's late 1977 peace initative toward Israel. With oil assuming an increasing role in world politics, Egypt has been forced into a relatively less important role vis-à-vis Saudi Arabia and Kuwait and has had to rely on these oil states for financial and political support. Hence, there are internal pressures to use nuclear arms as a source of prestige. But again the costs and risks of going nuclear may be greater than the hoped-for benefits of regional prestige and political clout. As the big nuclear powers have learned, it is difficult to translate nuclear capability into diplomatic muscle.

On the domestic front, it is questionable whether Egypt's plans for substantial investment in nuclear energy can be fully justified in view of the considerable generating capacity of the Aswan Dam. In Egypt, as in India, Iran, and elsewhere, the energy argument is probably used in part as an excuse to acquire external resources that can eventually be used for conducting a nuclear explosion, though Egypt does plan to use the reactors to power desalting plants.[50]

Egyptian leaders have also speculated about the potential gain in domestic morale and cohesion that would result from the development of a nuclear weapon, but they have observed that such gains, like those from spectacular achievements in space, tend to be short-lived. The prestige generated by dramatic events erodes quickly and is not easily translated into usable political coinage. The diversion of scarce resources into a weapons program is likely to be opposed by development-minded Egyptians as well as by ordinary citizens who see little to be gained. Domestic prestige factors, therefore, appear to carry little weight in Cairo's policymaking circles. Both the Egyptian leaders and their people, insofar as the latter are aware of the issues, are likely to view nuclear arms policy primarily in terms of its probable impact on national security and foreign policy.

50. Bernard Gwertzman, *New York Times*, August 3, 1976.

Future Relations of Israel and Egypt

Any plausible future for the relationship between Israel and its hostile Arab neighbors will be significantly influenced by the interests and behavior of the Soviet Union and the United States in the Middle East and the fundamental relation between the two superpowers. Under probable circumstances, a high level of tension and political conflict between Israel and the Arab states will continue and a fifth war is always a possibility. Such a war could involve nuclear arms.

The United States and the Soviet Union have had an essentially adversary relationship in the Middle East, but with varying degrees of hostility and accommodation. The United States will continue to be the chief patron of Israel and the Soviet Union the principal backer of the militant Arab states; both superpowers will probably maintain some supportive relationship with Egypt, though American influence appears to be increasing at Russia's expense. At times, U.S. pressure on Israel to make concessions in the interest of a comprehensive Arab-Israeli settlement has strained relations between the two.

Under these changing circumstances, both Israel and Egypt have sought to chart a more independent and self-reliant course. This has clear implications for their respective nuclear decisions. In fact, Israel has always pursued an almost wholly independent nuclear policy, albeit with technical assistance from France and the United States, under the fundamental assumption that in the ultimate crisis of survival Israel could not depend on the United States to come to its rescue. Israeli leaders with increasing frequency have emphasized to their people that in the final analysis Israel must depend on its own courage, will, and resources, though this determined political stance does not preclude attempts to get all the military assistance possible from the United States. Such assistance is regarded as essential for providing the resources necessary for Israel to consolidate its independent course.

Egypt is also attempting to become more independent, primarily by diversifying the sources of external diplomatic and material support. It will continue to receive substantial aid from Saudi Arabia. Though Soviet military assistance has been cut off, it could resume. In the meantime, the United States is providing some economic aid and arranging to sell nuclear power reactors to Egypt. But Egypt is not likely to become an ally of the United States, much less a beneficiary of a U.S. nuclear guarantee.

Within this context there are three broad alternative nuclear futures short of war for Israel and Egypt: continuation of the Israeli monopoly, a nuclear arms race, or a balance of terror. Until the mid-1980s, and perhaps well beyond, Israel will probably continue to enjoy a nuclear monopoly. During these years it would probably increase the size, quality, and range of its bomb force. The monopoly would be maintained because of Israel's substantial lead and Egypt's relatively less advanced state of nuclear development. Israel would probably use its nuclear capacity with restraint, holding it in the background, not boasting or threatening, or even acknowledging its existence. Under certain circumstances, however, Israel might threaten its use. While Egypt might prefer to balance Israel's force with one of its own, the material and political costs would outweigh the problematical benefits of its becoming involved in a nuclear arms race. The result of Israeli monopoly could be a kind of imposed stability. But it could serve to unite the Arab states in a massive conventional war against Israel.

Egypt might decide to challenge the Israeli monopoly by building a nuclear force of its own, taking all the necessary measures to develop the technical capabilities for exercising the nuclear option as rapidly as resource limitations and political constraints permit. Even a determined effort, with maximum external assistance from Arab and industrial states, would not be likely to yield a bomb-making capability much before 1985. At that point, Egypt would have to abrogate its safeguard agreements or otherwise violate the spirit or letter of the constraints that surround international commerce in nuclear technology and materials. Depending on many unpredictable factors on both sides, Egypt could not expect to catch up with Israel much before the year 2000. Egypt's effort could not be hidden and would certainly unleash anxieties in Israel and elsewhere. Egypt's aim would be to build a counterforce to balance Israel's advantage, to create a mutual deterrent system.

While a mutual deterrence subsystem in the Middle East could result in war, it might bring stability, which would not depend on a general political settlement having been achieved between Israel and the Arab states. Stephen Rosen, among others, advocates "a regional balance of terror as a path to stabilization. . . . A stable system of mutual deterrence may be entirely possible, and such a system may make a positive contribution to the political deescalation of the Arab-Israel conflict."[51] However, nonnuclear factors, such as the military intervention of a great power, which determine the consequences of nuclear acquisition could change abruptly; almost overnight the deterrent value of Egypt's nuclear capability could be transformed into a dangerous provocation.

A nuclear arms race between the two countries seems a more likely future course than either the establishment of a deterrent system or the indefinite continuation of the Israeli monopoly. It seems implausible that Israel will freeze its nuclear force at its present level. Whether the force remains static or is further strengthened, it would appear that, at the very least, Egypt will seek to develop the capacity to exercise the nuclear option. As with Pakistan and Iran, keeping open the nuclear option offers Egypt advantages of ambiguity and flexibility that a crash program to develop a nuclear force would not enjoy.

A continuation of Israel's monopoly or the achievement of a balance of terror is possible, however, within the next twenty-five years. Each of the alternative directions has certain assets and liabilities as far as Middle Eastern stability is concerned. Any one could lead to nuclear war. In theoretical terms, a system of mutually assured destruction seems to offer the best hope for military stability, but the process for getting there—a crash program by Egypt—carries many risks. Under any plausible circumstances, it is impossible to predict that an Egyptian deterrent would improve the situation over the present one in which the Israeli capability may impose a degree of stability in a complex and volatile situation. Hence, acquisition of nuclear arms by Egypt is more likely to be destabilizing than stabilizing and thus would run counter to U.S. interests.

For years Israel has enjoyed certain benefits of deterrence without suffering the political costs of being an open nuclear arms state. But this strategy always carried the risk that convincing disclosure of Israeli nuclear power could prompt countermeasures by Egypt or, under certain circumstances, by the USSR or the United States. Israel's force is not likely, however, to draw the Soviet Union and the United States into a nuclear confrontation. The past record of the superpowers in the Middle East and elsewhere suggests that each has developed certain disciplines and safeguards to prevent either from providing the other with a plausible reason to launch a nuclear attack.

51. "Nuclearization and Stability in the Middle East," p. 157.

CHAPTER FIVE

South Korea and Taiwan: Allies under Siege

We have no plan or active research at this time for development of [nuclear] weapons.

PRESIDENT PARK CHUNG-HEE, 1975

We have both the facilities and the capabilities to make nuclear weapons and actually considered to build up a nuclear arsenal last year.

PREMIER CHIANG CHING-KUO, 1975[1]

THE Republic of Korea and the Republic of China have in common several salient characteristics in addition to their location in Northeast Asia. Each state is a portion of a former state whose territory is claimed by a rival regime. Living in a condition of contested sovereignty, each of these states is under political and military siege by a communist government with a powerful military establishment. Both South Korea and Taiwan have strong central governments and viable and growing economies. The per capita income of South Korea in 1976 was about $700 and of Taiwan $1,050. Between 1963 and 1973 the per capita growth rate for South Korea was 11.0 percent and for Taiwan 8.3 percent.[2]

In the struggle of great power interests in Asia and the Pacific, South Korea and Taiwan have played active roles. Each is an ally of the United States and each relies heavily on this relationship for its survival. In the mutual defense treaty between the United States and the Republic of China, which entered into force on March 3, 1955, "each Party recognizes that an armed attack in the West Pacific Area directed against the territories of either of the Parties would be dangerous to its own

1. Don Oberdorfer, *Washington Post*, June 27, 1975; and *Daily Report: Asia and Pacific* (Washington: Foreign Broadcast Information Service), September 24, 1975, p. B1.
2. U.S. Central Intelligence Agency, *National Basic Intelligence Factbook*, July 1977 (Library of Congress, 1977), pp. 40, 107–08.

peace and safety and declares that it would act to meet the common danger in accordance with its constitutional processes."[3] The U.S. treaty with the Republic of Korea, which has a virtually identical operative clause, came into force on November 17, 1954.[4] Since U.S. military action under either treaty could involve a nuclear response, both Korea and Taiwan have an implied U.S. nuclear guarantee. Both countries have received large amounts of American economic and military assistance.

Taiwan is significantly more isolated from the larger diplomatic world than South Korea, though Taiwan has a substantial and growing volume of foreign trade. The Republic of China was expelled from the United Nations when the People's Republic of China was given China's permanent seat on the Security Council in 1971. Many governments withdrew their diplomatic recognition from Taiwan shortly thereafter. South Korea has far wider diplomatic recognition, but neither it nor North Korea has been admitted into the United Nations.

South Korea with a population of 35.2 million has a formidable military establishment supported by a large contingent of U.S. combat troops. In 1977 its defense budget totaled $1.9 billion,[5] maintaining 635,000 men under arms. Its 560,000-man army included one battalion of Honest John surface-to-surface missiles and two battalions equipped with Nike-Hercules surface-to-air missiles, both of which can be armed with either conventional or nuclear warheads. The South Korean air force had 30,000 men and 335 combat aircraft, including three 18-plane squadrons of F-4D and F-4E fighter-bombers which are capable of delivering nuclear payloads.[6] The total authorized strength of U.S. forces in South Korea was 40,000 personnel in early 1978. Included in the U.S. units were an air defense artillery brigade armed with Nike-Hercules, Hawk, and Chaparral/Vulcan anticraft weapons, a missile command armed with Sergeant and Honest John missiles, and a tactical fighter wing equipped with 69–70 F-4 aircraft.[7] Several of the American units were equipped with tactical nuclear weapons.[8]

3. 6 U.S.T. 433.

4. 5 U.S.T. 2368.

5. CIA, *National Basic Intelligence Factbook, July 1977*.

6. International Institute for Strategic Studies, *The Military Balance, 1977–1978* (London: IISS, 1977), p. 60; and Barry Wheeler, comp., "World Air Forces 1977," *Flight International* (London), vol. 112 (July 2, 1977), p. 64.

7. For a description of these forces, see IISS, *Military Balance, 1977–1978*, pp. 6–7.

8. Statement of Secretary of Defense James Schlesinger, quoted by Murrey Marder in *Washington Post*, June 21, 1975.

Taiwan also has an impressive military establishment to protect its population of 17.2 million. It had 460,000 personnel under arms in 1977 and a defense budget for fiscal 1978 of $1.67 billion.[9] As of early 1978 there were no U.S. combat forces in Taiwan, but some 1,400 American military personnel remained there; their principal tasks were to advise Taiwanese forces and to gather intelligence. The U.S. Seventh Fleet patrols the area. The United States withdrew its last combat unit, a squadron of 18 F-4 Phantom jet-bombers along with 450 support personnel, from Taiwan in 1975.[10] This withdrawal and the gradual reduction in the size of the U.S. military mission took place in accord with the U.S. pledge to Communist China during President Nixon's February 1972 visit there. In the Shanghai communiqué issued at that time, the United States said its "ultimate objective" was the withdrawal of all U.S. forces and the closing of all U.S. military installations.[11] At the time, there were about 9,000 American military personnel in Taiwan.[12]

South Korea and Taiwan face powerful, hostile, and determined adversaries who maintain that the governments in Seoul and Taipei are illegal and reactionary puppets of the United States. The Democratic People's Republic of Korea, with less than half the population of South Korea, in 1976 had 500,000 men under arms and a defense budget of about $1 billion.[13] The North Korean armed forces are largely equipped by the Soviet Union which has provided Frog-7 surface-to-surface missiles, MIG-21 tactical aircraft, a small number of modified MIG-21s, and other systems capable of delivering nuclear warheads. Western observers believe none of these systems is fitted with nuclear explosives. The hostility and militancy of North Korea are demonstrated in its constant military pressure on the demilitarized zone that divides the two Koreas. Its forces have dug through solid rock several deep underground tunnels to facilitate infiltration and possible invasion of the South. Its rigidly Stalinist government carries on a global propaganda program against the United States and its South Korean "lackey."[14]

Taiwan's implacable, if somewhat more prudent and patient adver-

9. IISS, *Military Balance, 1977–1978*, p. 57; and CIA, *National Basic Intelligence Factbook, July 1977*, p. 40.

10 Bernard Gwertzman, *New York Times*, June 8, 1975.

11. *U.S. Department of State Bulletin*, March 20, 1972, p. 438.

12. Bernard Gwertzman, *New York Times*, June 8, 1975.

13. IISS, *Military Balance, 1977–1978*, p. 60.

14. See David Rees, *North Korea: Undermining the Truce* (London: Institute for the Study of Conflict, 1976).

sary is the People's Republic of China with its massive population of 965,937,000 and a military establishment, largely army, numbering 3,950,000.[15] Red China is a nuclear power with a growing arsenal of warheads and delivery vehicles: in 1976 it had 200 to 300 atom and hydrogen bombs, and in 1977 30 to 40 each of nuclear-tipped intermediate-range and medium-range ballistic missiles.[16] China has about 80 TU-16 medium bombers capable of delivering nuclear arms. It has a growing navy, with a naval force equipped with more than 600 shore-based combat aircraft. Its regular air force of 400,000 men has 5,200 combat aircraft.

South Korea's Nuclear Status

Only recently has South Korea been seriously considered a plausible candidate for nuclear arms.[17] The 1974 Indian nuclear explosion, the global oil crisis, the fall of South Vietnam in April 1975, and an uneasy feeling that the American commitment to South Korea may be weakening are all instigating factors in this changed estimate. The steep rise in the price of imported oil accelerated Korean interest in acquiring reactors to produce nuclear energy. The defeat of the Saigon government awakened North Korea's ambition to conquer the South. Some observers fear that, under these circumstances, South Korea's substantial and active interest in acquiring nuclear technology and equipment may be motivated as much by the desire to bring nuclear arms within reach as by the need for nuclear energy.

South Korea's official policy toward nuclear arms is unclear and ambiguous, reflecting changing circumstances. When the substantial U.S. military presence, including nuclear weapons, was taken for granted, the issue of South Korea's acquisition of nuclear arms was dormant. But with the prospect of an eventual withdrawal of U.S. troops, an

15. CIA, *National Basic Intelligence Factbook, July 1977*, p. 53.

16. IISS, *Military Balance, 1975–1976*, p. 48, and *1977–1978*, p. 53. For further details on the development of China's nuclear force, see Harry Gelber, *Nuclear Weapons and Chinese Policy*, Adelphi Paper 99 (London: International Institute for Strategic Studies, 1973).

17. South Korea was not included among eight Third World candidates for the nuclear option discussed in Andrew Caranfil and others, "Briefing Notes: Nuclear Proliferation After India" (Croton-on-Hudson, N.Y.: Hudson Institute, November 1, 1974).

erosion in the U.S. security commitment, or both, South Korea has seriously contemplated the nuclear option. When President Park Chung-hee said that his government had no plans for development of nuclear weapons, he pointed out that South Korea had recently ratified the nonproliferation treaty. He added, however, that South Korea would do everything in its power to defend its security, including the manufacture of nuclear arms if necessary, if the U.S. nuclear umbrella were withdrawn, a contingency he regarded as unlikely.[18]

The nonproliferation treaty had been ratified in late April 1975 under quiet pressure from the U.S. State Department. Ratification followed shortly after a joint congressional resolution[19] was introduced, calling on the Export-Import Bank to "defer approval" of financing for a second nuclear power reactor for South Korea; it was aimed in part at inducing South Korea to ratify the treaty. In the fall of that year, South Korea arranged with France to purchase a plutonium reprocessing plant that, along with the training of Korean specialists in related areas, would eventually have given South Korea the capability to produce nuclear weapons.[20] Again the United States threatened to withhold Export-Import Bank financing and export licenses for a power reactor.[21] This time South Korea responded by canceling the purchase agreement for the French plant.[22]

South Korea's active nuclear research program had begun in 1962 when the United States provided the Atomic Research Institute near Seoul with a two-hundred-and-fifty-kilowatt research reactor. In 1971, a two-megawatt reactor, also of American design, was added for the institute's exploration of the biological and agricultural uses of isotopes and radiation. Development of the industrial applications of nuclear power was put in the charge of the Korean Institute of Science and Technology when it was established in 1966. (A semiautonomous subsidiary of the institute—Korean Nuclear Engineering, Inc., established in 1977—took over responsibilities for plant construction, component fabrication, and industrial applications.) In 1970, the Korean Electric Company signed a contract with Westinghouse to construct Korea's first

18. Don Oberdorfer, *Washington Post*, June 27, 1975.
19. H. J. Res. 298, March 10, 1975.
20. *New York Times*, October 29, 1975.
21. *The Export Reorganization Act—1975*, Hearings before the Senate Committee on Government Operations, 94 Cong. 1 sess. (Government Printing Office, 1975), pp. 224–28.
22. *Washington Post*, January 30, 1976; and *New York Times*, February 1, 1976.

atomic power plant, Ko-Ri I, located northeast of Pusan. Though it was originally scheduled for completion in 1975, it only began operating in 1977. Ground was broken for a second U.S. plant, Ko-Ri II, in April 1977. Each of these plants has two reactors. The global oil crisis, which in 1974 quadrupled Korea's 1973 import bill for petroleum, prompted South Korea to accelerate its nuclear power program. In May 1974 the government revised its energy plan, increasing its reliance on water and nuclear power. Nuclear energy was to provide 24 percent of the power by 1981 and 40 percent by 1986, at which time nine power reactors were to be in operation. Negotiations were opened immediately with Atomic Energy of Canada, Limited, for the supply of two six-hundred-megawatt natural-uranium power reactors to be located at Napori. In 1976 South Korea opened discussions with France on construction of a fifth and a sixth nuclear power reactor.[23] South Korea's nuclear power ambitions have been seriously curtailed, however, by construction delays and spiraling capital costs. The final cost of Ko-Ri I, originally estimated at $167 million, will probably be more than $250 million. The cost of Ko-Ri II, which will not be completed before 1981, has been estimated at $673 million. The first of the Canadian reactors is expected to cost $700 million.[24]

If South Korea decided to manufacture nuclear arms despite the financial costs and political risks, it would be possible to adapt them to the country's existing airborne or missile systems. South Korean F-4D fighter-bombers or surface-to-surface Honest John missiles fitted with nuclear warheads would provide a significant deterrent to North Korean forces. The South Korean government in December 1975 purchased a complete Lockheed facility for manufacturing solid-fuel rocket motors along with a program to train Koreans in "how to manufacture solid rocket propellant, the kind used in Minuteman and Polaris missiles."[25]

Taiwan's Nuclear Status

In 1970 Taiwan ratified the nonproliferation treaty, among the earliest states to do so. For some years, however, it has been considered a plausible candidate for nuclear arms development, because of its ad-

23. See New York Times, *Index*, p. 116.
24. Richard Halloran, *New York Times*, February 9, 1975.
25. Robert Lindsey, *New York Times*, December 17, 1975.

vanced industrial base, including a relatively sophisticated nuclear technology, and because its adversary, Communist China, is a nuclear power.

Ratification of the nonproliferation treaty (on January 27, 1970) was wholly consistent with Taiwan's declaratory policy of pursuing only civil uses of nuclear energy and nuclear research generally. But Taiwan's expulsion from the United Nations in 1971 isolated it from many states that switched their diplomatic and economic ties to Communist China. Taiwan was also ousted from the International Atomic Energy Agency in 1972, but with U.S. encouragement it has continued to accept the full range of IAEA safeguards, including on-site inspection of all its nuclear facilities and materials. The Communist Chinese, who insist that all ties, however informal, between Taiwan and the IAEA be severed, have not yet assumed Taiwan's place in the IAEA.

The most authoritative public statement on Taiwan's nuclear arms policy came from Premier Chiang Ching-kuo in September 1975. It reflects a degree of past ambiguity, but comes down on the side of non-acquisition. Noting that his government had begun research on nuclear arms seventeen years before and had considered building up a nuclear arsenal, he said, "When I broached the idea to the late president, he rejected it flatly on the ground that we cannot use nuclear weapons to hurt our own countrymen."[26]

The United States views all reactors and nuclear materials in Taiwan as adequately safeguarded. American-built reactors are safeguarded by a trilateral U.S.-Taiwan-IAEA agreement and a bilateral agreement of June 22, 1972, that would come into effect if for any reason the IAEA no longer had jurisdiction to inspect the facilities.[27] A Canadian-built reactor is safeguarded only by a bilateral arrangement between Taiwan and the IAEA, which is not backed up by a bilateral agreement between Canada and Taiwan. This leaves a loophole through which materials for weapons uses could be diverted if IAEA inspection were terminated. The United States undoubtedly would take measures to rectify that situation and to assure that two research reactors designed and built in Taiwan were inspected.

Taiwan's nuclear technology and supporting infrastructure are considerably more advanced than South Korea's. Its nuclear power effort has also reached a higher stage of development. Nuclear research is

26. *Daily Report: Asia and Pacific* (Washington: Foreign Broadcast Information Service), September 24, 1975.
27. 23 U.S.T. 945.

carried on at two principal centers, the Institute of Nuclear Science and the Institute of Nuclear Energy Research. The former, located at National Tsing Hua University in Hsin-chu, has three small research reactors, including a 0.1-watt mobile educational reactor used for training and demonstration, and Taiwan's first reactor, a 1-megawatt enriched-uranium assembly supplied by the United States in 1961. The latter, Taiwan's major nuclear research and development center, was established in 1968 as a civilian offshoot of the military-operated Chung Shan Institute of Science with which it still cooperates closely. It operates the Canadian-designed reactor. This Canadian assembly is virtually identical to its counterpart in India, the 40-megawatt Trombay reactor. The Taiwan reactor, which has a maximum capacity to produce twenty-two pounds of plutonium a year,[28] has been in operation since April 1973.[29]

Taiwan's Atomic Energy Council, directly accountable to the premier, is charged with the responsibility for the country's nuclear energy program. The council plans to have in operation by 1985 three power plants of American design, each with two light-water reactors fueled by enriched uranium. The two 636-megawatt reactors for the initial plant were expected to begin operating before 1980, and those for the second plant by 1985. If this ambitious program succeeds, Taiwan will have an installed nuclear power capacity of approximately 5,500 megawatts by 1985. Since all of the projected power reactors are of U.S. design, Taiwan will be dependent on the United States for the enriched uranium to fuel them. The fuel contracts were signed by the two governments on June 14, 1975. When U.S. inspectors found that Taiwan had built a reprocessing laboratory during the early 1970s, the United States forced Taiwan to stop reprocessing of nuclear material.[30]

Should Taiwan eventually produce a small number of nuclear bombs, they could be delivered in properly adapted F-5E fighter-bombers to targets on the periphery of the People's Republic of China. Taiwan's air force had about a hundred F-5Es in June 1977 as well as a coproduction arrangement with Northrop for building additional ones.[31] Taiwan has no surface-to-surface missiles capable of reaching the Chinese mainland.

28. *Washington Post*, July 20, 1972.

29. See Melinda Liu, *Washington Post*, February 27, 1977.

30. See Edward Schumacher, *Washington Post*, August 29, 1976; David Binder, *New York Times*, August 30, 1976; Fox Butterfield, *New York Times*, September 5, 1976; and Don Oberdorfer, *Washington Post*, September 23, 1976.

31. Wheeler, comp., "World Air Forces 1977," p. 111.

South Korea's Nuclear Incentives

The incentives for South Korea to acquire nuclear arms must be regarded as stronger than those in most Third World states on the nuclear threshold. Many pressures for and against going nuclear are present, but the chief factor is a growing sense of insecurity and uncertainty in face of the continuing, if not increasing military threat from North Korea, and the gnawing fear that the United States may diminish its security support or abandon South Korea altogether. This anxiety has been aggravated by the fall of the Saigon government in April 1975, the imposition of a Marxist regime in Angola in 1976 by Russia and Cuba, and most important of all by President Carter's stated intention in March 1977 to withdraw all U.S. ground forces from South Korea within five years.[32]

Following the U.S. defeat in South Vietnam, President Ford and Defense Secretary Schlesinger reaffirmed America's commitment to South Korea. At one point Mr. Schlesinger suggested that the United States would not hesitate to use tactical nuclear weapons to defend South Korea. Later he pointedly praised "the self-help efforts" of the South Korean government, agreeing with President Park Chung-hee that in about five years reductions in U.S. forces could begin, but adding that "it is at least arguable that a U.S. presence will need to remain for the indefinite future."[33]

The South Koreans' fear of being abandoned by the United States and exposed to their implacable adversary has strengthened the proponents of nuclear arms in Seoul. They can argue with some plausibility that even a small arsenal of first-generation bombs could serve as a deterrent against a massive conventional assault from North Korea after there are no longer any U.S. troops in the South. Assuming that the North had no nuclear weapons, the South could hold the cities in the North in hostage, threatening a countervalue strike if there were a major violation of the demilitarized zone. Though it is reasonable to assume that the South would not use weapons of mass destruction against brother Koreans, this constraint might not hold in a massive attack. Cities might be ruled

32. Ernest W. Lefever, "Withdrawal From Korea: A Perplexing Decision," *Strategic Review*, vol. 6 (Winter 1978), pp. 28–35.
33. Quoted by Richard Halloran, *New York Times*, September 14, 1975.

out as targets, and the South's nuclear arms used only against airfields or directly against a massive mechanized invading force.

A more compelling argument against a nuclear buildup in the South is that it would provoke a conventional attack from the North before the South could develop an effective deterrent. A nuclear force in the South could also provoke a nuclear effort in the North, though it is unlikely that the Soviet Union or China would provide the necessary assistance. Either or both of the nuclear powers might intervene, however, with conventional or nuclear forces, to save the North and to reunite the peninsula by force under communist rule.

The foreign policy arguments advanced for going nuclear if the United States diminishes or abandons its commitment have considerable appeal. Nuclear arms are advocated as a supplement to the conventional military buildup designed to compensate for the loss not only of American firepower but of the implied U.S. nuclear guarantee. Without American help, it can be argued, the South needs a nuclear deterrent to buttress its international prestige and diplomatic leverage as well as to deter an attack. But nuclear-induced prestige has proved to be an ephemeral asset in India. And diplomatic muscle is the product of many factors, including conventional military strength, the productivity of the economy, and the quality of political leadership.

In South Korea, as in the other countries examined in this study, there are no sound economic reasons for developing nuclear arms. There is an economic case for the development of nuclear energy, but the diversion of technology, skilled manpower, or fuels for weapons would clearly detract from rather than add to a rational nuclear power program. Further, even a modest nuclear arms program would be a heavy drain on the economy. South Korea's decision about nuclear arms will probably be based primarily on its perception of external danger, not on economic or domestic factors. This perception will be greatly affected by the extent to which the government and people feel isolated, exposed to their chief adversary, and abandoned by the United States.

Taiwan's Nuclear Incentives

In Taiwan, security may have an even more pronounced role in a nuclear decision than in South Korea. Taiwan is far more isolated diplomatically than South Korea, and its implacable enemy is a nuclear power. Communist China's quiet pressure on the United States to ignore, dilute, or terminate its mutual defense treaty with Taiwan is considerable. If the United States should yield to this pressure, Taiwan would lose its only strong ally. It would then be virtually alone in the world, an island confronting a mainland colossus across the narrow Formosa Strait. The leaders of Taiwan fear the day when their country may be abandoned, and certainly some of them are advocating that Taiwan develop a nuclear force as soon as possible to deter a mainland Chinese ultimatum or military attack calculated to bring the island under communist control. Psychologically and politically, Taiwan's situation is quite similar to that of Israel—each feels its very survival as an independent state would be threatened if the United States withdrew its diplomatic and military support (though the United States has no formal security ties with Israel).

Given Taiwan's precarious situation, the "normal" constraints against acquiring a nuclear force may seem pale and ineffectual but they are, nevertheless, operative. Perhaps the chief constraint is the possible or probable ineffectiveness of a Taiwanese nuclear force against mainland China. How can a small force, created either before or after the United States withdrew its security guarantees, deter an attack by mainland China which has a much more formidable force? The French nuclear deterrent in the face of the Soviet Union may be an appealing model, but France does not border on the USSR and it is protected by the American nuclear umbrella. At most, the French deterrent is a supplement to the U.S. strategic deterrent.

The role of the United States is crucial. It opposes nuclear arms acquisition by Taiwan and also opposes the conquest of Taiwan by Communist China. But if U.S. normalization with the People's Republic is achieved at the price of dissolving the mutual defense treaty with the Chinese Nationalists, the latter will be compelled to make a difficult choice. It is possible that the formal treaty would be replaced by an informal American commitment to protect Taiwan against attack. Presumably, the Seventh Fleet would still be patrolling the Formosa Strait. Even if Taiwan had no assurance of U.S. assistance, the Chinese Communists would not find it easy to conquer a determined people armed heavily with conventional weapons. To attempt to augment this strength with a nuclear force would carry the risks of preemption from the mainland, alienation of the United States, and diversion of resources from conventional military power.

South Korea's Nuclear Future

Until 1985, and indeed until 2000, the key external factor in determining the security and territorial integrity of South Korea will be the behavior of the United States. American troops have been in Korea more than a quarter of a century and some units may stay for another twenty-five years. As long as they do remain, even in reduced numbers, and as long as the United States keeps its mutual defense pledge to Korea, the security of that embattled country will probably be assured. Under continued U.S. protection, South Korea may very well be constrained from going nuclear. Given these circumstances, a nonnuclear South Korea would probably be able to hold its own militarily against North Korea as long as there were no substantial increase in military aid to the North from Russia or China. Drastic political changes in the North or in the big-power climate might make it feasible for the two Koreas to normalize their relations or even unite peacefully on terms acceptable to each.

In spite of President Carter's determination to pull out U.S. ground troops, firm schedules have not been set for U.S. ground or air units to leave South Korea. The timing, character, and pace of withdrawal will have a significant bearing on South Korea's security position. Even more important will be the nature of the U.S. security pledge during and after the withdrawal. The 1954 pledge to "meet the common danger" is general, and its provision to do so "in accordance with constitutional processes" opens the way for U.S. congressional involvement in any decision to come to South Korea's aid.[34] The United States probably would be more likely to come to the aid of an endangered ally if U.S. troops on its soil were also threatened. But the United States might well aid an ally if significant U.S. interests were perceived to be seriously endangered and if it appeared that U.S. help would be effective and feasible, whether or not U.S. troops were stationed in the country. The character of U.S. aid would depend on circumstances. The United States has never used nuclear weapons to defend an ally, although the implicit threat to do so has doubtless had a moderating influence on Soviet military and political behavior toward West Berlin, Western Germany, other NATO countries, and to some extent the Middle East. After the last U.S. soldier has departed, the U.S. commitment to South Korea presumably

34. 5 U.S.T. 2368.

will change, as will the deterrent effect of the 1954 treaty on North Korea.

The root question is the extent of the U.S. interest in South Korea, which, in turn, reflects the importance attached to Japan in the larger strategic picture. The general assumption is that South Korea is important because the security of Japan is regarded as vital to U.S. interests. In 1950 the United States fought to defend South Korea without a prior commitment to do so. Ten or twenty years from now South Korea may not be considered vital. If the U.S. assessment of its significance should be downgraded significantly, it would create a pronounced sense of insecurity in South Korea which proponents of a nuclear force there could play on.

South Korea is capable of building a small deterrent nuclear force by 1985 and a more significant one by 2000. A determined effort to build a force by 1985 would inject a new power factor in the Korean equation which would exacerbate tensions and could lead to conventional or nuclear war. Ironically, in a period of declining U.S. interest, the very threat by South Korea to go nuclear would have an ambiguous impact on the United States, inducing an implicit counterthreat of U.S. withdrawal and a U.S. reaffirmation of a strong security commitment.

In South Korea, President Carter's pullout policy has decisively strengthened the forces calling for an independent nuclear deterrent. A firm South Korean decision to go nuclear in a period of ambiguous or declining U.S. support would tend to be highly destabilizing because it would tempt North Korea to launch a preemptive conventional attack. The danger would be greater if U.S. forces were being withdrawn and still greater if they had been removed altogether. It is not likely that the North would attack as long as U.S. ground troops were deployed in the South and as long as the North assumed that air units of the Seventh Fleet would respond to such an attack.

Any assault from the North would mean war which could end in another stalemate or could reunify Korea by force. South Korea could probably, without nuclear arms or U.S. combat involvement, deter or throw back a North Korean assault if it maintains an effective and ready conventional military establishment and if North Korea receives no active combat assistance from either China or the Soviet Union. But the United States and North Korea's two nuclear patrons each would be tempted to support its ally, thus raising the specter of superpower involvement. If the South reunited the country without U.S. assistance, this would presumably be a net plus for stability and U.S. interests. Russia and China would not look with equanimity on such an outcome and either might be tempted to intervene. If either supported the North and the United States did not intervene to help the South, the country would doubtless be reunited by the North. American failure to defend South Korea would cast doubts on the U.S. commitment to Japan and thus jeopardize both the security of Japan and stability in the Pacific generally.

If in the face of a declining U.S. security commitment and the withdrawal of all U.S. forces by 1980, South Korea should undertake to build a small independent nuclear force, it could turn out to be either a deterrent or a provocation, depending on how it was perceived in the North. This would be determined by military, political, and psychological factors not directly related to nuclear weapons as such. It is unlikely that the North's response would be nuclear. The North is neither as technically advanced nor as wealthy as the South. Recent history suggests that neither Russia nor China would look with favor on helping a small client state to secure an independent nuclear capability and that both would probably attempt to dissuade, or even prevent, it from doing so. Further, each of the communist powers would be opposed to the provision of such assistance by the other. In the unlikely event that the North should undertake a small nuclear effort, there is little chance that it could match the South Korean program.

The real problem in Korea is not nuclear arms as such, but rather political and conventional military realities, the chief counters being in the hands of external powers. The two Koreas are and are likely to remain for some years client states, and their behavior will be limited though not wholly controlled by their patrons. The uneasy stability that exists would be likely to disappear if the U.S. commitment to the South were to diminish, whether or not a nuclear factor were introduced. If nuclear arms were developed to compensate for a declining or departed U.S. presence, even greater instability would result, unless circumstances were so propitious that the South's new capability could deter as effectively as the earlier U.S. military presence.

It seems doubtful that South Korea would ever get to the point of developing a significant, war-fighting nuclear force. The beginning of even a token capability would probably set in motion countermeasures that would preclude a straight-line development in South Korea from a nuclear explosion to a force of twenty or more small nuclear bombs with a supporting delivery system. But should a militarily significant force be developed, its impact on stability in Korea and the region would be as indeterminate as that of a smaller force. Again, the outcome would be dependent on the response of the North, Russia, China, and the United States.

The central factor remains the United States, the strength of its military posture in the South, and the extent of its interest and commitment. Since South Korea is not convinced of the steadfastness of the American resolve, it seems likely that its leaders are engaging in research and development designed to create a nuclear arms option that could be exercised or rejected at some future time. Maintaining the option is not the same as a crash program to develop a bomb. It is an investment in keeping open a future decision which, depending on circumstances, could go either way.

Taiwan's Nuclear Future

Despite America's long, costly, and often controversial relationship in support of the Republic of China, most observers regard the defense of Taiwan as less central to vital U.S. interests in the Pacific than the defense of South Korea. This is due largely to the importance of Japan to the United States. The withdrawal of U.S. troops from South Korea "would cause the Japanese to question the firmness of the U.S. commitment to Japan. There is no satisfactory substitute for a significant U.S. combat force stationed in Korea as an earnest of U.S. intentions."[35]

The future of Taiwan as a tentative but independent state has been clouded since ties between the People's Republic and the United States began developing in 1972. The pressure for normalization of the two powers' relations appears to be growing, with the U.S. ambassadors in Peking and Tokyo urging diplomatic ties. The fate of Taiwan is thus bound up with the changing balance of power and interest among the

35. Ralph N. Clough, *Deterrence and Defense in Korea: The Role of U.S. Forces* (Brookings Institution, 1976), p. 61.

great powers. Looking toward 1985 and 2000, the future for the island republic could be simply a continuation of the ambiguous status quo. Taiwan could go on being recognized diplomatically by the United States and some twenty other governments and continue trading with the United States, Japan, and other countries indefinitely. The issue of contested sovereignty may for some time be considered in both Peking and Taipei a less unattractive alternative than active military confrontation.

There is also the possibility that the mainland Chinese could launch an active military campaign to seize Taiwan. But this would not be likely as long as a U.S. security commitment, even in diluted form, remained on the books. Even if there were no formal pact, the very presence of the Seventh Fleet might deter an invasion from the mainland. And a successful invasion is not a foregone conclusion.

With the communist regime's continued pressure on the United States to recognize its claim over Taiwan, the nationalist government is deeply apprehensive about the steadfastness of the U.S. commitment. This sense of insecurity has prompted it to take measures to develop a nuclear arms option that could be implemented if Taiwan were abandoned by the United States. Any Taiwanese nuclear force would doubtless be designed to deter an attack from the mainland, not to mount one against it. Taiwan is capable of building a small airborne force by 1985 and a missile force by 2000.

The impact of a small deterrent force on Taiwan would depend largely on the character of Taiwan's relation with the United States, and, in particular, the status of the U.S. security guarantee. As in the case of South Korea, this relationship is more important than the nuclear factor as such. China is not likely to launch an attack to take the island as long as it is under a U.S. security guarantee, whether or not Taiwan has a nuclear force. If there were no such guarantee, China would probably seek to take the island by a combination of political, psychological, and military means.

The effect of a small deterrent force on U.S.-Taiwan relations and on stability would vary with circumstances. At present, an uneasy equilibrium exists between Taiwan and China and among the great powers in the region. It is not likely that this balance would be upset by the development of a small nuclear force by Taiwan as long as the U.S. security guarantee remained intact, but neither would it be strengthened by such a force. The withdrawal of the U.S. guarantee, whether abruptly or in accord with an announced timetable, would introduce instability by tempting China to incorporate Taiwan by force. This objective could not be won without cost because of Taiwan's formidable military defenses, but the cost would not be greatly increased if this conventional strength were augmented by a small nuclear force designed for deterrence. Hence, in a military confrontation, Taiwan would probably not use its nuclear bombs for fear of nuclear retaliation. In short, a small deterrent force would not be necessary with a continued American guarantee. Without such a pledge, a nuclear deterrent could increase Taiwan's bargaining power with the Peking government in any future negotiations. It could well facilitate a peaceful resolution of outstanding differences between the two Chinas.

If Taiwan should develop sometime a nuclear force of thirty to fifty medium bombs with a reliable missile delivery system capable of reaching major urban targets on the mainland, it is possible that it could deter a conventional attack. But it might provoke a nuclear attack, or at least a nuclear threat. If it succeeded in deterring all military efforts, such a force would have a stabilizing effect, but new military or political factors could upset this tense and uneasy balance. Since it is quite unlikely that China would remain still while Taiwan was developing this force, here, as in Korea, the problem would doubtless be posed at an early stage and a low level of nuclear capability.

Since the United States is continuing to draw down the size of its military presence in Taiwan, it seems likely that Taiwan is actively involved in research that could lead to the development of nuclear arms. It is undoubtedly operating within the political and physical constraints implicit in its security ties with the United States, its adherence to the nonproliferation treaty, and its acceptance of IAEA safeguards on nuclear facilities. But if it should feel abandoned and seriously threatened, Taiwan may feel compelled to exercise the nuclear option and thus abrogate the agreements that have limited its nuclear activities. Like South Korea, Taiwan is keeping its options open. Each is moving toward the threshold of a big and nearly irreversible decision by making a number of small and reversible decisions. In pursuing this course they are behaving very much like Pakistan, Iran, and Egypt.

If current big-power relations persist, it would be safe to assume that the United States would be more likely to intervene in behalf of South

Korea than in behalf of Taiwan, if for no other reason than to protect U.S. troops which are the visible symbol of the U.S. commitment to Seoul.

CHAPTER SIX

Brazil and Argentina: Regional Rivals

The system of security assurances proposed by the three nuclear weapon Powers does not represent a valid and balanced counterpart to what the non-nuclear countries are entitled to expect when they renounce the possession of nuclear weapons.

FOREIGN MINISTER OF BRAZIL, 1968

Whilst the arms race among the great Powers continues and is embodied in the production of ever more sophisticated weapons of mass destruction, those States which have a lower industrial capacity are to bind themselves to a discipline that inevitably spells new limitations on their sovereignty.

ARGENTINE REPRESENTATIVE TO THE UNITED NATIONS, 1968[1]

THE TWO GIANTS of South America, Brazil and Argentina, are traditional rivals for economic, political, and military influence within and beyond the region. Economically, Brazil is surging ahead of its southern neighbor. Its dynamic and productive economy is rooted in greater internal stability than is the economy of Argentina, a state torn by terrorism and insurgency. Brazil's spectacular economic growth since 1967 has been matched by increased military expenditures. Between 1967 when its gross national product was $52.5 billion and 1976 when it had increased to $116.7 billion (both in constan 1975 dollars), its average annual real growth rate was 9.4 percent.[2] During this period

1. "Statement by the Brazilian Foreign Minister (de Magalhães Pinto) to the First Committee of the General Assembly: Nonproliferation of Nuclear Weapons, May 3, 1968," and "Statement by the Argentine Representative (Ruda) to the First Committee of the General Assembly: Arms Transfers [Extract], December 3, 1968," in U.S. Arms Control and Disarmament Agency, *Documents on Disarmament, 1968* (Government Printing Office, 1969), pp. 280, 763.

2. Figures for Argentina and Brazil are from U.S. Arms Control and Disarmament Agency, *World Military Expenditures and Arms Transfers, 1967–1976* (ACDA, 1978), tables 2 and 4, pp. 34, 36, 77, 79.

Brazil's military spending rose from $1.18 billion to $1.56 billion (1975 dollars). Because of its large population, including millions of people in the underdeveloped Amazon basin, its 1976 GNP translates into only $1,061 per capita. Argentina, by contrast, had a per capita GNP of $1,367 in 1976. Between 1967 and 1976 its GNP grew from $29.5 billion to $36.1 billion (constant 1975 dollars), an average annual real growth rate of 2.3 percent. Its military expenditures (in constant dollars) of $590 million in 1967 were higher than Brazil's, but by 1976 they were much lower, at $861 million.

For more than three-quarters of a century, South America has not seen large-scale military conflict. There are contested borders and there has been insurgency in several countries, but there has been no war except for the one between Paraguay and Bolivia in the 1930s. While the region has been tranquil compared to the Middle East and Asia, interstate conflict is possible by 1985 and more likely by the year 2000. It is probable, however, that each state will seek to redress its grievances and achieve its objectives by a combination of diplomatic and economic measures, undergirding them with a threat of military force. In this drama Brazil and Argentina are destined to play major roles. The historic rivalry between Latin America's two most powerful states appears to many observers to have been resolved in favor of Brazil, or at least to have given way to a clearly dominant position for Brazil. In 1977, Brazil had 271,800 men under arms compared to 129,900 for Argentina[3] and a defense budget two and one-half times larger than Argentina's. The Brazilian air force had 42,800 men and 131 combat aircraft and the Argentine air force 17,000 men and 146 combat aircraft, but the latter's planes were less modern.

As Argentina's power declines relative to that of Brazil,[4] Argentina's comparatively weak regime, or its successor, may very well be tempted to redress the loss of power and prestige by developing nuclear weapons. This may be seen as the only way to catch up with Brazil and to recapture an earlier position of glory and leadership. The Brazilians, sensing this mood, may seriously contemplate the same course to insure Brazil's preeminence and guarantee it a position of hegemony. Thus, both countries appear to be lively candidates for the nuclear option.

Each country is allied with the United States under the Inter-

3. International Institute for Strategic Studies, *The Military Balance: 1977–1978* (London: IISS, 1977), pp. 67–68.
4. See Penny Lernoux, *Washington Post*, June 9, 1977.

American Treaty of Reciprocal Assistance (Rio Pact) of 1947 under which "an armed attack by any State against an American State shall be considered as an attack against all American States and, consequently, each one of the said Contracting Parties undertakes to assist in meeting the attack."[5] Thus each enjoys an implicit U.S. nuclear guarantee. Rio Pact members, unlike NATO members, Taiwan, and South Korea, have not had U.S. forces stationed on their soil, but each of them has received substantial military equipment, training, and advice from the United States. Though the United States remains the major military supplier for virtually all Latin American countries, some of them have turned in recent years to Western European suppliers, and Peru now buys from the Soviet Union and Eastern Europe. Cuba is entirely dependent on the Soviet Union.

In Brazil and Argentina there is a growing sense of nationalism, increasing apprehension about U.S. policies in Latin America, and a strengthening of economic and diplomatic ties with Western Europe, Japan, and various countries in Asia and Africa. Argentina has developed ties with the group of nonaligned states in an attempt to upgrade its Third World credentials, and Brazil has made gestures in this direction. On February 21, 1976, Brazil and the United States signed a consultative accord that provides for meetings every six months between the U.S. secretary of state and Brazilian foreign minister.[6] This confers status on Brazil as a big power similar to Japan and India, with which the United States has such arrangements.

In early 1977, tension between the United States and Brazil and Argentina increased over open U.S. criticism of the alleged violation of human rights by their governments. Both countries rejected specific offers of American military assistance because they viewed this criticism as unwarranted interference in their domestic affairs. Brazil went further and on March 11, 1977, canceled its twenty-five-year-old military assistance agreement with the United States. Another irritant for Brazil was the U.S. effort to have Brazil and West Germany rescind their nuclear assistance pact. One observer commented that U.S.-Brazilian relations in 1977 were "at an all-time low."[7]

Argentina and Brazil have the most advanced civil nuclear energy programs with the greatest military potential in Latin America. Chile,

---

5. 62 Stat. 1700, art. 3.
6. Joanne Omang, *Washington Post*, February 20 and 22, 1976.
7. John B. Oakes, *New York Times*, April 25, 1977.

Cuba, and Mexico trail far behind. The scope and depth of its nuclear program give Argentina a significant edge over Brazil, although this advantage will probably have diminished radically by 1985. Both countries have been acquiring the scientific and technical knowledge, the nuclear raw materials, and the industrial equipment required for the production of nuclear explosives and weapons. They oppose international controls that would limit their research and development programs for the peaceful use of atomic energy or prevent the construction of nuclear explosives for peaceful applications. Both have refused to sign the nuclear nonproliferation treaty. They regard the possession of advanced nuclear technology as an important aspect of their national scientific and economic development and as a badge of their independence.

Brazil's Nuclear Status

Brazil's nuclear policy reflects its rapid economic growth, its decreasing dependence on the United States, and its drive for global influence and status.[8] Its appetite for nuclear power reactors was stimulated, but not initiated, by the world energy crisis. Before oil prices were raised by the Organization of Petroleum Exporting Countries in 1973, Brazil was importing more than 70 percent of its oil. But as early as 1971, the National Nuclear Energy Commission of Brazil had planned to have an installed capacity of thirty thousand megawatts of nuclear power by the year 2000.

Brazil's nuclear policies are fairly well expressed by its membership in the International Atomic Energy Agency and its refusal to sign the nonproliferation treaty. One of its principal objections to the treaty is that it permits nuclear powers to keep and increase their arsenals while denying nuclear arms to other states, thereby discriminating against the nonnuclear states.[9] The treaty also prohibits nonnuclear states from conducting peaceful nuclear explosions, thus consigning them to a perpetual dependency on nuclear states. Moreover, Brazil believes that the treaty is weak because it fails to provide for sanctions against nuclear aggres-

8. See Riordan Roett, "Brazil Ascendant: International Relations and Geopolitics in the Late 20th Century," *Journal of International Affairs*, vol. 29 (Fall 1975), pp. 139–54.

9. "Statement by the Brazilian Foreign Minister," pp. 279–80.

sors, and that it cannot be effective until all states adhere to it.[10] Given these far-reaching objections, it seems unlikely that Brazil will sign the treaty in the foreseeable future.

Brazil has also expressed reservations about the Treaty for the Prohibition of Nuclear Weapons in Latin America, known as the Treaty of Tlatelolco, which was signed in Mexico on February 14, 1967. The treaty prohibits the introduction of nuclear arms into a region of 7.5 million square miles with a population of nearly 200 million. Its parties—all Latin American states except Cuba—pledge not to manufacture or otherwise acquire nuclear weapons. The treaty also prohibits the installation of nuclear weapons bases on Latin American soil, but does not prohibit the transit of ships carrying nuclear arms in the territorial waters of the member states. The treaty has been ratified, at least conditionally, by all signatories except Argentina. Brazil was an early leader in the Latin American movement for a nuclear-free zone and an active participant in drafting the treaty. But when ratifying the treaty, Brazil registered three reservations designed to maintain maximum flexibility for peaceful nuclear development. It insisted that the treaty was not yet binding on Brazil because it was to come into effect only after being ratified by all Latin American states (most Latin American governments waived that stricture when ratifying the treaty). Brazil insisted also that Protocol 2 was not binding until it was ratified by all nuclear powers (only Chile and Trinidad and Tobago have expressed a similar reservation). The protocol, which obligates the nuclear powers to respect the nuclear-free status of Latin America and not to use or threaten to use nuclear arms against states in this region, has been ratified in Washington, London, Paris, and Peking, but not in Moscow.

Brazil's third reservation about the Tlatelolco Treaty relates to the stringent constraints on peaceful nuclear explosions. Brazil has long shown an interest in nuclear explosions for excavation projects. Any signatory planning such an explosion, according to article 18, must provide

10. Ibid., pp. 280–81. See also "Statement by the Brazilian Representative (Azeredo da Silviera) to the Eighteen Nation Disarmament Committee: Nonproliferation of Nuclear Weapons, March 14, 1967," *Documents on Disarmament, 1967*, p. 140. For a discussion of Brazil's position on the nonproliferation treaty, see H. Jon Rosenbaum and Glenn M. Cooper, "Brazil and the Nuclear Non-proliferation Treaty," *International Affairs* (London), vol. 46 (January 1970), pp. 74–90; and H. Jon Rosenbaum, "Brazil's Nuclear Aspirations," in Onkar Marwah and Ann Schulz, eds., *Nuclear Proliferation and the Near-Nuclear Countries* (Ballinger, 1975), pp. 255–77.

well in advance detailed information on the size, character, force, and expected fallout from the intended explosion to the Agency for the Prohibition of Nuclear Weapons in Latin America and to the IAEA. Both agencies may send technical personnel to "observe all the preparations, including the explosion of the device, and shall have unrestricted access to any area in the vicinity of the site." Brazil has also opposed a recommended safeguards agreement in which the two agencies cooperate. Instead it insists on the right to negotiate its own safeguard agreements with the IAEA and the supplier state[11] and has entered into such arrangements with the United States, France, West Germany, and other states providing nuclear technology or fuels.[12]

All these indicators add up to a remarkably consistent policy. There is heavy emphasis on Brazil's right to use nuclear energy for power and possibly for peaceful explosions. It appears that Brazil also seeks the capacity to conduct a nuclear explosion in order to produce a bomb—an achievement that would be seen as dramatic evidence of Brazil's political and military leadership in the region and beyond. The only indication that its nuclear policy might be motivated by defensive security considerations is its rhetoric about "the Argentine threat." One student of Brazilian affairs concludes that Brazil will develop nuclear explosive devices, " if it has not done so already."[13]

Until recently, Brazil was largely dependent on the United States for external nuclear assistance. In August 1955 the two states signed a bilateral agreement on joint nuclear research. In 1968 they signed an agreement on research and development that was superseded in 1972 by a new thirty-year agreement.[14] All U.S. nuclear assistance to Brazil is safeguarded by trilateral arrangements with the IAEA.

Brazil established a National Nuclear Energy Commission (CNEN) in 1956 within the Ministry of Mines and Energy for the coordination of all nuclear activities. The commission consists of five members, all of whom are appointed by the president. Three government-owned companies operate the country's nuclear program. The general direction and implementation of the program are the responsibility of Nuclebras, the

11. See John R. Redick, *Military Potential of Latin American Nuclear Energy Programs,* International Studies Series, vol. 1 (Sage Publications, 1972), pp. 28–29.

12. Brazil's position is spelled out in a 23-page white paper signed by President Ernesto Geisel; see Federative Republic of Brazil, *The Brazilian Nuclear Program* (1977).

13. Rosenbaum, "Brazil's Nuclear Aspirations," p. 271.

14. 23 U.S.T. 2477.

Brazilian Nuclear Corporation. Electrobras, the federal power utility, is particularly concerned with production of nuclear power, and CPRM, the Mineral Resources and Prospecting Company, with the mining of uranium.

Brazil's oldest nuclear research reactor, the American-designed IEA-R1 located at the Institute of Atomic Energy near São Paulo, has been in operation since 1957; it is a five-megawatt reactor fueled with enriched uranium from the United States. A second research reactor, Triga 1, began operating in 1960. Also of American design and fueled with enriched uranium, it is located at the Institute of Radioactive Research near Belo Horizonte and can produce one hundred kilowatts of power. Brazilian plans call for an increase in the power capacity of both reactors. A third research reactor, Argonaut, located at the Institute of Nuclear Engineering in Rio de Janeiro, was built primarily by Brazilian technicians, but based on a U.S. design. This ten-kilowatt reactor, which has been in operation since 1965, utilizes fuel elements fabricated at the pilot facility of the Institute of Atomic Energy. All three reactors are covered by IAEA safeguards.

The country's first two nuclear power reactors, with a total generating capacity of eighteen hundred megawatts, are to supply Rio de Janeiro. Both are Westinghouse-designed, light-water reactors. Angra 1, supplying a third of the generating capacity, was scheduled to begin commercial operation in 1979 and Angra 2 to be built after 1981. The power plant at Angra dos Reis will be safeguarded by the IAEA.

In their effort to develop a broader base for an indigenous nuclear industry, Brazilian scientists have been pursuing research in more advanced nuclear technologies. They have concentrated on acquiring expertise in fast-breeder reactor and uranium-enrichment technology since Brazil lacks significant known reserves of uranium ore but has the world's second largest reserves of thorium, an element that has been experimentally used in nuclear reactors to produce fissile U-233. In May 1967 Brazil signed an agreement with France to assist in uranium exploration in Brazil's interior regions and in research in fast-breeder reactor technology. A June 1969 agreement with West Germany provided for cooperation in uranium-enrichment research, notably centrifuge separation techniques, as well as assistance in planning for Brazil's longer-range nuclear energy development.

Brazil's dependence on external uranium sources, especially enrichment services, led to strained relations when the United States in 1975 refused to supply Brazil with uranium-enrichment technology that would have enabled it to embark on a large-scale nuclear power effort.[15] This incident, which provoked disagreement among U.S. policymakers, reflected divisions between those who advocated U.S. nuclear assistance as a means of restraining the recipient's behavior and others who sought to control the spread of nuclear weapons by denying the technology to produce them.[16] The debate was apparently resolved, at least temporarily, in favor of the technology restrictors. As a result, Brazil turned elsewhere for its assistance.[17] On June 27, it concluded an agreement with West Germany providing for construction of as many as eight enriched-uranium, light-water reactors, each with a capacity of twelve hundred to thirteen hundred megawatts. Four would be built by 1986 and four more by 1990. In addition, the West Germans agreed to provide Brazil with a fuel fabrication plant, a plutonium reprocessing facility, and a uranium-enrichment plant, giving Brazil a full fuel cycle and the basic capability to manufacture nuclear bombs. Total cost estimates of the agreement ran as high as $8 billion, to be financed, in part, by eventual Brazilian deliveries of enriched uranium to Germany.[18] The projected enrichment plant would be based on a nozzle process rather than gaseous diffusion, which is used in the United States and in all other nuclear weapons states. Brazilian scientists have worked on this process in collaboration with West Germans, but the process has not yet proved commercially feasible.

Within a fortnight of the signing of the West German agreement, the Brazilian government announced the conclusion of a nuclear accord with France,[19] like that with Germany a continuation of earlier collaboration. Under its terms, France agreed to sell an experimental fast-breeder reactor to Brazil and to assist Brazil in the exploration and development of its uranium deposits. Significantly, an announcement of a major uranium discovery by a French-Brazilian team was made ten

15. David Burnham, *New York Times*, December 11, 1975.

16. See "Nuclear Exports: A U.S. Firm's Troublesome Flirtation with Brazil," *Science*, July 25, 1975, pp. 267–69.

17. Dixie Lee Ray, chairman of the U.S. Atomic Energy Commission, strongly favored providing the technology to Brazil. See her testimony in *The Export Reorganization Act—1975*, Hearings before the Senate Committee on Government Operations, 94 Cong. 1 sess. (GPO, 1975), pp. 124–39, 156–60.

18. For details, see "Nuclear Proliferation: India, Germany May Accelerate the Process," *Science*, May 30, 1975, pp. 911–14.

19. *New York Times*, July 6, 1975.

days before the announcement of the new agreement.[20] Brazil's ambitious nuclear plans had by this time risen to an installed nuclear power capacity of seventy thousand megawatts by 2000.

Because of the nuclear weapons potential that the sale of West German enrichment and reprocessing technology would confer on Brazil, the United States sought to insure that adequate safeguards would be applied to the new facilities. It was concerned partly because of the secrecy surrounding the details of the Brazilian-German arrangement and Brazilian statements on the utility of peaceful nuclear explosions. At U.S. urging Brazil and West Germany agreed on comprehensive safeguards with the IAEA which would preclude "the production of either nuclear weapons or other nuclear explosives"[21] and would require the further application of safeguards to future Brazilian facilities "which incorporate any of the sensitive technology originally supplied to them."[22]

If present plans were completed between 1985 and 1990, Brazil would have an independent capability to produce nuclear weapons. To follow this course, Brazil would have to abrogate certain of its safeguard agreements. It already possesses a nuclear-capable weapons delivery system in fifteen Mirage 3 supersonic fighters purchased from France. It also has taken the initial deliveries on an order of thirty-nine F-5E and F-5B fighters from the United States. And before the year 2000 it may be possible for Brazil to develop nuclear warheads for missiles. Brazil has been actively engaged in rocket research with West German assistance and since 1965 has conducted over four hundred test launches.[23]

Argentina's Nuclear Status

Since 1950 Argentina has been engaged in an active program of nuclear research which, as in the case of India, has been directed toward developing the civil uses of nuclear power while simultaneously keeping

20. Marvine Howe, *New York Times,* June 26, 1975.

21. Niels Hansen, chargé d'affaires, embassy of the Federal Republic of Germany, letter to the editor, *New York Times,* July 7, 1975. See also Edward Wonder, "Nuclear Commerce and Nuclear Proliferation: Germany and Brazil, 1975," *Orbis,* vol. 21 (Summer 1977), pp. 277–306.

22. Myron B. Kratzer, "International Cooperation in Nuclear Energy and Nonproliferation," *Current Policy* (U.S. Department of State, Bureau of Public Affairs), November 1975, p. 4.

23. Andrew Caranfil and others, "Briefing Notes: Nuclear Proliferation After India" (Croton-on-Hudson, N.Y.: Hudson Institute, November 1, 1974), p. 43.

open a weapons option. The arms potential not only satisfies Argentina's self-perception as a continental power, but increasingly allays a sense of strategic and political inferiority vis-à-vis Brazil.

Argentina is not a signatory of the nonproliferation treaty nor is it a party to the Treaty of Tlatelolco, which it has signed but not ratified. Like Brazil, Argentina regards the nonproliferation treaty as discriminatory against the nuclear "have nots" and wants to preserve the right to conduct peaceful nuclear explosions. "Those who already have nuclear weapons are free to keep developing them without any restrictions but the others are prevented from getting them, and this is completely unfair from the point of view of energy politics," Jorge Sabato, a former member of the Atomic Energy Commission of Argentina, has complained. "It is not that we in Latin America are doing anything yet to produce weapons, it is just that we also wish to have our own capacity to judge, our own technical autonomous capability to decide what is best for our countries in that matter. For that reason we try to learn and develop as much as possible."[24] Argentina obviously wants no restrictions on its right and capacity to exercise the nuclear weapons option. This is not to say that it is determined to acquire nuclear arms, but rather that it is unwilling to foreclose the possibility of such a powerful symbol of national strength and prestige and presumably a ticket to the councils of the mighty.

Successive Argentine governments, beginning in the early 1950s during the Peron regime, have implied an interest in nuclear weapons manufacture. Indeed, when the Atomic Energy Commission was established in May 1950, it was given a responsibility "to propose to the chief executive the necessary provisions to be adopted for the defense of the nation."[25] Since its creation, the commission has been headed by an active or retired military officer, usually from the navy.

Argentina has an extensive nuclear infrastructure which includes five research reactors and a power reactor that as late as 1978 was the only one in operation in Latin America. Argentina's experience, technology, and level of nuclear expertise are considerably more advanced than Brazil's, although the gap is narrowing rapidly.

Argentina's largest research reactor, a 7.5-megawatt assembly lo-

24. Jorge Sabato, "Energy Options for Latin America," *Anticipation* (World Council of Churches, Geneva), no. 21 (October 1975), p. 36.

25. Redick, *Military Potential of Latin American Nuclear Energy Programs*, p. 15.

cated at the Ezeiza Atomic Center near Buenos Aires, was designed and built by its Atomic Energy Commission in 1967. Two smaller reactors, both with power capacities in the kilowatt range, are located at the nuclear research center at Constituentes, a suburb of Buenos Aires. A fourth, with a capacity of 0.1 watt, is located at the University of Rosario and a fifth, 0.5-watt reactor, at the University of Cordoba. All of the research reactors operate on enriched-uranium fuel supplied by the United States, but the fuel elements for the Ezeiza reactor are fabricated at a pilot facility at Constituentes. In addition, a pilot plutonium processing plant that has been in operation since 1967 is capable of reprocessing the spent fuel from the larger of the two Constituentes research reactors. The reprocessing plant, the fuel fabrication facility, and all of the research reactors are safeguarded by the IAEA.

In January 1974 Argentina's first nuclear power plant began operating. Located at Atucha, sixty miles northwest of Buenos Aires, this 318-megawatt, natural-uranium reactor was built by Siemens, a West German firm. The choice of natural-uranium technology has the advantage of relieving Argentina from dependence on an external source of enriched-uranium fuel—which would have been the case if it had purchased an American-designed reactor. Further, Argentina has the largest known reserves of uranium ore in Latin America. The Atucha plant, which supplies 5 percent of the power for Buenos Aires, is safeguarded by IAEA. The nation's second power plant, at Rio Tercero near Cordoba, was contracted jointly to Atomic Energy of Canada and the Italian firm of Italimpianti for completion before 1979.[26] It also is of natural-uranium design, with a power capacity of 600 megawatts.

Argentina probably has taken additional steps toward the completion of an independent nuclear fuel cycle based on natural uranium. France reportedly is cooperating in the construction of a pilot plutonium reprocessing plant, presumably larger than the one at Constituentes.[27] Moreover, some reports have stated that Argentina intends to build its own heavy-water plant.[28] The May 28, 1974, agreement on nuclear cooperation with India may well reflect Argentina's interest in acquiring expertise in heavy-water and plutonium-reprocessing technologies, areas

26. As a result of India's 1974 nuclear test, Canada sought explicit assurances from Argentina that the Rio Tercero reactor would not be used to produce a "peaceful atomic explosion." *New York Times,* June 29, 1974.

27. Spencer Rich, *Washington Post,* June 4, 1975.

28. Redick, *Military Potential of Latin American Nuclear Energy Programs,* p. 18.

in which India has had considerable success. The similarity of the two countries' fuel cycles provides impetus for their cooperation. An independent capability would not only have significant military implications, but would considerably reduce Argentina's reliance on external sources of technology and other nuclear assistance.

The choice of a natural-uranium fuel cycle has the advantage, for possible military application, of employing a reactor that yields more weapons-grade plutonium than an enriched-uranium reactor. And the reactor need not be shut down when fuel elements are changed, which means that spent fuel can be more easily diverted for weapons uses. Should Argentine scientists succeed in perfecting plutonium reprocessing technology and in building a sufficiently large heavy-water plant, then Argentina will be in a situation roughly analogous to that of India in the mid-1960s.[29]

When construction of its third natural-uranium power reactor was being negotiated with Canada in 1976, Argentina projected six nuclear power plants for the country, with a total capacity of thirty-seven hundred megawatts by 1985, a somewhat optimistic goal. The Atucha plant took six years to build, two more than projected. Further, Argentina's economic problems and uncertain political situation raise doubts about its administrative and financial capacity to carry through a concerted nuclear effort. On the other hand, the high level of nuclear expertise and an embryonic nuclear fuel cycle make it technically feasible for Argentina to conduct a nuclear explosion by 1980. Dr. Jorge Sabato said in 1975 that the country could build a bomb "in four years at a very reasonable cost—say $250 million, which is 10 months of deficit on the Argentine State Railways."[30] A militarily significant nuclear force would require a substantially higher level of plutonium-reprocessing technology than Argentina now has. If by 1980, Argentina could produce enough unsafeguarded plutonium (which also means producing heavy water which it now purchases from the United States) for two fifteen-kiloton bombs per year (India's level in 1975), by 1985 it could have an arsenal of ten such bombs. This generous projection does not take into account technical, administrative, or political obstacles. It is noteworthy that India paused on the nuclear threshold for approximately four years before conducting its explosion.

29. India's first heavy-water plant began operating in 1962, a plutonium plant in 1964.

30. Robert Lindley, *Washington Star,* October 6, 1975.

Existing Argentine military technology is sufficient to meet the demands of a small force that would be militarily significant with regard to Brazil, and especially to the southeastern region where there is a high concentration of industry and population. The Argentine inventory of nuclear-capable aircraft includes French Mirage 3 fighters, American A-4 fighter-bombers, and British Canberra bombers.[31] And research is under way on surface-to-surface and surface-to-air missiles.

Brazil's Nuclear Incentives

Brazil is in a dynamic and expansionist period, expansionist not necessarily in a territorial sense, but in the attempt to be the dominant economic, political, and military power on the continent and to project its influence in the larger world. The Brazilian government, with the support of the major military and economic elite groups, appears to many observers to be seeking to establish a position of unchallengeable hegemony in the region and to become a "world power." Brazil has long been motivated by a sense of destiny, a sense of mission, and a commitment to regional leadership. This doctrine has been developed and promoted among a large number of military and civilian leaders who have passed through the Superior War College of Brazil where equal emphasis is given to national security and political development. As in most Latin American countries, military leaders in Brazil think of themselves as having a "dual mission"—to defend the state in a security sense and to save the state in a political sense. They are prepared not only to act against dangers to the physical security of the state but against the dangers of subversion, alien ideology, and the weakness of inept civilian politicians.

Brazil's present military regime has pursued this dual mission with vigor and considerable success. The economy has boomed and law and order have been maintained. Externally, Brazilian influence has expanded, notably over neighboring Chile, Uruguay, Bolivia, and Paraguay. Brazil, for example, supports the claims of Bolivia for a corridor to the Pacific Ocean. Whether deliberate or not, Brazil's foreign policies have had the effect of isolating Argentina from its neighbors and placing it in an increasingly inferior position of power and influence.

Unlike the other nuclear candidates examined in this study, Brazil

31. IISS, *Military Balance: 1977–1978*, p. 67.

faces no plausible military challenge from its neighbors or beyond. It has clear military superiority in the region and is not heavily dependent on U.S. military support. Hence, any incentive within the ruling elite to acquire nuclear weapons is not rooted in a feeling of insecurity, but rather in the ambition to see Brazil become a great power. This imperial motivation contrasts sharply with the security motivation of India, Pakistan, Israel, Egypt, South Korea, and Taiwan and is more akin to the motivation of Iran.

Since rivalry and jockeying for position always feed on fear and uncertainty, Brazil must take one major potential security factor into account—a decision by Argentina to go nuclear to shore up its deteriorating position, to establish approximate military parity with Brazil, or even to achieve superiority. Argentina may attempt to upstage Brazil by developing a token or militarily significant nuclear force.

There is no evidence of how vigorously the political and security arguments for going nuclear have been advanced within Brazilian ruling circles, or what effect they have had in countering arguments for nuclear abstention. The cost argument would not weigh heavily on either side. Brazil has the resources to finance the marginal expenditure needed to add a modest program of military application to its growing nuclear energy effort. A nuclear arms program would be only a small portion of its nearly $2.1 billion defense budget (for 1977) and would not divert significant resources from the civilian economy. The argument that a nuclear capability enhances international prestige could be defended by proponents of nuclear arms as a means of assuring the supremacy of Brazil in South America, but opponents could argue that Brazil already enjoys a hegemonial position by virtue of its economic and military strength.

The most consequential arguments are likely to revolve around the risks of pursuing a nuclear course—the risk of military confrontation with Argentina, the risk of isolation, and the ultimate risk of nuclear war. The knowledge or expectation that Brazil would go nuclear would be decisive for Argentina—it would almost inevitably follow suit. The resulting technological and prestige race could increase political tension and end in conventional military or nuclear confrontation.[32] The deci-

32. C. H. Waisman deals with the relationship of "reciprocal uncertainty" between Brazil and Argentina and concludes that for Argentina the external incentives for going nuclear are more significant than internal ones. "Incentives for Nuclear Proliferation: The Case of Argentina," in Marwah and Schulz, eds., *Nuclear Proliferation and the Near-Nuclear Countries,* p. 292.

sion to go nuclear or an actual explosion by Brazil could alienate its neighbors, though it could draw closer those that wished to take refuge in Brazil's protection.

In the final analysis, Brazil's decision to conduct a nuclear explosion or to go further will be determined primarily by considerations of its fundamental national aspirations for greatness which are expressed externally by a foreign policy designed to gain and hold a position of hegemony in South America and to preclude Argentina or oil-rich Venezuela from assuming this role.

Argentina's Nuclear Incentives

In many respects, but not all, Argentina presents the converse of the situation in Brazil. The same observers who see Brazil as an ascendant power regard Argentina as a declining power in relation to Brazil, if not in absolute terms. Brazil is characterized by internal order and rapid economic growth, Argentina by turbulence and slow economic growth. More significant than economic indicators is the sharp decline in Argentina's political cohesion, self-confidence, and international reputation, all of which have tangible consequences that further erode the country's power and capacity to influence external events. Argentina's regime, or elites who want to replace it, is seeking means to reverse the situation. There appears to be little hope of an early political solution to fragmentation and demoralization. Argentina is also overshadowed by Brazil's superior and growing military power. While the government in Buenos Aires may not fear a Brazilian invasion, it may well look with apprehension on Brazil's unmatched influence on various unsettled regional disputes, some of which bear on Argentina's interests.

In dire circumstances, the Argentine government would naturally consider the dramatic, perhaps drastic, approach of manufacturing nuclear weapons. This possibility has doubtless been under discussion for some time, and the decision to keep the option open may have been followed by a decision to press ahead. The primary incentive would surely be political, with the central objective of shoring up Argentina's national position, especially vis-à-vis Brazil, but there would be a significant security incentive as well.

The view that a nuclear arms capability can transform a weak country into a powerful one is not convincing. It takes more than an explo-

sion or a few bombs to weld a fragmented political order into a viable
state that earns the respect of either neighbors or the international community. The hard-won nuclear prestige of the Indian explosion proved
to be a wasting asset. The chief justification given in Buenos Aires for
going nuclear—internal chaos and fractured authority—may itself be
the chief barrier to the solution. It is sometimes less difficult, however,
to solve complex technical problems than "normal" political problems.
Again, India provides a good example. Its government achieved a nuclear explosion, but it has not been able to cope effectively with internal
political dissension.

Argentina faces the same range of risks as Brazil, including that of
provoking Brazil into going nuclear or accelerating the pace of imple-
menting such a decision. Any effort by Argentina to preempt would
speed up the nuclear race and increase the chances of confrontation.
Even if it succeeded in conducting an explosion first, it could hardly rest
in the confidence that Brazil would be far behind. In sum, it is clear
that the decision in Argentina will rest on the weight given, on the one
hand, to the claimed benefits for the restoration of power and prestige
and for deterrence against Brazil's feared nuclear acquisition and, on the
other, to the risks of stimulating a nuclear arms race and precipitating a
confrontation with Brazil. Problems of financial cost will have little
bearing on the decision, though they may affect the timing.

The Future for Brazil and Argentina

Both Brazil and Argentina have said they have no intention of manufacturing nuclear arms, but each has kept open the legal, political, and
technical options to do so. Each is moving ahead in the development of
nuclear power and in the various technologies essential to conducting
an explosion. Each has the skills and resources to produce first-generation bombs and the systems for delivering them to plausible targets
within South America. It seems reasonable to conclude that both Brazil
and Argentina have already decided on a minimum policy of keeping
their nuclear arms option open and that each has undertaken the necessary bureaucratic and technical steps to this end. Either government
may have already decided to move ahead toward a nuclear explosion.
Argentina is more likely than Brazil to have reached such a decision
because the basic political and psychological needs of the rulers and the

nation are more compelling. Desperation is usually a more powerful engine than success.

Both governments' decisions presumably relate to the pace of acquiring the facilities to make a nuclear option possible, the timing of a decision to go nuclear, the level of nuclear capability sought, and the resources devoted to achieving this capability. These kinds of decisions will continue to be determined far less by the behavior of the superpowers than is the case for South Korea, Taiwan, Israel, or Egypt where the conflicting interests of the United States and the Soviet Union are directly involved. Brazil and Argentina each will be affected primarily by its perception of its own security and political needs as they relate to the external behavior of the other. Their decisions will be made within their own bipolar regional system which is only tangentially affected by their small neighbors or the policies of the United States or the Soviet Union. They will probably not be seriously constrained by embargoes on technical goods and services because there are always supplier states that do not adhere to such arrangements.

Thus the future nuclear behavior of Argentina and Brazil will be determined largely by the historical rivalry and power relations between them. All indicators suggest that Brazil's dynamism, Argentina's internal turbulence, and the power disparity that divides them will persist with little significant change for the next decade and perhaps until the year 2000. Unexpected events in either country could alter the present balance of forces, but any near-term development would be more likely to widen than narrow the power differential.

Nuclear policy would probably be affected most by an abrupt change of government in Brasilia or Buenos Aires. There is little reason to assume that in Brazil a successor regime, whether of the left or right, civilian or military, would be less dedicated to economic development and a leadership role for the country than the present one. It is unlikely that a left-wing regime will be installed in the next decade, but if it were, its tenure would probably be brief. No plausible change in government would seem to carry the prospect either of a significantly weakened Brazil or a Brazil fundamentally hostile to the United States.

An abrupt and unscheduled change of regime in Argentina is far more likely, but it is improbable that any such change would in the short run greatly enhance the country's power position in relation to that of Brazil. It is possible that a new military regime could restore order and confidence and build up the economy of Argentina, but Brazil is already so far ahead in overall economic and military strength that the gap between the two would probably continue to widen rather than narrow. In the highly unlikely event that Argentina suddenly got a new regime as effective as the government that replaced Brazil's earlier inept and lackluster regime, the power gap could be narrowed and eventually the historic role of the two countries reversed. But any change in either country that could reverse the balance would have to last a decade or more—the minimum time for Argentina to catch up economically under optimum conditions.

History rarely changes drastically and abruptly without a major war —a contingency that appears to be unlikely—so it is reasonable to assume that the present Argentine-Brazilian balance of forces will persist with little fundamental change for the next twenty-five years. If this is the case, it is not unlikely that both Brazil and Argentina will develop a small nuclear force by 2000. This could constitute a regional mutual deterrent without eliminating the tensions and accommodations between the two powers. Or the worst could happen—nuclear asymmetry or political miscalculation could lead to nuclear blackmail or a nuclear attack. But the history of the nuclear era suggests that the risk of war is not high, though the number of nuclear actors could adversely affect the odds.

The impact of acquisition by either Argentina or Brazil would be felt preponderantly in South and Central America. If Brazil conducted the first explosion, this would tend to reinforce its dominant position and thus provide a hegemonial stability that would hold until it was effectively challenged. If Argentina were first, the immediate impact would tend to be unsettling because the lesser power would be challenging, at least in symbolic terms, the dominant power. Though a token Argentine force would not compensate for Brazil's superior power, Brazil would probably follow suit and soon surpass Argentina in the nuclear race. A race for status and leadership would not be seriously detrimental to regional stability. But either of the new nuclear powers could threaten the other, use blackmail tactics against smaller neighbors, or try to "solve" sensitive issues like border disputes by nuclear diplomacy.

If any of these improbable contingencies occurred, the United States would certainly attempt to exercise a restraining influence on its Rio Pact allies. But even this highly unlikely development would hardly lead to U.S. military involvement or to involvement by the Soviet Union.

CHAPTER SEVEN

Deterring Nuclear Arms Acquisition

The need to halt nuclear proliferation is one of mankind's most pressing challenges.

PRESIDENT JIMMY CARTER, 1977[1]

THE WIDESPREAD assumption that any new national nuclear force in Asia, Africa, or Latin America will automatically make regional conflict and general nuclear war more likely has often precluded serious analysis of the nonnuclear factors that must be taken into account. Every past acquisition of nuclear arms—whether American, French, Chinese, or Indian—was rooted in unique circumstances and has led to diverse consequences. Such acquisitions are not a monolithic phenomenon. Nuclear weapons share many of the basic characteristics of powerful conventional weapons; both are instruments of coercive force that can be measured and assessed by the same basic terms of reference. The fire bombing of Tokyo killed more people than the atomic bombing of Hiroshima. The small nuclear arms that Third World governments are likely to build are similar to conventional arms. Both kinds of weapons can be used to conquer, deter, defend, provoke, or blackmail. The impact of either depends on the political circumstances in which they are developed, held in readiness, or used. The weapons themselves are inert and neutral until they are given meaning by human volition in a political setting.

That nuclear arms can deter nuclear war and certain kinds of conven-

1. "The President's Message to the Congress Transmitting the Proposed Nuclear Non-Proliferation Policy Act of 1977," *Weekly Compilation of Presidential Documents,* vol. 13 (May 2, 1977), p. 611.

tional war is amply demonstrated by the effectiveness of the strategic balance between the United States and the Soviet Union. There has been no nuclear or conventional war between the superpowers since 1945, and the Soviet Union has not mounted a conventional attack against any member of NATO. The system of mutual deterrence did not, however, prevent conventional wars in Korea and Vietnam. The independent nuclear forces of Britain and France may not have contributed to strategic deterrence, but neither force has detracted from stability in the Northern Hemisphere. Not even China's nuclear force has had an adverse effect on strategic stability. In a perverse way, it may have enhanced the U.S. deterrent by forcing Russia to face a second nuclear adversary.

Though the effects of new acquisitions cannot be forecast with scientific precision or reliability, the chances of making categorical errors will be reduced if the major security, political, and psychological factors are taken into account. The decision of a technically capable government to conduct a nuclear explosion, build a token force, or develop a militarily significant capability will be based on a combination of unquantifiable, nonnuclear factors. The case studies presented here have thus emphasized the conventional military strength of the various nations, their sense of external threat, foreign policy objectives, alliance relations, and internal political and psychological stresses.

Nuclear proliferation is an untidy and imprecise term. The word *proliferation,* borrowed from biology, means "to grow by rapid production of new parts, cells, buds or offspring"; it often connotes an automatic, if not an inevitable process. Far from being automatic, the acquisition of nuclear weapons by any government is a profound and deliberate act of the will, a result of long and painstaking calculation of costs and benefits. The spread of nuclear technology—reactors, fuels, and skills— in the Third World does not mean that nuclear weapons are bound to follow, propelled by a kind of technological momentum or determinism. The view that the capability to manufacture bombs will almost automatically lead to fulfillment flies in the face of recent history. Half a dozen Western European states and Japan have long had this capability, but for political and other reasons they have not chosen to build bombs. It takes a combination of technology and political will to exercise the nuclear option.

There are, however, several important differences between the nuclear-competent European states and potentially competent states in the Third World that would affect the impact of new acquisitions on U.S. and Soviet interests. The strategic balance between the United States and the Soviet Union is most directly affected by states within the system—members of NATO and of the Warsaw Pact—and by important contiguous or nearby states. Nuclear China and nonnuclear Japan have a significant impact on this system, and some Third World states, notably South Korea and Iran, have an important influence by virtue of their location. Israel and Egypt have a bearing on the strategic picture because of the involvement of the two superpowers in the Middle East conflict. That proximity is important was dramatically illustrated by the 1962 Cuban missile crisis. More distant states, such as Brazil and Argentina, have little direct impact on the superpower system of mutual deterrence.

Any new acquisition of nuclear arms in the Third World would take place in a nuclear vacuum, unless it were by a state on the periphery of the central strategic system. If the chief rationale for acquiring nuclear arms is to deter a nuclear neighbor, it is valid only for states such as Mexico, Burma, Pakistan, India, and Iran that border on a nuclear power. If the aim of the acquiring state is to deter or conquer a nonnuclear neighbor, the absence of other nearby nuclear states would naturally be considered an asset.

Virtually any Third World state that decided to go nuclear would develop only a token or a small nuclear force. A state bordering on the Soviet Union would be likely to settle for a small minimum deterrent or trip-wire force designed to involve the United States should the Soviet Union move against it. However, the two superpowers have developed disciplines and mechanisms to avoid being provoked into accidental or deliberate nuclear responses. Each has met provocation in the Middle East with restraint. Hence, no new nuclear force in the Third World is likely to jeopardize strategic stability.

Third World nuclear forces will not only be much smaller but less well protected and hence more vulnerable than European forces. This is especially true of aircraft delivery systems. Such vulnerability tends to be destabilizing because it invites preemption.

American policymakers should keep these realities in mind in assessing the probable effects of nuclear acquisition by any particular Third World country. One of the key questions in determining U.S. policy toward each threshold state should be the state's foreign policy orientation—whether it is allied, friendly, or neutral to the United States, and what its relations are with the other great powers and states in the region. Its power and capacity to influence external events depend on the strength of its conventional military forces as well as on a nation's size, location, population, economy, technical level, and natural resources. Its behavior will be influenced by whether it is a rising, declining, or stagnant power—a condition reflected in the government's capacity to control its own territory and population. Internal stability and the extent to which a regime enjoys the consent of the governed are also important policy determinants.

The strength of the nuclear force a government is planning or is likely to achieve is an important element of any assessment. If it is to be a significant force, its capability must be judged in relation to its most plausible adversaries. The levels of capability may be roughly analogous to five identified for major nuclear powers confronting each other: minimum deterrence, massive urban-industrial retaliation, flexible response, denial of the other side's ability to win a nuclear war, and the ability to win a nuclear war.[2] The level and configuration of a planned force are a function of its purpose, available resources, and time. Even a small Third World nuclear state confronting a weak, nonnuclear adversary would be able to achieve a war-winning level, barring, of course, intervention or the threat of intervention by a nuclear ally of its adversary.

Range of U.S. Policy Options

The spectrum of U.S. policy responses to other states' nuclear undertakings is wide and diverse. Those addressed to a state preparing to acquire nuclear weapons may be quite different from those employed after that state has conducted a nuclear explosion or has manufactured a token or significant force. Policies may be designed to deter or facilitate acquisition, but always their objective must be to maintain or strengthen stability. In some instances the aim may be to avoid influencing a situation that is regarded as stable. The U.S. response to nuclear development in a particular state may be supportive, punitive, or passive, or a combination. For example, the United States may provide technical nuclear aid and materials to accelerate a power program or to facilitate the manufacture of nuclear weapons, or it might take actions

2. Paul H. Nitze, "Assuring Strategic Stability in an Era of Detente," *Foreign Affairs*, vol. 54 (January 1976), pp. 212–13.

ranging theoretically from a mild diplomatic rebuke to the bombing of nuclear facilities of an offending state. Policies may be carried out unilaterally, bilaterally, in collaboration with other supplier states, or in cooperation with international organizations such as the North Atlantic Treaty Organization, the International Atomic Energy Agency, or the United Nations.

The spectrum of theoretical responses is broad, but the particular response—for example, to the Indian explosion—is severely narrowed by circumstances, including the limits of U.S. power and influence. Even though the United States is a nuclear superpower, and in part because it is, there are finite limits to its capacity to alter the behavior of another government. All states, especially those most likely to exercise the nuclear option, are under powerful and contradictory external and internal pressures. At most, the U.S. response is only one factor in their calculations, though in delicately balanced situations it can be the decisive one.

U.S. Security Assistance and Guarantees

In its efforts to deter the development of new nuclear forces in the Third World, the United States has available three general approaches that can be directed toward threshold states. It can reduce the pressure on these states to seek nuclear arms by providing U.S. security assistance or guarantees, encourage nuclear abstinence by promoting international agreements, and increase the difficulty of making nuclear weapons by denying the technical capability to do so. Ironically, the most effective of these approaches—the provision of security assistance or guarantees —is the one that has been least seriously examined, in part because of the mood of withdrawal and disengagement that has affected U.S. foreign policy, especially related to military commitments in the Third World, since the end of the war in Vietnam.

In all threshold states, considerations of prestige, power, and security are important, but in the cases considered here, with the probable exception of Argentina and Brazil, and the possible exception of Iran, a sense of insecurity—whether already evident or likely to develop—appears to be the driving force for a nuclear arms option. The security factors are sometimes combined with hegemonial ambitions. Insecurity may be induced by the military buildup of a neighboring state, abandonment by allies, or other similar developments that diminish the coercive power available to the state in relation to potential adversaries. This sense of insecurity is strong in South Korea, Taiwan, Pakistan, Egypt, and Israel.

Any government's sense of security is a combination of objective and subjective factors and reflects both its military posture and its foreign policy objectives. A status quo state surrounded by hostile powers is objectively insecure. A state whose territory is not directly threatened, but whose government is bent on expanding its influence, such as Brazil, may describe its military buildup as an effort to bolster its national security. These self-perceptions and public declarations always contain an element of calculated and necessary ambiguity that must be shrewdly assessed in Washington to determine where U.S. interests lie.

If the United States decides that the security of a given friendly state should be strengthened in the interest of enhancing regional stability, it can advance this objective by providing a nuclear guarantee, by entering into an alliance or bilateral defense treaty, by giving military assistance, by offering economic aid, or by any combination of these measures. Moreover, a state that is considering going nuclear "may be dissuaded from that act by perceiving that its own security is not in jeopardy. Hence, alliance with, and confidence in, the United States may be decisive for some nations. . . . In Northeast Asia or NATO Europe, for example, . . . [U.S.] *efforts, which include conventional force deployments, security assistance, and nuclear guarantees, have contributed to regional stability and have provided strong incentives not to acquire nuclear weapons.*"[3] The U.S. policies that can decrease the sense of insecurity also provide an opportunity for the United States to influence the military decisions of the recipient government through aid and advice.

Policies designed to augment the resources of a Third World state, as opposed to policies that ignore or deny what that state wants, tend to create a positive atmosphere between the United States and that state. The advice of the senior partner is likely to be taken seriously, particularly if it emphasizes the mutuality of the association and insists that the interests of both are being served. A categorical denial of security assistance urgently sought by an allied or friendly government, regardless of

3. Statement of Assistant Secretary of Defense Robert F. Ellsworth before the Subcommittee on Arms Control, International Organizations and Security Agreements of the Senate Foreign Relations Committee, 94 Cong. 1 sess., October 24, 1975.

the merits of the U.S. position, tends to create a climate of coolness or anger. A classic case was the U.S. denial of the sale of jet fighters to Brazil in the late 1960s, which so angered the Brazilians that they promptly ordered French Mirages. The U.S. denial also had two other negative effects—it eroded the U.S. capacity to influence Brazil's security policies and, less significant, it lost the balance-of-payments benefits from the sale of the aircraft.

This is not to say that assistance always provides an opportunity for influence and that denial has the opposite effect. The carrot and stick are sometimes quite effective. Further, close partnership and assistance have their own forms of tension, as NATO has proved. But, on balance, aid generally creates a better chance for influence than does denial.

The simplest and most effective way to deter a nuclear attack and to enhance the security of a state or group of states would be for the United States to provide, alone or with other nuclear powers, a security guarantee. In practice, however, the efficacy of such guarantees varies with circumstances. Six of the nine states in this study are covered by an implicit U.S. nuclear guarantee—South Korea and Taiwan by bilateral mutual defense treaties, Argentina and Brazil by the 1947 Rio Pact, and Iran and Pakistan by mutual defense agreements. Each of the instruments provides that in the event of an attack or serious threat to the other party, the United States will take appropriate action, including military force, by agreement with the other party and in accordance with U.S. constitutional processes. If the attack should come from a nuclear power, a nuclear response might be deemed appropriate by the President and the affected ally or friendly state. Most presidential decisions would require the support of Congress.

Though the U.S. nuclear umbrella is often described as full of holes, this less-than-perfect shelter has served as an effective deterrent against certain categories of Soviet conventional and nuclear military action in Western Europe and Asia. The Soviet Union has never launched a direct attack of any kind against any state having a U.S. mutual defense treaty or agreement, all of which embrace the possibility of nuclear protection. Nevertheless, it is difficult to ascertain the extent to which the nuclear umbrella enhances the security of the various states under it. Each recognizes that the United States cannot give an ironclad pledge that will be automatically honored in any future crisis and that it will respond in terms of American vital interests, but each hopes that U.S. interests will be defined broadly enough to take into account the interests of its ally as well.

The circumstances that will determine the U.S. response include the character, magnitude, and source of the threat or attack and the nature of the U.S. commitment, the latter being a partial reflection of the degree of U.S. interest. The United States would certainly respond differently to a Soviet nuclear attack against West Germany than to a small conventional Soviet attack against Iran. Germany is a major member of NATO, is strategically located in terms of America's most vital interests, and is host to a large U.S. military force. The extent to which a U.S. security treaty, including a possible nuclear guarantee, encourages a sense of security is determined by objective strategic factors not directly related to the form of the guarantee. Probably the most important is the presence of substantial U.S. combat forces in the country concerned. Within the Third World, U.S. combat troops are present only in South Korea and the Philippines (two fighter squadrons), but South Korea fears that the American forces will be withdrawn before its own conventional forces become strong enough to deter effectively an attack by a Soviet or Chinese backed North Korea. The availability of U.S. nuclear power in the Sixth and Seventh Fleets and in the Indian Ocean is also reassuring to the states in these areas covered by the U.S. guarantee.

The United States supplemented its bilateral security guarantees in 1968, when it signed the UN Security Council Resolution on Security Assurances to Non-Nuclear Nations. All permanent members of the council voted for the resolution except France, which abstained along with Algeria, Brazil, India, and Pakistan; there were no negative votes. The resolution declares that the nuclear powers have special responsibilities to the nonnuclear powers that are parties to the nonproliferation treaty and that may become victims of nuclear "aggression" or be threatened by such aggression and welcomes the "intention expressed by certain States" to "provide or support immediate assistance" to such victims.[4] The resolution is a weak reed, however. Secretary of State Dean Rusk pointed out that it in no way binds the United States to move against a future nuclear aggressor. A decision on what to do would have to be made "in terms of the total interests of the United States and the judgment of the President, in consultation with the leaders of the Con-

4. SC Res. 255 (1968), June 19, 1968.

gress."[5] Mr. Rusk acknowledged that it would be difficult to gain Security Council agreement in the event of nuclear aggression since every nuclear power is a permanent member of that body and has the right to veto. Thus, a U.S. bilateral guarantee is more likely to create a sense of security than the Security Council resolution, though again the U.S. perception of its own interests in each particular situation would limit its guarantee.

The concept of a joint Soviet-U.S. nuclear guarantee has received some quiet attention over the years. The primary obstacle to such an agreement has been the lack of an identity of interest between the two superpowers strong enough to sustain this degree of security cooperation toward a particular state or region. The two governments can and do cooperate in efforts to avoid nuclear war between themselves and in efforts to deter the creation of additional nuclear forces, but this does not mean that they can agree on nuclear security policy toward Taiwan or Argentina, to say nothing of Israel, Egypt, or South Korea. There may be situations, however, where a country could enjoy a tacit and informal guarantee from both superpowers that a nuclear attack by one would evoke a nuclear response by the other. Perhaps India benefited from a tacit guarantee in the early 1960s.

A sense of security can also derive from being a U.S. ally. As in the case of security guarantees, the confidence of the smaller partner in the willingness of the United States to come to its defense depends on the total relationship. Obviously the United States has a stronger identity with its NATO partners than with Taiwan or Brazil. A treaty supported by the presence of U.S. troops and providing for joint military planning, nuclear consultation, and substantial military aid certainly engenders a greater sense of security than one that involves no tangible elements of U.S. support.

One highly visible form of support is military aid. It usually enhances the security of the recipient in objective and subjective terms, and its termination usually erodes a nation's sense of security whether or not it is a U.S. ally. Imagine how Israel would feel and act if U.S. military assistance and sales were abruptly terminated. Turkey reacted to the embargo on U.S. military aid in 1975 with the prime minister's threat that Turkey would "go nuclear."[6] By contrast, the end of a ten-year

5. *Nonproliferation Treaty*, Hearings before the Senate Foreign Relations Committee, 90 Cong. 2 sess. (Government Printing Office, 1968), p. 17.

6. Metin Munir, *Washington Post*, February 27 and 28, 1975.

embargo and the resumption of conventional military assistance to Pakistan in February 1975, nine months after India's nuclear explosion, was accepted as a move to bolster that country's sense of security.

Generally, U.S. economic assistance or any other substantial net transfer of U.S. resources enhances the security of the recipient because a stronger economy can support a more effective military establishment, and any augmentation of the economy theoretically releases resources that can be devoted to national defense. By its security guarantees and economic aid the United States can strengthen the security of a friendly or allied threshold state and thus diminish its motivation to manufacture nuclear arms. A state like South Korea which has received substantial military and economic aid is heavily dependent on the United States both for its objective security and for its sense of security. Fear that one or more components of U.S. support will be withdrawn has fueled the desire to compensate for an anticipated loss or erosion of the American commitment. The chief security responses to this prospect have been a buildup of South Korean conventional armed forces and a desire to create a nuclear arms option.

South Korea offers proof that one of the most effective ways for the United States to diminish the motivation for going nuclear is to provide greater security for the threshold states by mutual defense treaties with their implicit nuclear guarantee. In strategically important countries this guarantee may be buttressed by U.S. troops or by land- or sea-based nuclear weapons, by military assistance or sales, and by various forms of economic aid. The instruments employed and the magnitude of the effort would vary with circumstances, including the proximity of the state in question to China or the Soviet Union, the intrinsic strategic importance of the threshold state, and its capacity to provide for its own defense.

Promoting International Agreements

From the late 1950s until the early 1970s, the primary effort of the United States, the Soviet Union, and other states seeking to deter and prevent further nuclear acquisition was a multilateral, consensual-legal approach, manifested in the nonproliferation treaty and the associated IAEA inspection system. Though this system cannot prevent a determined government from constructing a nuclear bomb, in certain circumstances it can deter a weapons application of nuclear facilities or materials. Had India been a member of the system, accepting IAEA safeguards on all nuclear facilities, it would have had much more difficulty in conducting its test. Preparations for the test could have forced the government to reveal its intentions by withdrawing from the system or by refusing to admit IAEA inspectors. Yet even without violating the safeguards, governments can build "near bombs." "A nonweapon state can come closer to exploding a plutonium weapon today without violating an agreement" than "the United States was in the spring of 1947. . . . Research on bomb design and testing of nonnuclear bomb components are not prevented [by IAEA agreements] . . . and can proceed in parallel with the accumulation of fissile material."[7]

Even with its inherent weaknesses and imperfections, the safeguard system is worth preserving and strengthening. The United States should use it as one instrument for persuading governments whose acquisition it believes would be destabilizing to refrain from exercising the nuclear weapons option.

Nuclear-free zones are another potentially useful form of deterring nuclear arms, but there are few areas where the states concerned have sufficient common interest to underwrite such an effort. The Antarctic Treaty applies to an uninhabited region and the Treaty of Tlatelolco to an area where nuclear weapons have not been a crucial issue. The limited test-ban treaty, which takes a zonal approach, was arrived at only after years of negotiation between the United States and Russia. None of these treaties is a fully effective deterrent to the prohibited activity, in part because none is inclusive.[8] The Treaty of Tlatelolco is weakened by the failure of Argentina to ratify and Brazil's ratification with reservations. Two nuclear powers—France and China—have not signed the Antarctic and limited test-ban treaties, though both have signed Protocol 2 of the Latin American treaty which provides that the nuclear powers respect the denuclearized status of the zone and agree not to assist the parties to violate its provisions and the nuclear powers not to use or threaten to use nuclear weapons against the parties.

The idea of a nuclear-free zone has been proposed for Africa, the

7. Albert Wohlstetter, "Spreading the Bomb Without Quite Breaking the Rules," *Foreign Policy*, no. 25 (Winter 1976–1977), pp. 88–89.

8. The limited test-ban treaty, which bans nuclear tests under water, does not prohibit submarines that carry nuclear missiles. And the Treaty of Tlatelolco does not prohibit innocent passage of submarines or surface vessels carrying nuclear arms through the territorial waters of the signatories.

Middle East, South Asia, and the South Pacific, but the chances of further treaties on the Latin American model are not promising.[9] As India's response to Pakistan's 1974 suggestion for such a zone in South Asia underscored, the consent of all states in the area is a political, legal, and moral prerequisite to an agreement. Both superpowers acknowledged that fact in their abstentions on the UN committee vote.

Denying Technology for Nuclear Explosions

The United States has emphasized unilateral, bilateral, and international measures to deny nuclear arms technology and fuels to importing states. President Carter has called for legislation to control the export of technology. In his message of April 27, 1977, to Congress he promised that the United States would continue to be a reliable supplier of nuclear fuel under effective safeguards and called for "the establishment of common international sanctions" for states that violated any of the guidelines of the suppliers group.[10] His policy continues the U.S. "emphasis on controls or safeguards" and "restraint in the transfer of sensitive facilities and technologies, particularly enrichment and reprocessing."[11] Recognizing that the United States must "provide incentives for other nations to forego the sensitive technologies," the President's policy is designed to "provide [an] assured supply of nonsensitive nuclear fuels on a timely, adequate, reliable, and economic basis at the front end of the fuel cycle and to insure there is sufficient spent fuel and nuclear waste storage capacity at the back end of the fuel cycle." The President also would "ask other countries to study jointly how to avoid premature commitment to new technologies until they can be adequately safeguarded."[12]

The concerted U.S. effort to deny critical facilities and materials to nonnuclear states began in 1974. Congress has given the executive sub-

9. On December 9, 1974, the UN General Assembly adopted resolutions proposing that the Middle East be made a nuclear-free zone (GA Res. 3263[29]) and encouraging the denuclearization of Africa (GA Res. 3261[29]). On December 11, 1975, the General Assembly adopted a resolution supporting the establishment of a nuclear-free zone in the South Pacific (GA Res. 3477[30]).

10. For the text of his message, see New York Times, April 28, 1977.

11. Speech by Joseph S. Nye, Jr., undersecretary of state for security assistance, science, and technology, State Department release, June 30, 1977.

12. Ibid.

stantial support in this effort.[13] In the wake of the Indian explosion, Congress passed and President Ford signed a law directing U.S. representatives in the International Development Association "to vote against any loan . . . for the benefit of any country which develops any nuclear explosive device, unless the country becomes" a party to the nonproliferation treaty.[14]

In 1976, disclosure of the French and West German plans to sell highly sophisticated nuclear technology and facilities to Pakistan and Brazil prompted adoption of a Senate-sponsored amendment to the foreign aid bill. It provides that certain forms of U.S. assistance be withheld from countries that "deliver or receive any equipment, material, or technology for enriching uranium or reprocessing nuclear fuels" unless they place all their nuclear fuels and facilities under IAEA safeguards and place enriching and reprocessing facilities under multinational auspices and management when available.[15] The United States also began discussions with each of the parties to the proposed transfers, seeking to prevent the sales or to have stringent controls placed on the exported facilities. The U.S. initiation of the suppliers group in 1975 was aimed principally at institutionalizing procedures for controlling exports. The guidelines adopted by the group in 1976, demanding IAEA safeguards on exports and assurance of the recipients' nonmilitary intentions, were based in large measure on agreements arrived at in active bilateral negotiations by the United States.

In persuading South Korea not to purchase a French plutonium reprocessing plant,[16] the State Department threatened to withhold export licenses and Export-Import Bank financing for a nuclear reactor in early 1976. Reportedly also at U.S. instigation, Canada postponed the sale of a reactor to South Korea unless the order for the French plant was canceled. A year earlier, South Korea had ratified the nonproliferation treaty under quiet State Department pressure and in face of a joint U.S. congressional resolution asking the Export-Import Bank to defer financing of the reactor.[17]

13. See Warren H. Donnelly, *Indications of Congressional Interest and Concern Over Proliferation of the Ability to Make Nuclear Weapons* (Congressional Research Service, 1976), pp. 1–2.

14. P.L. 93-373.

15. P.L. 94-329.

16. Don Oberdorfer, *Washington Post*, January 30, 1976; and Richard Halloran, *New York Times*, February 1, 1976.

17. H.J. Res. 298, March 10, 1975.

The United States also sought to have the French impose strict safe-guards on any nuclear facilities or materials transferred to South Korea. The U.S. initiative, supported by the Soviet Union and other suppliers, resulted in what has been described as a model safeguards agreement. This trilateral pact among France, the Republic of Korea, and the IAEA, dated August 7, 1975, was tighter and more specific than any IAEA agreements negotiated before the Indian explosion. The general provision that transferred facilities not be used "to further any military purpose" has been replaced by more precise provisions that no material furnished by France shall "be used for the manufacture of nuclear weapons or to further any other military purpose or for the manufacture of any other nuclear explosive device." Not only do these prohibitions apply to facilities or materials provided by France, but to facilities "which are designed, constructed, or operated on the basis of or by the use of specified information supplied" by France and to "fissionable or other nuclear material" that may be derived from material or information supplied by France. These stipulations, obviously designed to plug the loophole made manifest by the Indian explosion, provided the pattern for the principles adopted by the suppliers group in early 1976.

American diplomacy has failed to prevent the comprehensive nuclear agreement between West Germany and Brazil that if fully consummated would provide the latter with a complete fuel cycle, but it has clearly had an influence on the quality of safeguards written into the pact, which are at least as comprehensive as those of the French-South Korean agreement. Pressure from the United States and other suppliers has resulted in a West German promise to make no further sales of sensitive equipment.[18]

The limits of pressure by a supplier state are apparent in Canada's attempt to prevent Pakistan from reprocessing wastes from the Canadian-supplied power reactor at Karachi.[19] Canadian officials failed to gain a commitment from Pakistan not to send the wastes to a plutonium reprocessing plant to be provided by France. When Canada threatened to cancel planned assistance to Pakistan, Prime Minister Zulfikar Ali Bhutto said Pakistan was not interested in conducting an atomic explosion and was "prepared to consider adequate safeguards, but we don't want to tie ourselves down body and soul." He added that he objected

18. Richard Burt, *New York Times*, January 16, 1978.
19. Robert Trumbull, *New York Times*, February 26, 1976.

to Canada's attempt to impose safeguards on a non-Canadian facility.[20] Though Pakistan and France signed a trilateral safeguards agreement with the IAEA covering the contemplated reprocessing plant, both Canada and the United States continued to express their disapproval of the transfer.

The United States appears to have been successful in putting pressure on Iran to abandon its embryonic plans to develop a national reprocessing facility. The shah has postponed indefinitely, if not canceled, the plans.

Reward and Punishment Policies

The arsenal of diplomacy is replete with positive incentives and negative sanctions designed to affect the behavior of governments. The strategy of the suppliers group is focused on the denial of nuclear explosive capability, as is that of the nonproliferation treaty through the IAEA safeguards system. There is a distinction between such denial measures and punitive policies. Denial involves refusal to give or sell something the other party wants. Punitive policies are more drastic and involve taking away something the other party already possesses, such as bombing a city, terminating a treaty of friendship, or suspending economic or military aid. The distinction between denial and punitive actions is blurred in the real world. Brazil, for example, probably felt that the U.S. denial of jet fighters in the 1960s and of certain categories of nuclear technology in the 1970s was punitive because it saw the denial as an affront to Brazilian sovereignty and dignity. Strictly speaking, U.S. refusal to sell uranium-enrichment technology is not punitive, but an abrupt cutoff of enriched uranium for a nuclear energy program would be. Canada's suspension of nuclear assistance to India after the 1974 blast was clearly punitive, a pointed interruption of an existing relationship of assistance accompanied by a statement disapproving India's behavior.

The United States has used denial to prevent nuclear arms technology going to nonweapons states and has threatened further denial, but it has not actually punished any threshold state. It issued a mild public rebuke to India for its nuclear test and suspended shipment of enriched uranium for two months, until it was reassured by India that

20. Ibid., February 26, 1976.

the fuel would not be diverted to weapons uses. It came close to punishing South Korea with its threat to suspend an expected Export-Import loan.

More often the United States has used positive incentives to induce nuclear arms restraint, including the continuation or promise of more nuclear, military, or economic assistance. In unusual cases, high-level statements or special agreements that confer status on the threshold state have been used as a measure of reassurance—for example, a consultative accord by Secretary of State Henry Kissinger and the foreign minister of Brazil in February 1976, and on the thirtieth anniversary of the bombing of Hiroshima, President Ford's reaffirmation of the U.S. pledge to use nuclear weapons to defend Japan.[21] After the defeat of the Saigon government in 1975, President Ford and Secretary of Defense Schlesinger carefully reaffirmed the U.S. security commitment to South Korea. Each of these actions offered the nonnuclear partner an inducement to trust the United States and to resist pressures to go nuclear.

Response to a U.S. policy may, of course, be unexpectedly bad—as was Turkey's reaction to the U.S. arms embargo imposed by Congress because of Turkey's military behavior in Cyprus. The Turkish government closed certain U.S. military bases and threatened to develop its own nuclear arms. In February 1975, the defense minister said, "We are acting from the presumption that we shall not receive military aid any more," and stated that Turkey would have to base its "national defense on national power and resources," adding that it was "working on nuclear energy." "There are plans to manufacture atom bombs and nuclear reactors. We have reached a fairly advanced state in rocket manufacture."[22] The next day the prime minister said, "Going nuclear is very dangerous for humanity, but if we have to go nuclear for our defense we will."[23] The punitive action by the United States also pushed Turkey, at least temporarily, closer to the USSR. That action was opposed by the President, and it was certainly not intended by its congressional backers to stimulate Turkey's nuclear aspirations. But the consequences of punitive measures cannot always be controlled.

The wide range of rewards and punishments the United States can

21. "Joint Announcement to the Press Following Discussions with Prime Minister Miki of Japan, August 6, 1975," *Public Papers of the Presidents: Gerald R. Ford, 1975* (GPO, 1977), p. 1115.

22. Metin Munir, *Washington Post*, February 27, 1975.

23. *Washington Post*, February 28, 1975.

use to deter threshold states and to mitigate the consequences of nuclear acquisition includes military, economic,[24] and political measures. The combination of rewards and punishments should be tailored to changing circumstances. For the most part, these policies will be pursued unilaterally, but in some cases they can be coordinated with the policies of the Soviet Union or other supplier states.

Encouraging Nuclear Abstinence through Security Aid

The provision of security assistance or support—by a nuclear guarantee, defense pact, or military assistance, and in appropriate circumstances the presence of U.S. combat troops—is the single most effective way to encourage nuclear abstinence. The opposite posture—withdrawing the nuclear guarantee and diluting the security commitment, or terminating military aid—is the most likely way to encourage nuclear acquisition among threshold states. Consequently, to deter key governments, the United States may have to extend additional security commitments, enter into more military pacts, provide more military aid, and in certain places, station new troops or enlarge U.S. forces abroad. This means more U.S. security commitments in the Third World, not fewer. America must turn outward and become involved selectively in the security of significant states that will otherwise be inclined to go nuclear.

For many nonnuclear powers, protection against nuclear threat or attack rests on American commitments. America's self-interest dictates that we sustain our alliances. If we withdraw our protection, or if confidence in it were shaken, strong internal pressures would arise in many countries to acquire nuclear armaments for their self-protection. Then, their neighbors would feel threatened and follow suit.

To the degree that we appear to turn inward, we encourage nonnuclear nations—from Asia to Europe and the Middle East—to create their own nuclear forces. We will thus make the future less manageable and eventually bring arms control efforts to a dead end. . . . Our alliances help protect both other nations and ourselves from the dangers of nuclear proliferation.[25]

The most effective approach to deter further nuclear force is to create a pattern of foreign policy programs, a defense posture, a network of security relationships and guarantees, and general strategies designed to develop,

24. The providing or withholding of U.S. agricultural exports is an instrument of diplomatic persuasion that deserves further consideration. See William Schneider, *Food, Foreign Policy, and Raw Materials Cartels* (Crane, Russak, 1976), chap. 6.

25. Fred C. Iklé, "The Second Nuclear Era," U.S. *Department of State Bulletin,* May 19, 1975, p. 643. Emphasis added.

maintain, or enhance conditions for regional and global stability (conditions wherein the disincentives for nuclear acquisition will be reinforced, and other countries will feel less need to move in that direction); and . . . specific policies, strategies, and tactics toward individual countries, which by design or otherwise help to reduce any possible incentives and reinforce any disincentives to their acquiring nuclear explosive capabilities.[26]

An "American recommitment" is needed to the security not only of Western Europe and Japan, but also to "countries like Israel, Iran and Pakistan."[27] Or put the other way, "American appeasement means nuclear proliferation on a massive scale."[28] These statements point to the inevitable relationship between mood, perception of external threat, and U.S. foreign policy. The weariness and isolation that followed in the wake of the fall of Saigon have abated somewhat and the American people are now more prepared to support, and perhaps increase, U.S. security commitments in allied and friendly Third World countries that feel especially threatened. If this mood is translated into specific U.S. security assistance policies, countries such as South Korea, Taiwan, Pakistan, and Iran will have less incentive to exercise the nuclear arms option.

26. Michael A. Guhin, *Nuclear Paradox: Security Risks of the Peaceful Atom* (Washington: American Enterprise Institute for Public Policy Research, 1976), p. 68.

27. Walter F. Hahn, "Nuclear Proliferation," *Strategic Review*, vol. 3 (Winter 1975), p. 24.

28. Irving Kristol, *Wall Street Journal*, February 12, 1975.

CHAPTER EIGHT

Restraining New Nuclear Forces

The impact on U.S. security depends upon both where and when nuclear proliferation occurs. . . . The problem . . . will require . . . comprehensive planning to adjust our country's defense in the eventuality of further proliferation.

ASSISTANT SECRETARY OF DEFENSE ROBERT F. ELLSWORTH, 1975[1]

NUCLEAR ACQUISITION, like nuclear war, poses two questions simultaneously—how best deter it, and how best deal with it if deterrence fails. Fortunately, the failure to prevent acquisition is not as catastrophic as the failure to prevent nuclear war.

Even in those cases where a militarily significant force is developed, the net effect of nuclear acquisition could be stabilizing, tending more to deter conflict than to provoke it. It is significant that since Nagasaki, no nuclear weapon has been exploded in war and that the policy of nuclear deterrence has been wholly successful. Throughout their history, nuclear forces have been more self-limiting than conventional arms; this characteristic might persist even if they should be developed or inherited by inexperienced or irresponsible regimes. Their only uses since 1945 have been for deterrence and political leverage.

There are now five or six nuclear states and there may be as many as ten by the year 2000, but an increase in number does not necessarily increase the probability of nuclear war. It would be difficult to prove that the likelihood of nuclear war increased with the advent of British or French or even Chinese nuclear forces. In fact, these forces within

1. Statement before the Subcommittee on Arms Control, International Organizations and Security Agreements of the Senate Foreign Relations Committee, 94 Cong. 1 sess., October 24, 1975.

the main strategic theater were probably more stabilizing than destabilizing. The number of nuclear actors is always a significant factor in the military calculus, but it is only one factor and an ambiguous one.

Each of the nine threshold states included in this study could, given sufficient external assistance, manufacture a small militarily significant nuclear force (of ten bombs or more) by 2000. Perhaps all but Pakistan could manufacture a token force (of about five small bombs) by 1985. But the costs and risks of doing so are so high that few of these governments will be sufficiently motivated to make the maximum effort.

Only two of the states are likely to have nuclear arms in 1985, and only three to have a militarily significant force by 2000. But all of them appear to be good candidates for acquiring some nuclear arms by 2000. Israel, which presumably already has a militarily significant force that can reach plausible targets in Egypt and Syria, will continue to have one in 1985 and 2000. India will probably have a token force by 1985 and may have a militarily usable one against Pakistan by 2000, but not against China. It will take some considerable effort for Pakistan to achieve even a token force before 2000. If the U.S. commitment to South Korea is withdrawn within the next decade, then South Korea will probably develop a militarily significant force against North Korea. This could be achieved as early as 1985 or 1990, depending on when the decision was made. The same can be said for Taiwan. Unless the security situation alters significantly for Iran, Egypt, Argentina, and Brazil, these states will probably not achieve a token force until after 1985.

U.S. Policy Options

American policies designed to mitigate the destabilizing effects of new nuclear arms acquisitions must be adapted to meet the particular requirements of each situation. Just as it is more important to deter some acquisitions than others, it is more important to attempt to freeze, slow down, or otherwise render less destabilizing certain new forces. Even in cases where acquisition may be judged by the United States to be stabilizing, U.S. policies must be designed to reinforce the political and security situation that sustains this judgment. The line between deterrence and provocation is thin and not wholly predictable. The signals sent out by the possessors of a new military capability to friendly and hostile neighbors are subjectively received, and they may reassure or cause anxiety.

All U.S. measures must be aimed at inducing the new nuclear state to pursue a moderate and nonaggressive foreign policy. Hence, policies directed toward all such states will focus on intentions and motivation, but in some cases there will be a concurrent attempt to slow down or limit the development of nuclear arms. For these reasons, U.S. policies calculated to support a stabilizing force may sometimes also be appropriate for limiting a force regarded as destabilizing. And with changing circumstances, the same force may at different times have a net stabilizing or destabilizing effect. Policymakers must weigh many probabilities in predicting the net effect of a new force on stability. Acquisition that is judged to be stabilizing in the short term may not appear to be so in the long run. There is always a risk of accident, miscalculation, or stupidity, but the history of nuclear arms suggests that none of these risks is high. Most Third World regimes, however, tend to be less stable than those of the five big nuclear powers, whose past restraint may not be a prologue to the future. If the government of a state possessing a small nuclear capability that was essentially stabilizing were replaced by one with a reckless or aggressive foreign policy, that state's power could be transformed into a destabilizing force. The reverse is also possible. But as regime changes in South Korea, India, Pakistan, Israel, Brazil, and Argentina suggest, continuity is much more likely in foreign policy than radical discontinuity.

The range and intensity of U.S. measures designed to deal with unwanted new forces should be geared to circumstances and take fully into account the anticipated severity of the impact on U.S. interests. Overreaction to the first nuclear explosion by a friendly government may confer prestige on the regime and encourage it to continue on the nuclear road. Punitive action by the United States may force the regime to rely more heavily on the Soviet Union, just as the U.S. cutoff of military aid to Turkey resulted in a visit to Ankara by Premier Aleksei Kosygin and a subsequent $700 million credit agreement between the Soviet Union and Turkey.[2] In 1956 U.S. punitive policies against Egypt prompted Egypt to rely on the Soviet Union to build the Aswan Dam and for military aid. There may be future cases, however, in which the USSR will find it in its interest to cooperate with the United States.

2. *New York Times,* July 5, 1975.

Most of the policy options for deterring acquisition discussed in chapter 7 can be used to mitigate the adverse consequences of new explosions or the building of a token or a significant nuclear force. They include security guarantees or military aid to the acquiring state and in some cases to its rival, legal instruments like the nonproliferation treaty and IAEA agreements, supplier-imposed constraints and other devices for denying technology, and bilateral or multilateral measures of reward or punishment. Policies to mitigate destabilization may be directed to the acquiring state, the potential victim of nuclear attack, a regional group, or supplier states.

The fundamental objective of all policies is to limit the negative impact of the new capability on regional and strategic stability—both in the token force phase and in the militarily significant force phase. This means that the United States should strive, in cooperation with other powers when feasible, to maintain or strengthen the conventional and nuclear balance in the region concerned and, failing this, develop disciplines to avoid big power nuclear involvement in any local conflict.

A Token Force—The Indian Case

By 2000, Pakistan, Taiwan, Iran, Egypt, Argentina, and Brazil may have token nuclear forces with about five small nuclear bombs, but without reliable means of delivery to plausible targets. India, which presumably does not yet have a token force, may have one by 1985. From the initial explosion or the first evidence that a country has acquired a nuclear bomb, the United States can undertake certain measures to discourage or slow down further nuclear arms development, ranging from diplomatic persuasion to the unlikely measure of military intervention.

The Indian case suggests that instruments at the lower end of the coercive spectrum are more likely to be used than those at the upper end to counter nuclear development. After the 1974 explosion a number of governments, including the United States, criticized India. Canada went further and ended nuclear assistance. The United States, after a three-month suspension, resumed sales of enriched uranium to India—which the Energy Research and Development Administration forecast would total $18.3 million by the end of 1979,[3] if they were not inter-

3. David Burnham, *New York Times*, March 3, 1976.

rupted. If India should persist in a nuclear arms program or start making nuclear threats and if this were regarded as a serious risk to regional stability, the United States could take stronger measures to dissuade—or even prevent—India from developing a nuclear arsenal. It could start with status-conferring measures, such as nuclear aid, other forms of technical assistance, and economic aid. It could even extend its nuclear umbrella to India so that India would not need an independent deterrent. It could also provide conventional military assistance. Theoretically it is possible, though unlikely, that the United States could join with the Soviet Union to provide a joint nuclear guarantee to protect India from China.

If these policies appeared to be ineffective, the United States could undertake measures of denial and punishment against India. Working with other parties to the nonproliferation treaty and the suppliers group, the United States could attempt to mount an embargo of all nuclear assistance. It could go still further by persuading other states to invoke sanctions against India. Senator John Glenn has suggested that the United States could treat states that refuse to cooperate in nonproliferation efforts "just as we treat criminal elements. . . . It may be necessary to seek commitments from *all* nations, suppliers or not, to impose drastic trade and even communications embargoes against *any* nation, signatory to the [nonproliferation treaty] or not, in the event of an unauthorized diversion of nuclear fuel for weapons purposes or a nuclear explosion of any sort." Such a commitment would "fail in the absence of strong U.S.-Soviet cooperation."[4] Senator Abraham Ribicoff went further, proposing that the United States cooperate with the USSR in threatening to cut off nuclear fuel to France and West Germany when they offered assistance to Pakistan and Brazil in 1976.[5] Secretary Kissinger pointed out that such collaboration with the USSR on nuclear exports was highly unlikely in view of Soviet-American tension and that "pressure, blackmail, or whatever," with Soviet concurrence, "would have the gravest foreign policy consequences."[6] In fact, collaborative

4. John Glenn, *Washington Post*, March 8, 1976. See also Warren H. Donnelly, *Indications of Congressional Interest and Concern Over Proliferation of the Ability to Make Nuclear Weapons* (Congressional Research Service, 1976), pp. 41–43.

5. *Export Reorganization Act of 1976*, Hearings before the Senate Committee on Government Operations, 94 Cong. 2 sess. (Government Printing Office, 1976), pp. 764, 789–90.

6. Ibid., p. 776.

action involving either the Soviet Union or certain NATO partners and designed to deny sales of nuclear technology is very difficult to arrange because different supplier states have different views of the costs, risks, and benefits involved. Perhaps the Soviet Union secretly approves of an Indian nuclear deterrent against China to deflect some of China's pressure on Russia's eastern front. And Pakistan, a U.S. ally, may well regard its possession of a reprocessing plant as a stabilizing force, a counterpressure against Indian nuclear developments. As one Pakistani put it, "The French plutonium plant by itself will serve as a deterrent to India by turning Pakistan into a potential nuclear power."[7]

Punitive action against a newly acquiring state may consist of rewards to the potential target of the embryo force. Just after the first explosion, for example, the United States could promise to provide compensatory assistance—conventional military aid or technical nuclear assistance— to the potential target state, as it did in resuming military aid to Pakistan shortly after India's 1974 explosion. The U.S. offer in 1974 to sell six-hundred-megawatt power reactors to both Egypt and Israel was in effect, if not intent, an equalizing device that would have eased the significant nuclear disparity between the two. The tender did not mean that the United States wanted Egypt to develop nuclear arms to match those of Israel; but it offered Egypt an opportunity, in terms of prestige and civilian nuclear capability, to come off better in this formally evenhanded export of nuclear technology.

Again, as in attempting to deter acquisition, the most effective U.S. policies are unilateral actions that do not depend on the collaboration or consent of other parties. The policies most likely to persuade a regime that has just exploded a nuclear device to stop there or to move slowly are supportive efforts designed to meet the need for security, reassurance, or prestige that motivated the explosion in the first place. Collaborative policies of denial are almost doomed to fail because of the elaborate structure of consent required and unilateral denial efforts can exert leverage only when the assisted state is heavily dependent on the United States for an essential service or technology. Denial or punitive measures would tend to backfire or to induce the regime they are directed against to rely more heavily on the Soviet Union, whose interests are often inimical to U.S. interests, or on an ally who then receives the

7. Zahid Mahmood, letter to the editor, *New York Times*, March 8, 1976.

commercial and balance of payments benefits, as West Germany did when the United States refused to sell fuel cycle technology to Brazil.

A Significant Force—The Israeli Case

Israel is the only state in the Third World that appears to have a militarily significant nuclear force of ten or more bombs and the means to deliver them to plausible targets. No other threshold state is likely to acquire one by 1985, though India, Taiwan, or South Korea, if highly motivated, could have a significant capability by 2000. Thus Israel provides a view of the problems the United States confronts in attempting to blunt the destabilizing effects of acquisition. The potential responses by the United States to a militarily significant capability depend on how threatening the nuclear force appears to be. Assessments of the strength of Israel's nuclear arsenal can vary enormously, depending on how the complex Middle Eastern conflict is viewed. It is clear that Israel's force has neither caused nuclear war nor provoked Egypt into building an independent nuclear force of its own. It probably has prompted Egypt to take measures to keep open the nuclear arms option. And it has, according to *Time*'s report on the 1973 crisis, caused Israel to exercise restraint.

Israel's regional monopoly is similar to the nuclear monopoly enjoyed by the United States before the Soviet Union's first explosion. But Israel's policy options are limited by the nuclear power of the Soviet Union. The impact of the force is as impossible to predict as ever. At best, its effect on regional stability will continue to be ambiguous. It could either induce the Arab states to seek a peaceful settlement or encourage Arab belligerency, but it is more likely to have a mixed effect of simultaneously encouraging a peaceful solution and inducing Egypt to build a compensatory force of its own. Whatever impact Israel's force may have within the region, it is not likely to draw the Soviet Union and the United States into a nuclear confrontation.

The general U.S. policy approach toward Israel and specific policy measures flow from a basic assessment of the net impact of Israel's nuclear force—or an assessment of whether Israel's force strengthens stability, mildly disturbs the balance, seriously jeopardizes stability, or makes little difference either way. Regardless of its assessment, the United States as the chief patron of Israel has an obligation constantly to press on Israel a moderate, nonbelligerent foreign policy and a willingness to negotiate a peaceful settlement of its conflict with the Arab states. This would be the case were there no force. To this end, giving, suspending, and withholding of economic and military aid should be used as leverage.

No special measures would be needed if Israel's force were held to be of little consequence and unlikely to be disruptive, or if it seemed likely to strengthen stability. That the U.S. government is apprehensive about Israel's nuclear power is indicated by its insistence on comprehensive safeguards for the reactor that is being sold to Israel. Consequently, the United States should undertake special measures to mitigate the dangers of this lopsided nuclear development in a region of unresolved conflict. The severity of the measures should reflect the seriousness of the perceived danger. If it is considered very serious, the United States should attempt to establish a nuclear balance in the area. This could be done theoretically by removing all nuclear arms or by helping Egypt to catch up with Israel. The first course would require Israel to destroy its nuclear weapons or surrender them to a credible international authority. The second would mean external aid to help Egypt develop a compensatory force so that a regional system of mutual deterrence could be established. Neither course appears feasible. The government of an imperiled state will not voluntarily surrender its ultimate weapon. And the United States, the chief advocate of the nonproliferation treaty, would hardly consider helping Egypt to build nuclear arms.

There are less drastic ways to help redress the nuclear imbalance, and the United States has already been pursuing several. The sale of reactors to Egypt and Israel on the same terms will help balance the nuclear equation, while the significant increase in U.S. military and economic aid to Egypt will help to establish a more equitable general balance, as well as to replace Soviet influence. The U.S. support of Jordan also tends to offset Israel's military superiority and nuclear monopoly. Under these unique circumstances, the United States should consider extending a nuclear guarantee to Egypt, Syria, and other Arab states. This would have the effect of deterring both the use of Israel's force for military purposes or blackmail and the acquisition of nuclear arms by Egypt.

Thus far, compensatory assistance to Israel's potential victims has not been sufficient to offset the bargaining advantage and war-making potential of the Israeli force, so the United States should pursue efforts to deter or prevent Israel from increasing its nuclear capability. In a sense it is already doing so through participation in the nonproliferation treaty, the IAEA safeguards system, and the suppliers group, but the effect on Israel is severely limited because its vital nuclear facilities are not safeguarded. The United States and other concerned powers could demand that Israel grant IAEA inspectors access to all facilities, but this demand is not likely to be met.

This raises the question of undertaking measures of denial or even punitive action against Israel. Should the United States withhold military and economic aid until Israel opens all its facilities to IAEA inspection, announces the size and character of its nuclear force, or makes a no-first-use pledge? Domestic political pressures in the United States would make it very difficult to invoke such denial measures, though both Senators Glenn and Ribicoff proposed measures of that severity to curb nuclear forces in the Third World. They recommended a ban on all nuclear exports to states that are not parties to the nonproliferation treaty,[8] and Israel is not a party.

The United States should undertake a series of measures designed to encourage Israel to pursue a moderate foreign and military policy and to refrain from brandishing a nuclear threat. They might well include the use of military and economic aid as a weapon to persuade Israel to join the nonproliferation treaty and to admit IAEA inspectors. These measures might be combined with compensatory efforts to bolster the security of Egypt and other Arab states subject to possible nuclear blackmail or attack. The efforts directed toward Arab states could include military and economic aid, civilian nuclear assistance, and a nuclear guarantee. These are the kinds of policy options available for mitigating the destabilizing impact of a militarily significant force.

Once a force exists and the United States accepts it as a fait accompli, regardless of how serious a threat the force poses, the United States should undertake efforts to encourage the adoption of responsible command and control measures over the force. Obviously this would be less difficult in situations where the United States had been providing military assistance. In a quiet advisory relationship undergirded by some technical dependence on the United States, American experts could help convey the mood, disciplines, and procedures of restraint and accountability developed over the years by the world's first nuclear power.

8. Glenn, *Washington Post*, March 8, 1976; and Abraham A. Ribicoff, *New York Times*, March 26, 1976.

Modest nuclear assistance compatible with the nonproliferation treaty is a small price to pay for helping to induce greater nuclear responsibility in a new nuclear state. Such aid, however, may be read by some threshold governments as an inducement for them to go nuclear to reap the benefits of U.S. assistance.

Policies toward Threatened States

As the Israeli case demonstrates, U.S. measures to mitigate the destabilizing effects of a new nuclear state must be addressed to potential target countries as well. Freezing or curtailing the military power of a new nuclear state has essentially the same equalizing effect as augmenting the power of its potential adversaries. For practical and political reasons it is less difficult to take compensatory measures to strengthen a newly threatened state than to diminish the power of the threatening state. The United States has taken modest compensatory measures in Pakistan against India and in Egypt against Israel to offset the psychological and military advantage of the acquiring state. The United States could also offer a security agreement to the neighbors of a new nuclear state, including a pledge to take appropriate military action if the allied state suffered a nuclear attack. The awareness of a deliberate U.S. compensatory policy toward a potential victim would tend to erode the incentive of a threshold state to go nuclear or a new nuclear state to engage in threats.

Compensatory measures are not appropriate in all situations—South Korea and Taiwan, to name two. If South Korea should go nuclear, it would be largely because the United States had withdrawn its security commitment and it faced an implacable adversary, North Korea, which has two nuclear patrons. Under these circumstances it is possible that a nuclear force in South Korea could deter an attack from the North and thus enhance rather than detract from stability in the area. The same line of argument may be advanced for Taiwan facing a nuclear Chinese mainland. Since a nuclear force in South Korea or Taiwan could also provoke an attack, the United States should calculate carefully before assisting those governments to develop a deterrent. The chief guide to U.S. policy should be regional stability, the components of which are many and ever shifting.

Security of the United States

It is unlikely that any new nuclear force developed in the Third World before 2000 will threaten directly the United States as it was threatened by the Soviet missiles in Cuba in 1962. Unless there is a radical change in U.S.-Soviet relations or a unilateral change in the Soviet Union's external policy, the Russians will not place their strategic arms on the soil of any other sovereign state, though the United States may continue to do so in a few places outside Western Europe. Nor is it likely that any Third World state will manufacture or otherwise acquire a force that could be relied on to destroy significant targets in the United States, though this would be technically possible for Mexico, and speculatively possible for Argentina or Brazil, if either acquired long-range missiles.

The overwhelming nuclear threat to the United States is from the USSR, with a secondary threat from China. An effective antiballistic missile system would make sense to deal with the Chinese threat, as it would also for missiles from Mexico or elsewhere in Latin America.[9] But a nuclear threat from Latin America is an unlikely contingency.

Catalytic war between the superpowers sparked by a nuclear attack on one of them by a state with a small nuclear force also seems unlikely because of the sophisticated command and control systems on both sides and the availability of the hot line between the two. The acquisition of nuclear arms by a Third World power is more likely to affect strategic stability by drawing the Soviet Union, the United States, or both into a local conflict, like that in the Middle East where they are already deeply involved. What can the two superpowers do to avoid being sucked or tricked into such a conflict? The hot-line agreement has since 1963 provided for communication and consultation in the event of a nuclear accident or any other nuclear explosion. And the Nixon-Brezhnev 1973 Agreement on the Prevention of Nuclear War provides a formal mechanism for exercising restraint and sober second thinking in the heat of a fast-moving crisis. As with all such legal instruments, the utility of the

9. Defense Secretary Rumsfeld called for continued research and development on U.S. ABM systems to provide for "missile defense against 'third' country attacks." See *Annual Defense Department Report, FY 1977: Report of the Secretary of Defense Donald H. Rumsfeld to the Congress on the FY 1977 Budget and Its Implications for the FY 1978 Authorization Request and the FY 1977–1981 Defense Programs, January 27, 1976* (U.S. Department of Defense, January 27, 1976), p. 91.

agreements depends on the willingness of each party to do what the agreement requires. Experience in the Middle East and elsewhere suggests that both the United States and the Soviet Union have a high incentive to avoid a nuclear confrontation. The disciplines of mutual deterrence and the mechanisms of command and control extend to areas outside the primary strategic arena because each party is determined not to give the other an excuse to launch a nuclear first strike, and each is deterred by the fear of an unacceptable retaliatory blow.

Despite many uncertainties and imponderables, it appears quite unlikely that any new national nuclear force in the Third World will seriously threaten strategic stability unless there is a drastic change in the outlook and behavior of either or both superpowers. The United States and the Soviet Union are unlikely to be drawn into a regional conflict because their compatible and conflicting interests in the Third World have been and can be pursued by nonnuclear means.

Index

Agency for the Prohibition of Nuclear Weapons in Latin America, 105
Agreement on the Prevention of Nuclear War, 6, 146
Akhund, Iqbal, 45n
Alexander, Tom, 14n
Alliances. *See* Mutual defense pacts
Allon, Yigal, 67n
Anderson, Raymond H., 73n
Arab-Israeli War of *1973*, 64–65, 76
Argentina: armed forces, 101; Canadian relations, 110, 111; delivery systems, 112; economy, 101; French relations, 110; future options, 115–17; Indian relations, 110–11; military aid, 102; nuclear aid, 110–11; nuclear arms capability, 111–12; nuclear incentives, 114–15; nuclear policy, 108–09; nuclear program, 109–11; U.S. relations, 101–02, 120; West German relations, 110
Armaments. *See* Nuclear arms
Armed forces, U.S., 51, 83, 84, 90, 93, 125, 134
Atomic Energy Act of *1954*, U.S., 3
Atomic Energy Commission: Argentina, 109, 110; India, 25, 27; Israel, 66; U.S., 3, 36, 56
Atomic Energy Council, Taiwan, 89
Atomic Energy Organization, Iran, 54, 55

Baruch plan, 3
Batchelder, Robert C., 21n
Beaton, Leonard, 28n, 73n
Berger, Marilyn, 71n, 72n
Bhabha, Homi J., 27
Bhutto, Zulfikar Ali, 25, 37, 43, 44, 131

Bilateral security agreements. *See* Mutual defense pacts
Binder, David, 1n, 5n, 13n, 89n
Bombs. *See* Nuclear arms
Borders, William, 38n
Branigan, William, 49n
Brazil: armed forces, 101; delivery systems, 108; economy, 100–01; French relations, 106–08, 130; future options, 115–17; military aid, 102; nuclear aid, 102, 105, 106–08; nuclear arms capability, 108; nuclear incentives, 112–14; nuclear policy, 103–05; nuclear program, 105–08; U.S. relations, 101–02, 105, 106–07, 108, 120, 131; West German relations, 106, 107, 108, 131
Brezhnev, Leonid, 6, 146
Buchan, Alastair, 73n
Burnham, David, 16n, 65n, 68n, 107n, 139n
Burt, Richard, 5n, 46n, 131n
Butterfield, Fox, 89n

Cahn, Anne Hessing, 47n, 54n
Canada: Argentine relations, 110, 111; French relations, 131–32; Indian relations, 28, 32–33, 36–37; nuclear aid, 28, 43, 87, 110; Pakistani relations, 43, 45–46, 131–32; South Korean relations, 87, 130; Taiwanese relations, 88; U.S. relations, 130
Caranfil, Andrew, 16n, 85n, 108n
Carter, Jimmy, 1, 74, 90, 93, 118, 129
Central Intelligence Agency, U.S., 64, 65
Central Treaty Organization (CENTO), 43–44
Chiang Ching-kuo, 82, 88
China, People's Republic of: armed

149

FIC   Babson, Marian.

Reel murder

R·E·E·L
MURDER

Also by Marian Babson

R·E·E·L
MURDER

A Mystery by
MARIAN BABSON

St. Martin's Press
New York

F / C

R 00550   45487

Library of Congress Cataloging in Publication Data

Babson, Marian.
  Reel murder.

  "A Thomas Dunne book."
  I. Title.
PS3552.A25R4 1987   813'.54   86-27939
ISBN 0-312-00227-0

First published in Great Britain by William Collins Sons & Co. Ltd.

First U.S. Edition

10 9 8 7 6 5 4 3 2 1

R·E·E·L
MURDER

CHAPTER 1

There are certain decisions you regret from the moment they are made. By then, it is usually too late.

I knew better. Every time I had fallen into her net, I had lived to regret it. I refused to admit to myself the number of years—decades—it had gone on. It seems that bitter experience teaches us nothing. Or can it be true that some of us are born victims?

'You're an idiot, Mother.' My beloved daughter did not hesitate to point this out to me at the airport. (Much too late.) 'You know there's trouble every time you have anything to do with her. *She* rushes ahead and does all sorts of awful things—and then you're left holding the baby.'

'It's only a trip to London,' I defended, glad that she could not read my mind. Poor Martha, she didn't know the half of it. 'Two weeks . . . a civilized city . . . everybody speaks English. What trouble could we possibly get into?'

'Practically anything,' she said severely. 'I'm against this whole trip. I have been since the beginning.'

So had I. But I could not possibly admit it now. Besides, Martha was usually against practically anything you could mention.

'Nonsense, dear,' I placated. 'We'll have a lovely vacation and we'll be back before you know it. You'll see.'

'I hope so.' There was no hope in her voice, only a grim certainty that I was on a collision course with disaster and about to bring disgrace upon myself and everyone connected with me.

'*Dear* Martha. Still the little ray of sunshine, I see.' The bone of contention was upon us. In a *sotto voce* aside to me, she murmured: 'So like her father. I always warned you *that* was a mistake.'

She had her brazen nerve, but there was no time to take issue with her; they were calling our flight. I kissed Martha hurriedly, promised faithfully to write every single day and tell her *everything*, then uncrossed my fingers and followed Evangeline Sinclair into the Departure Lounge.

It was just like old times. First, there were the sideways glances from our fellow passengers, then the furtive nudges, the whispers, and . . .

'*Is* it?' . . . 'It can't be' . . . 'It *is*—it's *her!*' . . . 'She's on our flight! Wait till I tell—' . . .

Evangeline lifted her head higher and passed through the crowd which parted respectfully to allow her passage. She smiled graciously as she met timid eyes, nodded regally to those bolder ones who murmured a greeting. It was an auspicious beginning to our journey.

'My God! Is *she* still alive?' Then some fool spoiled it. 'I thought she'd died long ago.'

'*Shhhhh!*' But it was too late. There was nothing wrong with Evangeline's hearing. Her lips tightened, her eyes snapped—she'd retained every bit of her legendary temper, too.

'Trixie!' Without turning her head, she summoned me to her side.

'I'm right here.' I spoke quietly, both to avert a scene and to counteract the impression she was trying to convey that she was the *grande dame* and I was the walk-on maid.

'Trixie? . . .' I needn't have worried; the whispers started again. 'Trixie Dolan?' . . . 'Sure, didn't you see her movie on TV last week? *Gold-Diggers of the Great White Way*—that's what they used to call Broadway, back when Broadway *was* Broadway.'

Now it was my turn to nod graciously and smile. This was not what Evangeline had intended at all.

'*Dear* Trixie—' I knew I was in trouble. You're always in trouble when Evangeline begins *dear*ing you.

'*Dear* Trixie, it's so kind of you to accompany me on this

trip to England. I can't tell you how much it means to me to have one of my *oldest* and dearest friends by my side as Britain honours me.'

'It's just a private cinema doing a restrospective season,' I said. She could always make me nervous, the way she inflated any attention shown to her. She was making this sound like the female equivalent of a Knighthood, at least. Audiences always did that to her.

'In conjunction with the London Film Festival!' She beamed upon me. 'And affiliated with the National Film Theatre. I'm deeply honoured that they should want to do a retrospective of *my* films! I can't think of any Body in the world whose accolade I would treasure more.'

And so much for the Metropolitan Museum of Art, which had been annoying her for years by digging up everyone else's films and making a to-do over them.

'Such recognition means *so* much more than the paltry re-runs on the Late Show—'

And so much for me, too.

'Naturally—' she added hastily—'that is not to say that I denigrate television. It has a right and proper place in the scheme of things but—'

The loudspeaker cut across her, requesting that we proceed to the Boarding Gate and board our flight. Not even Evangeline Sinclair could compete with that. Her audience abandoned their fascinated eavesdropping and returned to their own affairs. The pushing and jostling regained its normal level as we struggled forward and eventually found ourselves decanted into the narrow aisles of our prison for the long hours of the flight.

'I can't get over it . . .' Someone was still marvelling. 'Evangeline Sinclair and Trixie Dolan—on *our* plane. And travelling together! I mean, wasn't there some big feud? I thought they stopped speaking back in the 'thirties. Or was it the 'forties? There was some hushed-up scandal, anyway. And they had a knock-down drag-out fight and nearly killed each other . . .' The voice dropped, going into gory details.

There'll always be a film buff. Rumours, half-truths, whispers—they thrive on them. How they love to repeat them with the air of being in the know. I had someone's flight bag knocking the back of my knees and Evangeline immediately in front of me, so I couldn't turn around to see who was speaking. Not that it would have made any difference. This was neither the time nor the place for explanations or corrections.

Especially not the place. We had reached our seats and Evangeline was frowning. I didn't blame her. I could already feel claustrophobia wrapping its tentacles around me.

'Do they seriously imagine—' her voice rose indignantly —'that anyone larger that a malformed dwarf could endure this seating?'

The appreciative titters of her listeners did not placate her. Her righteous wrath went beyond any satisfaction at providing entertainment. For once, she was oblivious of an audience.

'I'll take the inside seat—' I couldn't stand a scene—not so soon. I pushed past her and curled into the inadequate space. 'You can sit on the outside.'

'To think—' she mused loudly—'that the French boxcars of World War One were considered so inadequate that soldiers inscribed "*40 hommes, 8 chevaux*" on them. What, one wonders, would those same doughboys say if they could see modern transportation—and realize that people actually *paid* for such accommodation?'

It was no time to remind her that when those same doughboys had left the ground they had often gone up in far worse machines. Not for nothing had they been known as 'crates'. In fact, looking around, I could see one or two elderly gentlemen who looked as though they might have pioneered air travel—in crates that allowed them little more space than our seating.

'Oh, Ms Sinclair . . . Ms Dolan . . .' A flight steward

rushed down the aisle towards us. 'This is such an honour
. . . I'm so pleased to meet you—' He looked at our seats with
horror. 'But there's been some mistake. Will you come this
way, please?'

We struggled out of the seats and followed him to the First
Class section. Another film buff doing his bit of homage? Or
had he instructions from someone to upgrade us if there was
room? It didn't really matter. We settled into seats that were
luxurious by comparison with those we had left.

The flight steward bustled behind a curtain and we heard
the discreet pop of a champagne cork.

'This is more like it.' Evangeline nodded approval.

'Here we are—' The steward was back with two glasses of
bubbling Veuve Clicquot. 'We'll finish the bottle after take-
off, but that will get you going. You're very lucky. David's
piloting this flight. His take-offs are so smooth no one has
ever spilled a drop.'

'How nice.' Evangeline took a deep swallow, making it
clear that there wasn't going to be anything left to be spilt on
take-off. It seemed like a good idea and I did the same. I
don't like take-offs.

'I'll top you up just as soon as we're aloft,' our steward
promised, leaving us to usher some genuine first class passengers to their seats. Some of them glanced at us with
interest, envy and—perhaps—surprise. We were a bit over
the usual age for hurtling ourselves around the world.

It seemed no time at all until the engines revved up and we
went taxi-ing down the runway, gathering speed. The plane
tilted and we were airborne, deep into that first frightening
thrust that lifted us into the clouds, leaving—in my case
—my heart, stomach and courage still on the ground behind
us.

'We're off—' Evangeline drained her glass—'on the Great
Adventure.'

I wished abruptly that I had never played the lead in *Peter
Pan* that season so long ago. As the plane seemed to hesitate

and gather itself for the final great thrust into the strato-
sphere, my mind presented me with that classic finale: the
darkened auditorium, the spotlight tight on my face as I
lifted my head and 'Peter' said,

'To die . . . might be the greatest adventure of all.'

CHAPTER 2

I don't mind landings quite so much. Intellectually, I know
that they're just as dangerous as take-offs; emotionally, I feel
that every foot closer to the ground is a foot closer to safety. I
hadn't realized I'd been holding my breath until I expelled it
as the wheels touched the tarmac.

'You just stay where you are, ladies, until we get the first
rush out of the way,' our steward told us. 'We have special
transport laid on for *you*.'

It was sweet of him to make it sound as though this was
going to happen because of our fame and not our decrepi-
tude. Whatever the reason, I was thankful to be spared the
long, tedious trudge to the Customs Hall.

'I'm afraid this isn't quite what you're accustomed to,' the
driver apologized as we sat on the back of his strange little
vehicle, gliding past the jet-lagged lines of shuffling tra-
vellers.

'Not at all.' After a preliminary narrowing of her eyes,
Evangeline had decided to be gracious. 'I spent a large part
of World War II entertaining troops all over the world and
jouncing over battlefields in jeeps. This is a far smoother
ride.'

In fact, I had done a lot more entertaining of troops in
far-flung outposts than she had. While she had been mostly
behind the lines in the European Theatre of Operations, the
USO had assigned me to the Far East—and my jungle jeep
rides had been a lot jouncier and more dangerous than

anything she had had to face. Both of us had made several tours with Bob Hope; but then, who hadn't?

Someone had collected our luggage from the carousel and it was piled waiting for us in the Customs Hall. It had been a long time since I had had this kind of service. Maybe it was going to be worthwhile travelling with Evangeline, after all.

I changed my mind again when we rolled through the final door, making our entrance to the crowd behind the barrier, a sea of anxious faces straining to watch for the appearance of their own personal star. I heard Evangeline draw in her breath with a hiss of displeasure.

'What's the matter?' My heart sank. It had never taken much to set off that famous temperament of hers.

'Look!' She waved her hand towards the waiting crowd. 'Just *look* at that frightful man!'

It took me a moment to spot him; quite a few of them looked frightful to me. Ours was the three-piece-suit, short-back-and-sides generation; multi-hued cockscombs and rag-bag raiment held no attraction for me. Then I saw him. No wonder she was furious.

MISS SINCLAIR said the neatly-lettered sign he was holding above his head.

Otherwise, he was a quite unexceptional early-middle-aged man. His suit was conservative, his hair was neatly trimmed, his smile was ingratiating—but he was for ever damned. He had betrayed the fact that he did not expect to recognize Evangeline Sinclair on sight.

Just then, he saw us. His face lit up with relief and he lowered the sign quickly. As he came forward to meet us, he detoured swiftly to drop the sign into a large refuse bin, not knowing it was already too late, poor creature.

'Miss Sinclair, Miss Dolan—' He rushed up to us. 'This is a great honour—'

'Yes-s-s-s,' Evangeline said.

'How nice of you to think so.' I covered quickly, giving Evangeline a dirty look. 'And you are—?'

'Oh, forgive me. Hugh. Hugh Carpenter. Let me take your things.' He took control of our luggage trolley, swinging it towards one of the exits. 'The car is over this way.'

I trotted along beside him, trying to keep up a steady stream of small talk in the hope that he wouldn't notice that Evangeline was stalking along behind us in stately silence. Unfortunately, he did.

'Oh, I'm sorry—' He slowed to a snail's pace and gave her another of his ingratiating smiles. 'Am I going too fast for you, Miss Sinclair?'

If looks could kill, he would have dropped on the spot.

'Oh, I'm sorry. I didn't mean to imply—' He had already broken off in confusion before I nudged him.

'We're nearly there—' He wheeled the trolley through sliding doors and had second thoughts. 'Why don't you ladies wait here and I'll bring the car round? It will be easier now that I know you— I mean, you stay here with the trolley and— I won't be a minute.' He abandoned us and the trolley and loped off.

I hoped he was better at driving than he was at diplomacy.

He narrowly escaped being hit by an airport bus and three taxis as he crossed to the car park. I looked up at the towering structure, with its hairpin curves looping up to each level and hoped that he was on the lowest level. It was all too easy to picture him losing control of his car, careering down those steep curves, crashing from side to side until, at ground level, denuded of its fenders and bumpers, the car shot out into the road to collide with a double-decker airport bus.

'Perhaps,' Evangeline said thoughtfully, 'we ought to take a taxi.'

'We can't, really.' How I wished we could. 'Not after he's gone to all the trouble of meeting us.'

'He reminds me of a director I worked with once. We lost three stunt men on that picture.'

'Well, he's not directing us, he's only driving us in to town—and here he is now.'

He drew up to the kerb smoothly and leaped out to come round and open the rear door for us. He handed us into the car, getting it right on the first take, then resumed his seat behind the steering-wheel. It was the first indication that there might be hope for him yet.

'Nice car,' Evangeline allowed, as we sank back cautiously against the rear seat.

'It's a Rolls-Royce,' he pointed out, just in case we hadn't noticed. 'Mr Sylvester has three of them. This is the newest.'

'Not . . .' The information seemed to give Evangeline pause. 'Not *Beauregard* Sylvester?'

'The one-and-only.' Hugh Carpenter turned to beam at us over his shoulder. Three oncoming cars swerved abruptly as we verged perilously near the white line dividing the road and several cars behind us sounded their horns in varying degrees of alarm and indignation.

'I didn't know he was still—' Evangeline broke off and resumed, 'How *is* dear Beauregard? I haven't seen him since . . . it must have been . . .'

'*Slaves of Passion*,' Hugh supplied cheerfully. 'That was the one the Hays Office tried to ban—' The sudden frost in the atmosphere made itself felt, even to him.

'Yes-s-s . . .' Evangeline said distantly. '*Dear* Beauregard. He taught me so much. But then, he was so much older than I. How *is* he these days?'

'Flourishing,' Hugh said. 'Surely you must have followed his career, even though your paths divided?'

'Oh, of course . . .' Evangeline said vaguely.

'I'm afraid I lost track of him a bit,' I said quickly, knowing Evangeline would never admit to it. We'd never find out anything if I didn't do a bit of tactful grovelling. 'Please, just refresh my memory, if you wouldn't mind.'

'You probably lost track of him during the war,' Hugh said forgivingly. 'A lot of people did. He and Juanita Morez—'

'His third wife, I believe.' Evangeline remembered that much.

'That's right—and his last.' There was a trace of acid in Hugh's voice, perhaps he wasn't as unworldly as he seemed. 'They came here in 1937 to make a film for Sir Alexander Korda. An historical romance—'

'He was always at his best with costume dramas,' Evangeline murmured. It was not clear whether she meant Sir Alexander or Beauregard Sylvester.

'Was that the one where he played a Cavalier?' A dim memory stirred in my mind. 'It kept turning up on the Late Show in the early days of television.' In fact, it was one of the group of pictures off-loaded on to the early television companies that had done so much to give English films a bad name.

'That's the one!' Hugh spun the steering-wheel expertly and we slid into the fast lane. '*He Laughed Last*—great, wasn't it? It was such a success that they signed him for another straightaway and rushed it into production. That was *The Merry Highwayman*.'

'Ah yes,' I said reminiscently. That had shown up on the late-night shows, too. The reviews had been nearly as pungent as the film.

'He enjoyed working in England—they both did. Juanita was starring in a West End musical comedy. Neither of them really believed there was going to be a war. Even after it was declared, there was that long interval when nothing happened—the Phoney War. Beau signed for another film. Even when Juanita's show was closed when all the theatres were shut down, she didn't care. By that time, she'd discovered she was pregnant and they were so delighted about it, they decided to have the baby here in England and settle permanently. They bought a Regency villa beside the Thames, near to the film studios where Beau was working. Then, of course—'

Evangeline stifled a yawn loudly.

'Forgive me—' He was instantly contrite. 'You're both exhausted after your trip and I'm rambling on. Lean back and try to get some rest. We'll be there soon.'

'I am not tired,' Evangeline said coldly, leaving the implication *merely bored* hanging in the air. She had a low threshold of boredom when the conversation didn't centre on her.

Outside, the fields and factories had given way to little houses, thickly clustered together. As we drove farther in towards the centre of the city, the houses joined together in neat little rows lining the road. Then came concentrations of shops and pubs, each with its own post office and church, set off by yet more little houses. It made me realize the truth of the assertion that London is a collection of villages.

Evangeline was paying no attention to the scenery. Her hooded gaze and withdrawn expression began to make me uneasy. I knew that attitude of old; she was scheming again. And we hadn't even unpacked.

We were passing familiar landmarks now, readily identifiable from stock shots and postcards. Finally, we came to the most famous of all: Buckingham Palace.

'Just a little detour here,' Hugh spoke over his shoulder. 'I thought you might like to see Buck House.'

'Not unless we're staying there,' Evangeline said coldly.

'Ha-ha!' He decided to take it as a joke. 'I'm afraid we couldn't quite arrange that. Not this time. Perhaps for your next visit.'

'Ha-ha,' Evangeline echoed bleakly, reminding him that he was lucky she had made it this time. To expect any more trips was tempting fate.

'Yes . . . well . . .' He stepped on the accelerator and we shot down the Mall at a speed I'm sure wasn't allowed. We veered and veered again, skirting Trafalgar Square and heading north.

'Young man—' Evangeline leaned forward suspiciously. 'Where are you taking us?'

'To your flat. We'll have you settled in no time.'

'You mean . . .' Her eyes narrowed in a danger signal.

'We're not staying at the Savoy?'

'Er, no . . .'

'The Dorchester, then.'

'Er . . . actually, as you're here for a fortnight, we thought you might be more comfortable in your own flat. A service flat, of course. You'll have everything done for you, just as though you were in a hotel.'

'I see . . .' Evangeline looked out of the window and did not appear to like anything she was seeing. 'And just where *is* this service flat?'

'Not far now.' He swerved round another corner. 'St John's Wood, actually.'

'St John's Wood?' From Evangeline's tone, it might have been Siberia.

'It's not that far out,' he said defensively. 'It's just above Baker Street.'

'I *know* where St John's Wood is,' Evangeline said severely. 'It's where Victorian merchants kept their mistresses. In love-nests.' She made it sound as though we were being carried away into the White Slave Trade. As though anyone would be interested, at our ages.

'That was a long time ago.' Hugh caught the implication; the back of his neck crimsoned. 'It's quite respectable now.'

'Hmmmph!' Evangeline said.

I wouldn't have thought it possible, but the back of his neck got even redder.

We drove the rest of the way in icy silence.

CHAPTER 3

We turned into a carriageway and pulled up in front of a Victorian edifice, too imposing to be called a mere house, although it must have been once.. One of those houses designed to accommodate a family of ten children, assorted elderly relatives and enough servants to ensure that they led the most comfortable of lives.

Today a discreet array of pushbuttons beside an entry-phone grille testified that it had been divided up into apart-ments—or 'Service Flats', as Hugh Carpenter had called them.

I saw the curtains twitch at an upstairs window as we stopped, then Hugh was out of the car and bustling round to open the door for us and help us out.

The front door burst open and a gangling youth stumbled down the steps and lurched to a halt beside us. Evangeline closed her eyes briefly. I managed a smile, but I'd almost forgotten they came so young.

'Help with the luggage, Hugh?' he offered eagerly.

'Good-oh, Jasper.' Hugh waved his hand vaguely towards the rear of the car. 'It's all in the boot—not locked. Just bring it along, will you?'

Evangeline stood on the paved walk looking up at the house as though all her worst fears had been confirmed.

'Just a few steps—' Unerringly, Hugh Carpenter put his foot in it again. 'Not too much for you, is it? Here, take my arm.'

Deliberately and ostentatiously, she did not hear him. She drew herself up and mounted the steps swiftly, not even touching the railing. Someday she'd do herself an injury, showing off like that.

I followed her quickly, before Hugh could offer his arm to me. I held on to the railing, but only because I was wearing new shoes with slippery leather soles. Otherwise, I wouldn't have bothered, either.

Evangeline gave an exclamation of annoyance and stop-ped short. There was a reception committee lurking in the entrance hall. A gaggle of young people in varying stages of what passed for fashion these days were looking welcoming and hopeful as we pushed open the door.

Drama students. I could spot them anywhere.

From behind me, Hugh Carpenter's exclamation of annoyance matched Evangeline's. 'That's the flat-share from the top floor,' he said. 'I've told them not to disturb you. Get along, you lot—' He flapped his hands at them ineffectually, like a man shooing away chickens. 'Clear out of here!'

'Weally, Hugh!' A small girl who seemed to have a disintegrating orange haystack, decorated with cerise ribbons, slipping off her head and trailing down her back, spoke haughtily. 'I was only passing through on my way to post a letter. There's no need to be wude!'

'I'm not the rude one,' Hugh said. 'You might at least wait until they were inside the door before you pounced on them.'

'Did I pounce?' Haystack quivering perilously, setting cerise ribbons fluttering like exotic butterflies, she turned to us indignantly. 'I was mewely on my way out to the postbox. Are we no longer to have access to our own fwont door fwom now on?'

'Be reasonable, Hugh.' A young man in a Mohican scalplock hairdo with three earrings running up the side of one ear and a multi-zippered black leather outfit, spoke earnestly. 'Gwenda's right. We have to live here, too.'

'I'm on my way to work—' This one was sleekly-coiffed, her black urchin cut framing her face. Black circles framed her eyes so enthusiastically that she resembled a Panda bear. 'Should I have climbed out of the window?'

'I'm not denying your right of access, Ursula,' Hugh said reasonably. 'I'm simply pointing out that you all might have chosen a better time to converge on the front door. Not very subtle, you know.'

Since when had drama students been expected to be subtle? I'd never met any who were and, for my sins, I taught the occasional course at the local night school. Grabbing attention was the name of the game—and the chance to attract the attention of Evangeline Sinclair must be well-nigh irresistible.

'You're being positively churlish, Hugh.' Now a thin wiry

boy whose hair stood up in multi-coloured spikes, chimed in. 'Leaving these ladies standing in a draughty hallway while you start a *brawl* with the legal tenants. Who do you think you are, the landlord?'

'Des is wight,' Gwenda said promptly. 'It's disgwaceful of you—and after they've twavelled all this distance. They must be exhausted. The least you could do is let them into their flat before you begin bewating us!'

'Oh, I do apologize.' Hugh's tendency to grovel, never far from the surface apparently, rose to the occasion. 'What must you think of me? Here. In here—' He fumbled with keys and unlocked a door beside us. 'I—I hope it's all right. I mean, you should be comfortable here.'

We entered a large drawing-room, dripping with the opulence of a stage setting. Long dark red velvet drapes at the windows, small Persian and Chinese rugs tossed carelessly on top of a wall-to-wall broadloom, huge overstuffed chairs upholstered in matching velvet, a glorious white marble fireplace and, above it, a gilded Chinese Chippendale looking-glass.

'Aaah,' Evangeline said appreciatively. '*The Second Mrs Tanqueray*, I presume? Or possibly, *Lady Windermere's Fan?*'

'A bit of both,' I agreed, just to keep my end up. She knew perfectly well that I'd never acted in a revival of either. You don't get those parts when you have a snub nose and freckles, you have to settle for cute roles. I'd been cute through so many B-pictures I'd made myself sick. She didn't have to rub it in.

'Hmmm . . .' She began strolling around the room, touching the fringe on a lampshade, straightening a silver Art Nouveau picture frame on a rosewood side-table. She looked at the picture in the frame, did a double-take and moved hastily to the mahogany sofa-table behind the sofa. She reached into a silver rose-bowl and stirred the potpourri inside, releasing a cloud of fragrance into the air.

There was no doubt about it, this room was going to take

some living up to. And me without a full-length, bare-shouldered white satin evening gown to my name, let alone in the luggage I'd packed for this trip. Oh well, you can't win 'em all.

'Cwumbs, Hugh!' Gwenda and her friends appeared in the doorway. They had had the forethought to possess themselves of a selection of our luggage and they staggered into the room helpfully. 'You've done a gweat job! I wouldn't wecognize the place.'

'Now, see here—' Hugh began threateningly.

'How sweet of you, my dears.' Evangeline decided to be gracious. Perhaps the room, reeking as it did of *noblesse oblige*, had got to her. More probably, she was doing it to spite Hugh, against whom she had taken one of her unfortunate dislikes. 'My bags—thank you so much.'

'Where do you want them? The bedwooms?' Gwenda led the way, the others bounding in her wake like overgrown puppies. Evangeline's acceptance of their help had given them new status; if they had tails, they would have been wagging them.

'Where's Jasper?' Hugh called after them. 'I thought he was bringing in the luggage.'

'Just here, Hugh.' Jasper must have kicked the door. It flew open and banged against the wall. He lurched into the room, a suitcase in each hand, a smaller case under each arm. 'There's an awful lot of it. I was glad to have some help.'

Most of it was Evangeline's, of course. She had made most of her Atlantic crossings in the era when seven to ten days on a luxury liner was par for the course, dressing for dinner every night, plus several changes of costume during the day, plus a spectacular costume for the ship's concert. And that was just the cabin baggage. The serious part of her wardrobe, to be worn once she reached shore, had been packed in cases marked 'Not Wanted On Voyage' and stowed away in the hold. There had also been a maid or two to pack and

unpack, iron, re-sew buttons, mend torn lace, not to mention
waiting on Evangeline hand and foot.

Those days might be gone, but old habits die hard.
Evangeline still packed as though for a year at Court. I'd
thought my poor Martha was going to have a seizure when
she heard how much we were being charged for excess
baggage weight.

'Through there,' Hugh directed unnecessarily. Jasper was
already heading for the bedrooms. Our upstairs neighbours
seemed quite familiar with the layout of the flat. I wondered
who had last occupied it.

'Suppose—' Evangeline moved forward. 'Suppose *we* inspect the rest of our quarters?'

'Good idea.' I was behind her immediately. If we didn't
make some decisive move ourselves, it was obvious that
Hugh Carpenter was just going to stand around dithering for
the rest of the day.

'Oh, I'm sorry. So sorry.' By a series of intricate sidesteps,
he managed to get ahead of us. 'The study—' He snapped a
switch and a green-shaded desk lamp glowed on to the
gilt-tooled red leather top of a teak desk. Booklined walls,
armchairs and reading lamps, another, smaller fireplace,
and an enormous window, which didn't seem to let in much
light, on the far wall.

'The conservatory—' Another switch snapped and a
jungle of foliage sprang into view on the far side of the French
windows. White-painted wrought-iron chairs and a table
clustered in a small clearing. 'It's a bit hot and muggy for my
taste, but you might like to sit out there occasionally.'

'It looks lovely,' I said.

'There's another French window in your room that opens
out into it. Your room—' he turned to Evangeline—'opens
into the garden itself, although it's rather chilly at this time of
year. You might prefer to sit in the conservatory, too. It
might remind you of California.'

'The California climate does not equate to a steamy,

overheated greenhouse.' Evangeline's tone effectively lowered the temperature about ten degrees. 'Despite the untutored opinion of some people. Have you ever been to California, Mr Carpenter?'

'Er, no. Not yet, that is. I hope to—'

'You must go sometime. You'll learn a lot.'

'Then my room must be through here.' I moved ahead hastily, trying to distract Evangeline from her hostilities. It wasn't fair for her to pick on a man she barely knew. I must admit, though, that I had no great faith that Hugh Carpenter would improve on further acquaintance.

My bedroom was plain but pleasant. A faint odour of fresh paint explained Gwenda's surprised reaction on entering the drawing-room. The place had quite obviously been re-decorated recently.

'Now—' Hugh looked at the pile of suitcases in the middle of the room. 'Are all your bags here?'

'Most of them are Evangeline's,' I said. 'Those two are mine, but I have two more. Somewhere.'

'They must be in Miss Sinclair's room.'

'I wouldn't be surprised,' Evangeline said. 'Everything else seems to be.' Everyone else, she meant. We could hear a discrete hubbub from across the hall.

Well! It was definitely the star dressing-room. It had everything but the actual star on the door. By comparison, I was billeted in the broom closet. No wonder the youngsters couldn't tear themselves away from it.

It was twice the size of my room, also freshly painted and wallpapered with a pale gold Regency stripe design. The bed was lengthwise against the lower end wall, framed by pink satin curtains draped Napoleonic-style from a gilt crown just below the ceiling. White-and-gilt-painted bergère chairs with gold velvet cushions, an elaborate chaise-longue, a secrétaire . . . the works! I tried to think what play could have had this for the setting, but was unable to think of any. Unless there'd been a little farce called something like, *Ooh*

La-La, Joséphine! which had escaped my attention. There were nearly enough doors for a farce, too.

'This part of the room used to be the morning-room.' Hugh moved upstage, to a portion of the room roughly across from the study. 'But we knocked down the wall to turn it into one large room. We, er, thought that it might make it more comfortable for—for *you*.'

Hmmmm? That foot was hovering perilously near his mouth again. Just for Evangeline, was it? I began to wonder who might be destined to occupy the star dressing-room after her departure. The flat, in fact. It would make a very nice little love-nest. Was the St John's Wood tradition lingering on?

'Oh, Hugh—it's fabulous!' Ursula exclaimed.

'Thwilling!' Gwenda glowed with excitement, prowling eagerly around the room. She stopped at the dressing-table, a proper stage dressing-table with the mirror surrounded by light-bulbs. 'Where do you—? Oh, I found it!' The bulbs sprang into life and Gwenda bent to pull her hair into yet more separated strands and fluff up her chiffon ribbons. 'So this is what all the banging and cwashing was about. Aren't you just wild about it, Miss Sinclair?'

Gwenda? If Hugh had amorous intentions towards her, they certainly didn't show. His face darkened with irritation.

'See here, you lot,' he said. 'You're becoming tedious. I told you yesterday you weren't to disturb Miss Sinclair —and Miss Dolan. You promised. So much for your promises!'

'Oh, don't be such a wotter, Hugh!' Gwenda pouted.

'*If* we are disturbing anyone—' Ursula spoke with icy grandeur—'we shall leave instantly.' She made no move to go.

'We were only helping,' Mick, the Indian brave, said defensively.

'We're still helping.' Des turned to me. 'Point out your cases and I'll carry them to your room for you. Then you can show me which cases belong to Miss Sinclair and I'll bring them back here.'

'That's wight!' Gwenda pounced on the idea triumphantly. 'We only want to help. We'll do anything at all for you, Miss Sinclair. We'll fetch and cawwy for you, make tea, wun ewwands—' She clasped her hands dramatically. 'Just don't send us away!'

'Dear children,' Evangeline beamed. 'I wouldn't dream of it.'

Hugh winced. 'On your head be it,' he muttered. 'You'll have them underfoot day and night.'

Precisely what I was afraid of, but Evangeline had the bit in her teeth and there was no stopping her. The double delight of thwarting Hugh and basking in the admiration of young fans was raising her spirits faster than champagne. Besides, it wouldn't be on *her* head, I'd watched her operate before. Evangeline's head was very well trained and could be relied on to produce a shattering headache which required her to go away and lie down quietly whenever a situation became difficult, leaving someone else—anyone else—to cope with the problem. Leaving me.

Again I wondered what momentary madness had led me into agreeing to accompany her. I wasn't in desperate need of a free trip. I could afford to pay my own fare. This way, I was in danger of paying excessively through my nerves. Financially would have been preferable.

'Perhaps they'd like to see the kitchen, Hugh,' Jasper said doubtfully. He glanced at us obliquely, as though to make sure we recognized the word.

'Ooh, yes! You must see what they've done with the kitchen.' Gwenda led the way eagerly.

'It's quite small,' Hugh said apologetically. Just as well. It was the room behind my bedroom and, if it had been much bigger, my bedroom really would have been a broom closet.

'Of course—' Hugh brightened—'you won't be using it much. There are plenty of restaurants nearby and there are also places you can ring up to have a meal delivered. You'll find some numbers by the telephone in the study.'

The kitchen seemed even smaller by the time everyone had crowded into it. The youngsters stood looking around avidly, not missing a trick.

'Do you have everything you need?' Gwenda dived for a cupboard beneath a formica work counter. 'Pots and pans, yes. Fwying-pan, tea-kettle—' It stood on one of the electric hobs. 'Toaster—' It was at the back of the counter. 'Supplies —' She opened the fridge. It seemed that quite a domestic heart beat beneath that somewhat bizarre exterior.

'I can assure you,' Hugh said frostily, 'they have everything they're likely to need.'

'Milk, butter, eggs, bacon, ice cubes—' Gwenda called out the inventory, not taking his unsupported word for it. 'Well, you have enough for bweakfast, anyway. And if there's anything else you need, you can always bowwow it fwom us. We're wight upstairs—but you don't have to climb them —just give a shout. One of us will hear you.'

'You'll have to shout rather loudly, I'm afraid.' Hugh gave us a stiff smile. 'They're two floors above you—in the maisonette. Jasper has the flat directly overhead.'

'That's all right,' Jasper said easily. 'I can lend them anything they want.'

'How kind of you all.' Evangeline bestowed approval indiscriminately. 'You're making us feel so much at home.'

They beamed and wriggled again. Even Jasper was not immune to the Sinclair charm, although he seemed a bit older and more sophisticated than the others. I was relieved to hear that he was directly overhead, it promised a measure of quietness. Of course, appearances were notoriously deceiving and he might play hard rock until three a.m., but somehow I didn't think so.

Des had located a store cupboard and I moved closer to look over his shoulder as he browsed through. We appeared to be well provisioned with tins, jars and boxes of food, including some long-life ready-made dishes. Then the label on one of the tins stood out like a beacon.

It had been a long exhausting flight, my internal clock was completely out of kilter, I was tired and hungry. That was what I wanted now: creamed chicken on toast, a cup of tea—and silence. Especially silence.

This time it was I who did not bother to stifle a yawn.

'There, you see.' Hugh rounded on the youngsters instantly. 'You're wearing them out. It really is time you left and let them get some rest. You shouldn't be here anyway. You don't see Anni behaving like this.'

'Anni's out,' Des said, 'or she'd be here, too. Anyway,' he added meaningly, 'she's already had a chance to see all the alterations.'

'P'waps we *should* go now—' Gwenda glanced uneasily at Evangeline, who was smiling bravely but seemed to be growing frailer before our eyes. I was still working on that one, but she had it down pat. On her better days, she could even go pale at will.

'Dear children,' Evangeline said weakly. 'You have been so kind. You must come down and have a glass of sherry with us some time. If we have any sherry . . .'

'If you haven't, we'll bwing some!' All the cerise ribbons fluttered wildly as Hugh herded them towards the exit. 'And don't forget—if you want anything, just shout.'

'I may even scream,' Evangeline said between clenched teeth as the door closed behind them.

'I'm terribly sorry about that.' Hugh was still inside with us. 'I *told* them they mustn't disturb you.'

' "Stand not upon the order of your going—" ' Evangeline fixed him with Lady Macbeth's demented gaze. ' "*But—*" '

He went. 'We'll be in touch tomorrow . . .' floated back over his shoulder.

I opened the creamed chicken and we had our light meal, did some unpacking, and roamed aimlessly through the flat in the restless jet-lagged state when you feel it's too early to give in and go to bed, but can't settle to doing anything useful.

'There must be a television set somewhere,' Evangeline grumbled, opening doors and drawers in her bedroom. 'There's everything else.'

'Let's try the drawing-room.' We roamed back there and stood looking around. 'Now, where would I hide a television if I were a set designer?' I crossed to a promising-looking cabinet and opened it. 'Nope, that's the bar.'

'That will do.' Evangeline revived a bit and began pulling out glasses and a decanter of brandy. I crossed to the matching cabinet.

'Ah—here it is!' It only took a few more minutes of experimentation before I found the proper switch and the set came to life. Meanwhile, Evangeline had poured our drinks, settled herself in an armchair and begun a dissection of our new friends upstairs.

'She's a sweet child, but seriously deluded, I fear. How can she hope to get anywhere in the theatrical field with a speech impediment like that?'

'. . . in the city. But we can expect—' On the television screen, a man in front of a weather map leaned forward and confided—'thwee degwees of fwost in the outlying suburbs.'

We stared at each other, dumbfounded. Evangeline shuddered and took a deep gulp from her glass.

'Forget I mentioned it,' she said.

I did, but I remembered something else I had intended to check out. Casually, I drifted over to the rosewood side-table and picked up the silver Art Nouveau picture frame. As I had suspected, the face was familiar.

'Isn't this Beauregard Sylvester?'

'I wondered how long it would be before you spotted that.' Evangeline took another deep gulp of brandy. 'We must face it: we have been delivered into the hands of the Enemy!'

CHAPTER 4

The cerise chiffon bows on my tap shoes kept coming undone and flapping all over the place. Busby Berkeley was furious with me. The rest of the chorus line was giggling and the star accused me of trying to upstage her.

'It won't do you any good,' she snarled. 'You'll just wind up on the cutting-room floor—where you belong!'

I was being my cutest, but it wasn't doing me any good. It was all a nightmare.

It was with relief that I heard the strange insistent noise summoning me back to consciousness and reality. I lay with open eyes staring into blackness while my mind caught up with me and told me that I was in England and the odd *brrr-brrr* noise that wouldn't stop was the telephone on my bedside table. I groped for it, knocking something unidentifiable off the table—I hoped it wasn't the lamp.

'Yes, yes. I mean, hello. Who is it—?' I groped again, this time connecting with the lamp and switched it on. 'Who—?' I blinked, covering my eyes against the sudden brightness.

'Who is it?' another voice demanded. It wasn't mine. 'Do you realize what time it is?' I recognized Evangeline's indignant tones.

'Get off the line!' Another indignant voice snarled back at her. 'I'm calling my mother. What are you doing answering?'

'Martha—' I groaned, finally identifying the distant voice. 'Why are you calling at this hour?' I blinked at my watch and it swam into reluctant focus. 'It's four o'clock in the morning. What's the matter? What's wrong?'

'Matter?' she wailed. 'Wrong? That's what I want to know. You never called me. Did the plane land safely? Are you all right?'

'Don't be absurd!' Evangeline snapped from her extension. 'If anything had happened to that plane, you'd have heard about it. It would have made headlines all over the world.'

'But anything could have happened after you landed. There could have been an automobile accident—'

'Nonsense,' I said quickly, before Evangeline could. 'Hugh is a very careful driver. We were perfectly safe.'

'Hugh? Who's Hugh?'

'Hugh,' Evangeline said icily, through clenched teeth, 'is an English gigolo who swept your mother off her feet the moment she arrived. I had to forcibly remove him from her bedroom just a few hours ago. All your worst fears are realized. If you value your inheritance, you will rush over and join me in the unequal struggle to keep your lust-ridden mother from the arms of this fortune-hunting monster.'

'Mother!' Martha wailed. 'Mother—!'

'For heaven's sake, Martha, pull yourself together. How can you be so gullible! You can't possibly imagine—'

'Oh, can't she?' Evangeline chuckled wickedly.

'Mother—' Martha wailed again. 'Mother, don't do anything rash. Promise me—'

'Martha, don't be so stupid! You can't believe—'

'He's very handsome, I'll admit,' Evangeline said insidiously. 'And you know how susceptible your mother always was.'

'Mother—!'

'Evangeline—get off the line! This is my call!'

'I'll do my best, Martha, but you know your mother. There are times when there's just no holding her.'

'Mother—!'

'Evangeline—hang up!'

'You mustn't blame her, Martha. It's just the way she's made. *Made* being the operative word, of course.'

'Mother—!'

'Evangeline, I'm going to kill you!' At last, I was awake enough to realize the futility of shouting into a telephone when two raving egomaniacs were on the line. I set down the receiver on the bedside table, shuffled into my slippers and went across the hall into Evangeline's room.

'Oh yes, Martha. At your age, you may not believe it, but one is never too old to hope for romance. You have to face it, Martha—' Evangeline was still having her fun. 'A glamorous foreign city . . . away from all restraints . . . a young handsome man making eyes at her . . . She wasn't the first, and she won't be the last—'

'Mother—!'

'All right, that's enough!' I slammed my fingers down on the telephone cradle, cutting her off. 'You ought to know better! How dare you upset Martha like that? You know she's a bit naïve?'

'Naïve?' Evangeline snorted. 'Face it, Trixie—you're seventy-five years old and your only daughter is a gibbering middle-aged idiot!'

'I'm only sixty-eight,' I said coldly. 'And Martha is forty. That's hardly middle-aged these days. Besides, she means well. She has my best interests at heart.'

'Hmmph!' Evangeline settled back against the pillows. 'You should have beaten her more when she was a child.'

'If I had, she'd probably be writing a book about it now.'

'She may be doing that anyway.'

'You should talk! You're old enough to have outgrown the mischief-making stage. You must be eighty now—or is it eighty-five?'

'I haven't decided recently,' Evangeline said thoughtfully. 'Which do you think is more effective? Or maybe I should stick at seventy-six for a few more years?'

I snorted in my turn and stormed back to my own bedroom. The telephone was still projecting strange ululating noises. I picked it up carefully and held it to my ear.

'Mother—' Martha wailed. 'Mother—speak to me!'

'Oh, shut up!' I snarled and slammed down the receiver.

*

My second awakening was more peaceful. There was no
sound from Evangeline's room and the clock told me it was
ten a.m. With luck, I might have some time to myself before
she awoke. I rose and went into the kitchen to put the kettle
on.

A woolly white cloud seemed pressed against every window. When I got closer to a window, the cloud receded a bit
and I was able to look out into a hazy landscape which must
have been charming when the sun was shining. As it was,
blurred by fog and with droplets of moisture clinging to every
leaf and twig, it had an enchantment of its own. November
fog and an autumn garden, grey-green and brown, softly
evocative of loss, mystery, adventure—perhaps danger.
What a waste to have a setting like that and no camera to
capture it, no actors to begin the promised drama.

Abruptly, I remembered just what it was like to be acting
out-of-doors on location in a setting like that: the damp chill
creeping into your bones while you waited for the dozens of
technicians to arrange and rearrange their bits; the endless
retakes while you grew colder and wetter, until your fingers
were too numb to hold the props and your brain too numb to
remember the dialogue. No, the garden could remain an
empty setting, a lost location, for all I cared now. Those days
were long behind me. I hadn't thought of them in years.

The kettle began whistling shrilly and I rushed to turn it
off before it woke Evangeline.

'Hmmph!' Too late. She made one of her Entrances—so
she was in that mood today—drawing her heavy black velvet
robe closer around her and doing up the gold braid frogs and
clinching her waist (still a trim one) with the heavy gold
cord.

'Good morning, Evangeline.' She made me feel like a
frump in my quilted glazed cotton housecoat—so carefully
chosen for me by Martha last Mother's Day. It had been
easier to pack it, bulky though it was, than try to explain to
Martha just why I didn't want to bring it along. I resolved to

get to Harrod's at the first opportunity (preferably without Evangeline) and buy myself something decent.

Evangeline seated herself at the tiny table and looked around fretfully. When I didn't move, she got up again, found herself a cup and saucer, the jar of instant coffee and made her own coffee.

'Toast?' I asked as the toaster popped; there were two slices in there anyway.

'Oh, all right,' she said, doing me a favour.

I put two more slices of bread into the toaster. They were the thinnest slices I had ever seen, so thin that the two that had just popped up were crisped all the way through.

Evangeline munched absently, looking out at the fog-shrouded garden, thinking her own thoughts.

'The garden must have been lovely in the summer,' I said. 'It's sort of pretty and atmospheric now—in a spooky kind of way.'

'Spooky is right.' Evangeline frowned out at the fog. 'It looks like a good place to bury a body.'

'Trust you to think of that!' Evangeline's long and chequered career had starred or featured her in every possible kind of film—some of which she hoped everyone had forgotten. These days she had cornered the market in Ethel Barrymore-type roles. There wasn't a regal dowager fighting for what she believed to be right, a proud matriarch struggling to hold her family together against the odds, a society doyenne adrift in a new social order, an unforgiving dying millionairess surrounded by her unloving relatives, that Evangeline hadn't played in the past couple of decades. (We will draw a merciful veil over that 'sixties horror film where she prowled the dark old mansion as the psychotic aunt, despatching family and servants with an electric carving knife, and hurtled down the staircase to her well-deserved sticky end after tripping over the extension cord.)

'What's that?' There had been a sharp metallic click from somewhere at the front of the flat. My nerves weren't as on edge as Evangeline's appeared to be, but we both went to investigate.

At the end of the tiny vestibule, two square white envelopes lay just inside the door beneath an oblong slot in the door that I had not noticed last night.

'It's just the mail,' I said thankfully. I didn't feel strong enough to cope with anything more vital. From the hallway outside, we heard the front door close firmly.

I stooped and gathered up the envelopes while Evangeline went on into the drawing-room. There was one for each of us, but I noticed there was no stamp or franking on the envelopes. They had been delivered by hand, then; presumably by the person who had just left.

Evangeline was standing at one of the drawing-room windows, looking out at the circular carriageway. I joined her just in time to see a tall dark shape walk into the mist at the end of the carriageway and disappear on the other side of the wall that bordered the property.

'The one called Jasper, I believe,' Evangeline said. 'He looks different in the daylight.'

'If you can call this daylight.' The fog seemed even thicker at the front of the house. Disconcertingly, it seemed to be alive. It thickened and thinned capriciously, one moment giving us a clear view of the cluster of rose-bushes in the centre of the drive, the next moment obscuring the entire world. I began to appreciate the fine discipline of dry ice clouds wafting across a sound stage.

Heavy footsteps thundered down the hall stairs from the top floor, paused at the landing above, then descended more slowly and quietly. Someone had obviously taken sudden thought of the two elderly ladies in the ground-floor flat.

Again the front door closed quietly and a figure stood on the top step squinting into the fog.

'Who's that?' Evangeline frowned. 'How many people do they have living in that top flat, anyway? It must be crowded.'

'I think . . . Yes, it is. It's Des, but he's done something to his hair.'

'He must have. He looks quite normal.'

'Crestfallen, in fact.' He had washed the multicolours out of his hair and his spikes had been flattened down to a rather uneven, but unremarkable, style. 'So that's what they do with it when they want to go out to work.' He was carrying a clarinet case and would not now look out of place in an orchestra.

'He's the sensible one. There's not much that other boy can do about his Mohican cut—except wait for all the shaved parts to grow back.'

'Ah, the Indian scalplock!' Evangeline sighed reminiscently. 'I haven't seen a style like that since *The Revenge of the White Squaw*. How it takes me back. Now, *that* was a picture!'

'They don't make them like that any more,' I agreed. They wouldn't dare. The title alone would make it impossibly racist and sexist today. I wondered whether they would be showing it in the Retrospective or whether all that violence would rule it out. I'd heard the English were more sensitive than we were to things like that.

'It was a classic,' Evangeline said complacently. 'Do you know, even today I have people coming up to me and telling me that they can still hear the scream I gave when the Indian squaws threw the broken body of my little son at my feet. They don't realize that it was a silent film. They *heard* my emotion. *That* was acting!'

'You had faces then,' I said, but it went straight over her head.

'*And* we knew how to use them. We didn't rely on outrageous costumes and silly hairstyles. *Look* at him. You could pass him in the street and never notice him without his—his plumage.'

'Perhaps that's why he does it. This generation knows how to use its plumage.'

Walking down the carriageway, Des twitched uneasily

and looked back over his shoulder, as though subliminally
aware that he was being watched and discussed.

On impulse, I pulled back the curtain and gave him a
smile and a cheery wave. His face brightened instantly, he
returned the smile and wave and disappeared into the fog, a
jaunty spring now in his step.

'Well,' Evangeline said drily, 'that's your good deed for
the day.'

I got that impression myself. I was further bemused by the
discovery that Des had a lovely smile—and that this was
the first time we had seen it. Come to think of it, none of the
youngsters—for all their high spirits and eagerness to meet
us—had seemed especially happy yesterday.

'Well,' Evangeline said brusquely. 'Are you going to stand
around mooning all day, or are you going to give me my
letter? Our marching orders, I'll be bound. We might as well
know the worst.'

'Oh, it's not so bad—' I tore open the envelope and
scanned the brief lines. 'Lunch with Beauregard Sylvester at
the Ivy at one. I presume yours is the same. A car will call to
collect us.'

'Lunch . . . with Beauregard Sylvester . . .' Evangeline
made it sound like a date with the tumbrils. 'I do believe I'm
getting one of my splitting headaches. You'll have go go
without me.'

'Oh no you don't! She wasn't going to start getting away
with that again. 'He was *your* co-star in all those pictures.
You're going to have to meet him sometime. You can have a
couple of aspirins and lie down for a while—but we're both
going to that lunch!'

CHAPTER 5

There were palm trees growing in the forecourt of St John's Wood underground station. Even Evangeline took that as a good omen as we drove past, although she had to be snippy about it.

'A bit stunted, aren't they?'

'We used to have much bigger ones,' Hugh said, 'but we had an exceptionally severe winter a few years ago and they died. These are the replacements. They'll grow.'

'I think it's marvellous that you have any at all,' I said. 'I never thought the climate was tropical enough for palms.'

'It's not tropical, but it seldom gets so Arctic that they can't survive. The Gulf Stream, you know. It flows offshore and protects us from the worst of the cold and storms. Usually.'

'Good heavens.' Evangeline gasped. 'What's that?'

A gleaming gold dome was drifting in the fog, a tall stone minaret beside it. For a moment, it seemed that we might have taken the wrong turning and were approaching Baghdad.

'That's the Regent's Park Mosque.' Hugh identified it calmly. 'We have a large Islamic community now, you know.'

'London has certainly changed since the days when I knew it.' Evangeline was pensive. 'Perhaps I shouldn't have stayed away for so long. Everything seems so strange now.'

'Wait until we drive through the City,' Hugh said. 'Then you'll really see some changes.'

'At least,' Evangeline said with satisfaction, 'some things don't change.'

The Ivy was an opulent rendezvous in a side street off

Cambridge Circus. Across the street from it, a theatre proudly proclaimed that *The Mousetrap* had been running for four decades.

Inside, there were shaded lamps, oil paintings on the walls, small bronze sculptures in every niche and in front of the dark mullioned windows. It was quiet and luxurious, the food was delicious. You could look around and imagine that Binkie and Gertie and Noel were about to make an entrance at any moment.

Beauregard Sylvester was a poor substitute. I was beginning to feel a headache of my own coming on. I sat there wondering why I had misspent any of my early teenage years being madly in love with his inflated image on the screen at Saturday matinees.

His profile was just as devastating as it had been, despite the fine network of wrinkles. The shock of thick wavy hair had turned an impressive solid silver. The dark penetrating eyes still seemed to suggest that, if only he weren't an honest man and totally devoted to his wife, you might be the lucky lady he swept across his saddle horn and rode off into the sunset with. The deep haunting power of his voice had not waned with the years; you could listen to it for ever—if only you didn't have to pay any attention to what it was saying.

That was the trouble. I stiffened my jaw against another yawn. Beauregard Sylvester might have been a star, but he only twinkled when someone else had written the script. There were a lot of them about.

'Juanita's certainly going to be sorry she missed this lunch, but she's in the country, you know.'

We did know. At a conservative estimate, it was the fifth time he'd told us. If Juanita were going to be all that upset, it would have seemed that she might have made an effort to come up to town and join us.

'She doesn't get up to town much,' he said again. 'She's become a real little country mouse.'

If that were true, she had sure changed her spots since the

old days. On the other hand, it occurred to me that, if I had been married to Beauregard Sylvester for fifty years (which heaven forbid!) I might want to put some country miles between us, too.

'Dear Juanita,' Evangeline said absently. 'It will be so nice to see her again—after all these years.'

'She hasn't changed a bit,' he testified promptly. 'Of course,' he added belatedly, 'neither have you.'

'Dear Beauregard, always the Southern gentleman.'

'It's true, my little *Flower of the North*.' He gave her the same look he had given her in the film of that name when, as a nurse with the Yankee army, she had steadfastly tended his wounds, hiding the fact that he was a Confederate officer to save him from being shot as a spy, and they had fallen in love, defying the prejudices of both sides and, as the cruel Civil War ended, they married and joined a wagon train to start life afresh in the newly opened Western Territories.

'Mmmm.' The look left her considerably less moved in real life than it had on celluloid. I now suspected that had always been the case.

Even Hugh Carpenter seemed depressed. I caught him sneaking a look at his watch. It was probably a dirty trick, but I made a point of catching him. Anything to get us out faster.

'Are we keeping you from something, Hugh?' Beauregard Sylvester followed my gaze and noticed that part of his audience was restless.

'Oh, er, no—' Hugh jumped. 'No, er, that is, I was just wondering if the programme had started yet. I'm sure the ladies are anxious to see The Silver Screen in the Sky at Cinema City. It's quite impressive, you know.' He turned to us. 'And the afternoon programme starts in half an hour. We'd just have time to make it comfortably if we were to leave now.'

'But we haven't had our dessert yet.' Beauregard was close to outrage. 'It's part of the set lunch. We're paying for it.'

Evangeline closed her eyes briefly and I remembered that rumour had always had it that Beauregard Sylvester was the slowest draw in the West when it came to drawing a billfold instead of a gun.

'Oh, sorry. Yes, of course.' A waiter materialized beside the table and Hugh turned on him as though it was all his fault. 'May we have the sweet trolley?' he asked brusquely.

The waiter moved off and returned pushing a hostess cart loaded with luscious desserts. There was no question here of picking something at random from a printed menu, it was spread out temptingly before you.

There were profiteroles heaped beside a bowl of dark rich chocolate sauce, cakes crowned with towering peaks of whipped cream, and the golden mounds topped by glittering caramelized sugar of *crème brulée*. The most innocent item was a bowl of fresh fruit salad, but it was dredged deep in Kirsch and a pitcher of heavy cream lurked beside it. I could feel my waistline expanding even as I looked at it all.

'Beau, darling—fancy meeting *you* here!' Cecile Savoy —Dame Cecile of recent years—*grande dame* of the British stage, caught our host's neck from behind in a sort of modified half-Nelson and bussed him on the cheek.

'Hello, Cec,' he said without any great enthusiasm. 'You remember Eve Sinclair, don't you?'

'How could I forget her and that wonderful season when we lit up the West End in *Three On A Match*? How are you, Evangeline?'

'Very well, Cecile, and you?'

Their implied rebukes to Beauregard Sylvester at the way he had shortened their names went right over his head. He was frowning at the sweet trolley as though the decision he had to make was of vital importance to the world.

'And *how* is darling Juanita?' Dame Cecile asked, a wealth of private meaning quivering beneath her dulcet tones. 'Still cloistered away in the country?'

'You know she hates to come up to town these days.' Beau

was obviously having a struggle to answer politely. 'What are you doing here, anyway? I thought you were working.'

'Still in rehearsal, we don't open for another week. I *do* hope you'll all come to opening night?'

'We're already booked,' Hugh assured her. 'All of us.' He glanced at us. 'I haven't had time to mention it.'

'Why aren't you rehearsing now?' Beau wanted to know.

'Aah!' Dame Cecile trilled, waving a hand. 'Fortunately —for us, if not for him—the Director was struck down by a toothache. He's rushed off to the dentist, so the rest of us have a free afternoon. Isn't that lucky? Otherwise, we wouldn't have run into each other here.'

'Very lucky indeed,' Evangeline said, 'although I *was* planning to telephone you as soon as we got settled. We only arrived yesterday.'

'*And* we'll get together—soon. Well—' Dame Cecile paused and caught Evangeline's eye in what was obviously an old signal. 'Well, I must just go and fix my hair before I meet my nephew.'

'That's not a bad idea.' Evangeline rose to her feet swiftly. 'I'd like to freshen up myself. You can show me where it is.'

I struggled to get up, but Evangeline's hand was on my shoulder, firmly pushing me back into my chair. I got the message. I was supposed to stay here while they went and had themselves a grand old gossip in the powder room.

'But,' Beau protested, 'what about your dessert?'

'I don't want any,' Evangeline said carelessly. 'I'll just have a coffee when I get back.'

'Coffee is extra,' Dame Cecile murmured under her breath. They swept across the room and up the staircase in gales of laughter.

'Those two always were as thick as thieves.' Beauregard Sylvester stared after them broodingly. 'Aren't you going with them?'

'I'm fresh enough,' I said. It was a line from *Gold Diggers Strike It Rich*. I had brought the house down with it then, now only Hugh raised a wintry smile of recognition.

'She's a Dame now, you know.' Beau was still brooding. 'The Queen gave her that award.'

'She's English.' Hugh spoke with the patient weariness of one who had explained it many times. 'Those awards are given to British subjects.'

'Douglas Fairbanks, Jr got a knighthood—and he wasn't a British subject. He wasn't living in this country as long as I've been, either. How do you explain that?'

'I don't know how to explain it.' Hugh's spine abruptly stiffened. 'I don't *have* to explain it. It's nothing to do with me. Honours are bestowed at the discretion of the Government—'

I let my spoon do a little tap dance over the hard shiny shell of my *crème brulée*—it was probably the least caloric item on the trolley, especially if I cracked the shell and picked it off.

Complaint and counter-complaint droned on over my head; it was very boring. I would much rather be upstairs in the powder room listening to all the lovely gossip and intrigue. Anyway, I'd learned one thing from Dame Cecile's parting sally: Beauregard Sylvester had carried his West Coast reputation over here with him. He was obviously as slow with a pound as he had been with a dollar.

And Evangeline would never tell me all the juiciest bits of gossip, she never did. She'd only tell me the unimportant bits. Anything really interesting I'd have to find out for myself.

I was still in a modified sulk when Evangeline came back to the table looking as though she had eaten several canaries. If she'd hiccoughed, feathers would have floated from her mouth.

'Dear Beauregard,' she trilled. 'Are we ready to go now? I'm simply dying to see your dear little cinema. I've been hearing such fascinating things about it.'

Beau shot her a suspicious look. 'Like what?'

'Oh . . . things . . .' Evangeline had slipped into one of her most maddening moods.

'Like what?' Beau's nostrils flared dangerously and his eyes narrowed in the look that had struck terror to the hearts of evil-doers in every film he had ever made.

'*Interesting* things.' Evangeline was not an easy woman to terrorize, perhaps because she had done her own share of it in her time.

'Right.' Hugh lurched to his feet, nerves cracking under the strain. He showered cash upon the table while Beau was still trying to extract a credit card from his wallet. 'Let's be on our way.'

Naturally, this restored Beau's good humour. He replaced his wallet far more quickly than he had drawn it out and even held the door for us as we went out. If he had a momentary impulse to let it slam in Evangeline's face, he restrained himself. But the day was young yet.

Unwittingly, he got his revenge when we reached the cinema. I thought Evangeline was going to have a seizure on the spot. Obviously, this was one item of news Dame Cecile hadn't imparted to her.

We had pulled up at the entrance to Cinema City, an impressive skyscraper on the border of the City of London and Evangeline had stood on the pavement for a moment looking up at the building with a smirk of private knowledge. Then Beau had rushed us through the lobby, into one of the elevators and whisked us directly to the penthouse cinema on the roof.

The elevator decanted us into a large padded cell. On closer inspection, it turned into a lush foyer with thick carpeting—on both floor and walls. A ticket booth faced the elevator and—I blinked—several Mack Sennett Bathing Beauties in full costume lounged beside the refreshment concession.

It had stopped Evangeline dead in her tracks, too. While we absorbed this phenomenon, something suddenly struck me as very familiar about the straw-coloured locks escaping from the mob-cap style bathing hat of one of the Bathing Beauties.

'Oh, Miss Sinclair, Miss Dolan—' She rushed forward to greet us. 'Welcome! Welcome to the Silver Scween. We're so thwilled—so honoured! Come and see the stills—' She took Evangeline's hand and tugged her over to a display. 'See —you're the next attwaction.'

That was when I thought Evangeline was going to have a seizure. There it was, staring out at her from behind the glass:

> She put the SIN in Cinema! Eve Sinclair—as
> you've never seen her before . . . sins across the
> sky in . . . WHEN ANGELS FALL

Beneath the legend, in full blazing colour, sprawled Eve Sinclair (in the days before she had gone formal both as to name and as to decorum) in ripped bodice, displaying heaving bosom, cringing in wild-eyed terror with a flaring-nostrilled male (not, in this case, Beauregard Sylvester) looming over her.

Yep, there it was: the poster for the film her fourth husband had spent a large chunk of his fortune trying to suppress.

'You—' Evangeline gasped, her hand fluttering to her throat. 'You actually have a *print* of that? A *complete* print?'

'Almost complete—and restored in our own laboratory,' Beau affirmed proudly. 'We caught it just in time. All those early films on nitrate stock are disintegrating, you know.'

'So I'd heard,' she said faintly. She had hoped for nothing more. 'But *wherever* did you find it?' (She had thought that every available copy had been bought up by that fourth husband and burned or buried in the depths of an abandoned mine somewhere in Nevada.)

'It was sheer luck. Hugh discovered it on a trip to Hong

Kong. There were rumours that it had come from Mainland China. He bought it from the guy who had it and brought it back here where we started on the restoration work right away. Good Old Hugh.'

'Anyone would have done the same,' Hugh said modestly, blissfully unaware that he had nothing to be modest about.

'Isn't that a fantastic rescue story?' Beau, too, was inordinately pleased with himself. 'You'd hardly believe it—except that the print still has Chinese subtitles running down the side. Ursula—she's our archivist—did her best, but we couldn't get rid of them without ruining the print.'

'That's right,' Hugh chimed in eagerly. 'Ursula's the best we have at restoration work but even she couldn't do it. The only way would have been to black them out and then we'd have lost the action running underneath.'

'What a pity,' Evangeline said. Nothing would have suited her better than to have the entire film blacked out. She wanted everyone to forget the days when she had been billed as the sexpot who 'put the Sin in cinema'. (Not a few people opined that she had also done a lot towards putting Hays in the Hays Office.)

Still, I had some sympathy for Evangeline in this situation. There were certain of my own films I'd be happy to think had self-destructed, particularly a top contender for the Golden Turkey Award called *No More Sugar For Daddy*, complete with title song. I must admit that when I occasionally fell over the old 78 disc at a bazaar or flea market, I bought it up, took it home and had a smashing good time with my little hammer.

'Come and see the view from the roof garden.' Beau led the way to a door on the far side of the lobby. We stepped through it into an English garden—twenty-five storeys above the ground. The tables and chairs, when looked at closely, turned out to be heavy white plastic replicas of the usual wrought-iron garden furniture. At the moment, they were heavily beaded with damp and there were no customers for the small bar built out from the side of the cinema.

'We're getting one of those retractable plastic roofs, like they have on the QE2, to roll out when it rains, so that we can enjoy the garden in all weather.'

'What a good idea,' I murmured as Evangeline continued to brood over what she undoubtedly saw as a betrayal.

'Look over here.' Beau led us down a squidgy gravelled path between dispirited brown stalks with shrivelled leaves hanging here and there, to a rustic bower at one corner of the roof. 'Isn't that a view to end all views?'

We looked down on a bank of fog that seemed solid enough to step out on.

'It certainly is,' Evangeline said tartly. 'I haven't seen anything like it since the fog-making machine went out of control when we were shooting *Beast of the Barbary Coast*.'

'Oh well,' Beau said, 'I'm afraid it's not a very good day today. But when it's clear, you can see the Thames, the Tower of London, Tower Bridge . . .' He went on pointing out invisible sights while we shivered in the dank chill.

'Perhaps—' Hugh finally noticed a particularly convulsive shudder of Evangeline's—'perhaps we ought to go in now. It's cold up here.'

'And getting windy,' I said. The sooner they got that plastic roof, the better, although I wouldn't like to take any bets on how long it would last if the wind was often this strong. It wasn't going to do the flowers any good, either.

'I think the wind's blowing the fog away a bit.' Beau held his ground stubbornly. 'If you lean over the parapet just a little—' he illustrated; none of us rushed to join him—'and look over that way, you ought to be able to see the top of Tower Bridge.'

Evangeline looked wistfully at Beauregard Sylvester's broad back as he leaned out. Her hands twitched briefly and I saw the struggle as she got her impulses under control. Besides, there were too many witnesses.

'No, I'm afraid the fog isn't really clearing all that much.'

Unaware of his narrow escape, Beau straightened up and stepped back from the parapet into the precarious shelter of the rustic bower. 'Next time you come, the weather ought to be better.'

Neither of us answered. We were too busy racing each other across the roof, back to the warmth of the cinema lobby. I was through the door ahead of Evangeline, which was just as well because I'd never have had the nerve to let the door slam in Beau's face the way she did.

'You poor angels, you must be fwozen! Come and have some coffee. Would you like a little bwandy in it?'

I had liked that girl from the moment I saw her. Her hair might resemble an abandoned bird's-nest, but her heart was in the right place—and there was nothing wrong with her brain, either.

'We'd love some,' I gasped, checking to see whether my fingers had actually turned blue or just felt as though they had.

'With a *lot* of brandy in it,' Evangeline amended, flexing her own fingers. 'On second thought, you can forget the coffee.'

'Sorry—' Hugh grimaced apologetically—'but we're ruled by licensing hours. Not only that, but the matinee is about to let out. If people think the bar is open—' He grimaced again.

'I see.' Evangeline plainly saw that the world was aligned against her. Her martyred heroine expression returned.

'There isn't *much* coffee.' Gwenda was back with a tray of coffee cups and saucers. She spoke the literal truth. There was only enough coffee to colour the brandy.

'Thank you, dear.' Evangeline sipped appreciatively. 'How this takes me back—' She looked into her cup reflectively. 'Just like a Speakeasy during Prohibition days.'

Two usherettes secured the doors back and the first stream of departing cinema-goers poured across the lobby towards the lifts, chattering, struggling into their coats and blinking

in the light. Several of them glanced at our little group and
nudged each other. I wondered if it were entirely fortuitous
that we were there at that time. Had Beau deliberately
lingered over dessert so that we could become an added
attraction for the matinee audience?'

'Drink up,' Beau said heartily. 'The next show starts in
fifteen minutes.'

I noticed now that the lifts were disgorging as many as
they had engorged. A queue was forming at the ticket office.
Gwenda had hurried away to help behind the candy counter,
where they were also selling hot coffee and some amorphous
lumps of healthfood cake.

'Dear Beau,' Evangeline said coldly. 'I'm afraid I can't
stay. I have the most frightful headache—'

'But it's *Sunset on the Rio Grande*—the first film Juanita and
I made together. That was when we met.'

'*Dear* Beau, much as I would love to see you again in the
full flush of youth and virility, I simply cannot. My headache
is worsening by the moment. I must get back to the flat and
lie down.'

'Well, then—' Beau turned to me—'*you'll* stay—?'

'Oh no,' I babbled. 'I feel terrible, too. That wind has
brought on my neuralgia. I'm in agony—'

We were both edging towards the lift. Hugh, recognizing
the inevitable, was right behind us, reaching for his car
keys. 'I'll tell you what—' Beau did not give up easily. 'I'll set
up a special screening for you in the morning. You can get a
good night's sleep and see it then.'

'I think not,' Evangeline said firmly. 'Tomorrow, I'm
planning to have laryngitis.'

CHAPTER 6

'Mortgaged to the hilt!' Evangeline announced with relish.

'What—everything?' I splashed more brandy into our glasses. In the background, the characters in a television serial mouthed at us; we had turned the sound off as soon as Hugh had left. 'You don't mean it!'

'Cecile told me all about it. Apparently, it's been the talk of the town. There were problems with the construction workers and the building wasn't finished anywhere near on schedule. Costs ran way over budget, they had a couple of strikes, then one of the worst winters in years delayed progress still more. It seems that everything that could possibly go wrong went wrong.

'Poor Beau—but the cinema seems to be doing well.'

'That won't go very far with his debts—and the running costs alone have doubled since the building opened a year ago. He'd hoped to empty half of Wardour Street into it, that's why he called it Cinema City. Along with all the office space, there are six private screening rooms and two film processing labs. He kept the Silver Screen in the Sky to run himself, thinking that the rents from the rest of the building would finance it, but the building is only half rented and he's losing money hand over fist.'

'Poor Beau—that must be killing him. You two didn't waste any time in the powder room, did you?' They must have made fascinating eavesdropping if anyone else were around.

'We've barely scratched the surface.' Evangeline was complacent. 'I'm lunching with Cecile tomorrow—she has a late rehearsal call—and she's going to fill me in on the *real* dirt.'

'How nice. You really *will* have laryngitis by the time you're through.'

'You don't mind, do you? We're such old friends and we have a lot of catching up to do. You wouldn't know most of the people, anyway.'

'I don't mind,' I lied calmly. 'I have plans of my own for tomorrow, you needn't worry about me.'

There was a sudden crash over our heads, followed by a series of heavy thumps. The ceiling shook. Jasper was either practising a dance routine or he had started throwing the furniture around.

'And we thought *he* was the quiet one,' Evangeline said bitterly.

'Oh, Tewwific! You weally mean it? You're not just being kind?'

'It's you who has been so kind,' I assured her. 'I really feel I'm imposing on you—'

'Oh no! No! I'd love to! Honestly!'

'Good. Get dressed then—' She was still in surprisingly practical woollen dressing-gown, neat and serviceable but not gaudy. Presumably she only wore her bizarre costumes for public display. I tried not to think what she might consider suitable to conduct a guided tour of the High Street and surrounding district followed by lunch in one of its best restaurants. I would almost have preferred the dressing-gown.

'Ten minutes!' she promised. I didn't believe her an instant; her hair was looking almost neat, it would take at least half an hour to transform it into its usual mess.

'That's fine. I'll wait downstairs.' I stepped over a cluster of dreg-stained coffee cups in the middle of the floor. 'Just come down when you're ready . . .'

However, I had wronged her. It was only slightly over ten minutes later when she tapped on the door. 'Good heavens, that was quick,' I said.

'I did two years in Pwovincial Wep—we had to make some weally fast changes in that.' She came through into the drawing-room, her clothes fluttering about her. She couldn't really have fallen into the ragbag and not quite managed to shake all the remnants off, but it certainly looked like it from where I stood. She was multi-layered with varying lengths and clashing colours. In contrast, her hair was a rigid beehive surmounted by rigid multi-coloured bees which, on closer inspection, turned out to be plastic Bulldog clips.

'I thought—' she was blissfully regardless of my reaction —'I'd show you awound Swiss Cottage, then come down to St John's Wood High Stweet and have lunch. It has some westauwants I've always longed to twy—but they're so expensive—'

'Don't worry about that,' I said briskly. 'You're my guest and I'm very grateful to you for giving up your morning to show me around. After lunch, I thought I might go to Harrod's and look for a dressing-gown.'

'Hawwod's . . .' she almost-echoed wistfully. 'But—' she relinquished the temptation with a sigh—'I have to be at the Silver Scween at thwee . . .' She sighed again.

'Another time, perhaps.' I forbore to mention that she had not been invited this time. 'We could have tea there some afternoon when you don't have to work.'

'Oh, Miss Dolan,' she squealed. 'That would be wonderful!'

'Please—' I felt guilty, seeing that I was about to start pumping the poor little wretch for all I was worth. But Evangeline had her sources of information, it was time I developed a source or two of my own. 'Please, call me Trixie.' Too late, I saw what I had let myself in for.

'Oh, Twixie—I'd love to!'

It's bad enough to be stuck with a name like Trixie, to begin with. Over the years, I have cheered myself with the thought that it could have been a lot worse. Hollywood never left a good plain name alone and everyone concerned got a bad attack of Terminal Twee when it came to naming new stars. The cutesy-poo awfulness of male names was bad enough, but they never rested from their excesses where the females were concerned. From Pola to Theda, through Bebe, Ginger, Osa, Lupe, Benay, Jinx, Piper and even Honey-Chile, the Hollywood Star-Making Machine did its worst, never considering what it would be like to be stuck with that name four or five decades on. Only Evangeline had beaten that rap, moving from Baby Evvie, to Eve, to Evangeline as advancing age and circumstances warranted.

'Let's get going, then,' I said quickly. 'I'm dying to explore the neighbourhood and get myself orientated. Don't—' I stifled a yawn nearly as ostentatiously as Evangeline—'don't mind if I yawn a bit. My sleep was a bit disturbed last night. Tell me, is Jasper a dancer or a choreographer?'

'Gwacious no!' Gwenda laughed merrily. 'Nothing so pwecawious as show business for our Jasper. He's a stock-bwoker!'

Well, talk about taking candy from a baby. I ought to have been ashamed of myself, except that I learned so much. As a prime source of information, scandal and general gossip, I'd back Gwenda against Dame Cecile any day of the week.

As the characters in *Scars On Her Soul*, the gangster quickie Evangeline and I made so that the studio could cash in on the success of *Scarface*, kept saying to each other, 'She sang like a canary.'

'Oh, go on, Twixie—' Right now, she was egging me on. 'Evewybody does it. I'll never tell. You'll never find another one like it, you know you won't.'

'Well . . .' I pirouetted before the looking-glass and let myself be tempted—especially if she wouldn't tell. Tell Evangeline, that is. I wasn't worried about anyone else. I didn't know anyone else here.

We were in the Oxfam Shop in St John's Wood High Street—a far cry from Harrod's, where I had intended to buy

a new dressing-gown. The irony was that I had found the
perfect one in here. I pirouetted again, the shimmering
kingfisher blue brocade flowed with my every movement. It
was a luxurious material and the colour was strong enough to
let me stand out on my own in that red velvet drawing-
room—and against Evangeline's black velvet gown. Should
I be such a snob as to let it matter that it was second-
hand?

'Oh, Twixie—it's *you*! You can't not buy it. You'd never
forgive yourself later.'

Damn it! She was right. And heaven knew, it was cheap
enough. Also, it looked as though it had never been worn
—or not very often. Bought and kept for best, or perhaps put
away in a closet and forgotten . . .

'It isn't faded at all—' Gwenda was scrutinizing the seams
with an eagle eye. 'And no fwaying. It's as good as new. I
weally think it *is* new. People just thwow things away
sometimes because they change their minds about liking
them, you know.'

'Oh, all right.' I gave in. 'I'll take it.' And may Martha
never find out where I got it. If she asked, I would tell
her—with perfect truth—that I had found it in a delightful
little shop in St John's Wood High Street.

However, my plans for the afternoon had to change. I
couldn't go to Harrod's carrying an Oxfam bag. I would
have to go back to the flat and leave my purchase there—and
also dispose of the Oxfam bag before Evangeline saw it. But
first . . .

'What time are you supposed to be at the cinema?'

'Cwumbs!' Gwenda looked at her watch and gasped. 'I
didn't wealize it was so late. I must fly!'

'You must take a taxi,' I corrected. 'No—no arguing.' I
opened my purse. 'I insist. You've given up so much of your
time and I've enjoyed every minute. I made you late—and
this is the least I can do.' I pressed a ten-pound note into her
unresisting hands. 'I shall want to call on your good services

again—and if you don't allow me to do this, I won't feel able to.'

'Oh, but I enjoyed it all, too—it was such fun. And it was such a delicious lunch—and so expensive—and the taxi won't cost nearly this much—'

'You just take it and shut up!' I folded her fingers over the banknote. 'When you're starring in your first West End hit, *you* can take *me* out to an expensive lunch.'

'Oh, I will, Twixie!' Her eyes shone at the thought. 'I pwomise you I will.'

Just as I turned the corner, a taxi drew up in front of the house. Just my luck—Evangeline was back early. I hid the Oxfam bag behind my back and approached in a sideways crablike scuttle.

Evangeline was too busy paying off the taxi to notice my approach. She was also juggling several small bags and I relaxed as I saw the name on them. I let her get inside the carriageway before I caught up with her and said, 'Hello, Evangeline.'

She jumped and tried to hide her own purchases behind her back, but there were too many of them and one of the bags slipped and fell at her feet.'

'Let me—' I rubbed salt in the wound by stooping quickly to retrieve the bag and handed it to her.

'Thank you.' She took a deep breath and said quickly, 'Cecile took me to the most amusing little shop in Kensington. I couldn't resist picking up a few things—and it's in such a good cause. It's a charity shop, you know.'

'I know.' I brought my own bag out from behind my back. 'Gwenda took me to the local one. She says *everyone* shops there and, if Dame Cecile took you, it seems to be true.'

'Snap!—as they say here.' Evangeline gurgled with amusement. 'I got some books—mint condition and about one-third of the original price—and a woollen scarf, a pair of gloves and a bit of old jewellery, just paste, but very sweet. What did you get?'

'Just what I wanted.' We were at the door and, unhampered by as many parcels as Evangeline, I inserted my key in the lock. We stepped inside.

'Just wait till you see—' I broke off. We both gaped at the scene before us.

We had caught Mick descending the stairs. Our entrance had been too sudden to allow him time to turn and flee—or even to think. He stood there, yellow cockscomb quivering, eyes wide with fear and despair, clutching the inert girl in his arms and staring back at us.

'Young man—' Evangeline spoke in a voice that would have brought Ethel Barrymore to her knees. 'Is that a *body*?'

CHAPTER 7

It was obvious that he would have given anything in the world to be able to say 'No'. With a little more nerve, he might have tried the Jimmy Durante ploy in *Jumbo* when, stopped by a policeman as he led away the stolen elephant and queried about it, he replied, 'What elephant?'

But we had him dead to rights and, unfortunately, it looked as though the operative word was 'dead'.

'Well, don't just stand there,' Evangeline said. 'Come down here.'

Numbly, he descended the remaining stairs. 'Look,' he said, his voice blank with shock, 'it's not the way you think.'

'Oh, isn't it?' Evangeline dropped her parcels on the hall table and moved closer to inspect the body. Unwillingly, I moved with her.

The dead girl was no one we had seen before, not that that meant much. I sometimes had the feeling that the house was full of people we had never seen. She was lying across his arms in the Scarlett O'Hara position for the staircase scene, but there were bruises on the bare dangling arms. There were more bruises on her forehead, one cheek and throat. A thin dark red thread of dried blood streaked from one corner of her mouth. She was very beautiful—and very dead.

Unnervingly, her streaked blonde hair seemed to have taken on a life of its own, it moved and quivered. Then I realized that the young man holding her was trembling violently.

'We can't stand here like this,' Evangeline said. 'You'd better come inside.'

'No!' I recoiled instinctively. I didn't want that . . . that *thing* in our lovely little flat.

'Oh, perhaps not.' Evangeline caught my thought. She looked at Mick sharply. 'Just what were you planning to do with her?'

'I thought . . . the back door . . . the garden. Leave her there. After midnight . . . when no one's around . . . move her somewhere else . . . where she could be found. Away from the house . . . away from us . . .'

'Yes,' Evangeline agreed, 'that might be best.'

'Evangeline!' Ever since she had appeared as the feather-brained young matron with an unexplainable body on her hands in *Disposing of Larry*, she had had an unfortunate insouciance towards dead bodies. It had been remarked on unfavourably at more than one Hollywood funeral. 'Why can't he just . . . just put her back where he found her?'

'No!' he choked. 'Please . . . I can't! You don't know what you're asking.'

It seemed reasonable enough to me, but Evangeline gave me an offended look.

'Of course you can't,' she soothed the agitated young man. 'Don't worry about *her*. Trixie always did see everything in black or white—and then she wonders where Martha gets it from.'

'I do not—and there's no need to drag my daughter into

this.' That was a low blow. 'And does he have to stand there holding her like that? He's giving me the creeps!'

'A good point. I suggest that you carry on with your original plan, dear boy. Go out and leave her in the garden, then come back and we'll give you a large brandy. You look as though you could use one.'

'Evangeline, you're crazy!'

She paid no attention to me. She calmly gathered up her parcels and went into the flat. 'I'm leaving the door open for him,' she told me. 'He'll be right back.'

'We'll get into the most awful trouble.' I followed her into the flat, still protesting. 'We're foreigners here. They—they could *deport* us!'

I could see it all: the grim-visaged official stamping my passport, then the long walk between lines of stern but sympathetic Marines as I was marched up the gangplank of the waiting ship. Just like in *Canal Zone Carrie*. Only then I unmasked the Axis Agent who had stolen the secret plans for the defence of the Canal Zone in the event of a sneak attack which was, even then, being planned somewhere out there in the middle of the Pacific . . .

'Don't be absurd.' Evangeline spoke as though she could read my thoughts. 'Once he gets rid of the body, no one will ever connect it with this house.' We stood by the kitchen window and watched our neighbour disappear into the fog, still carrying the girl's body.

'Take your coat off.' After a long moment, Evangeline turned away from the window. 'Let's go into the drawing-room. We'll give that young man a few stiff drinks and then we'll get to the bottom of this situation.'

'What makes you think he'll come back?'

'Where else is there for him to go?'

'That's right—he *has* to come back. We're the only witnesses. You know what happens to unwanted witnesses, don't you? And *you* left the door open for him.'

'Oh!' She glanced involuntarily over her shoulder. She

hadn't thought of that, although she'd been in enough of those movies herself. They were all the rage in the 'forties and had been having a vogue as *film noire* latterly. And now, here we were in the stock situation: all by ourselves in the big deserted house, thick fog outdoors and darkness falling. Outside was a strong ruthless teenager, possibly a psychotic, who had killed once and was disposing of the body before returning to kill again . . .

'You and your big mouth,' I said bitterly.

'Don't be silly.' She had recovered her nerve—of which, she had always had plenty. 'Anyone can see he's innocent. He'll be able to explain everything.' But I noticed that she picked up the brandy decanter and hefted it thoughtfully.

'Maybe . . .' I was more practical. I went over to the white marble fireplace, where the fire was laid ready to be lit, and helped myself to the brass-handled poker.

We met each other's eyes as we heared the slow footsteps returning along the hall, and prepared to sell our lives dearly.

We moved closer together, not quite standing back-to-back in the swordmen-at-bay stance. That would have been too pointed.

Unfortunately, we were pointed enough as we were.

'Oh no!' Mick halted in the doorway, staring at the poker, at the heavy decanter gripped ready for use as a weapon. 'Oh no! You don't think I— You're not afraid of me!'

To our horror, he stumbled forward, sank to his knees, buried his face in his hands and burst into tears.

It was amazing how guilty that immediately made me feel. I hadn't felt so guilty since—well, never mind. I looked at that bowed shaven head with its narrow improbable thatch and then at my poker. It would have been like bashing in an egg just as a little yellow chick was hatching out.

'It's all right, dear—' Hastily, I replaced the poker in the holder with the fire tongs and brush. 'Take it easy.'

'Of course we don't suspect you.' Evangeline unstoppered

the decanter and poured a generous measure. 'Would we have asked you to come back, if we did? Here, drink this.'

He groped for the glass blindly and she thrust it into his hand. He took a deep swallow and began choking.

'There—that's better.' I was patting his back as much as hitting it.

'Try again,' Evangeline urged. 'More slowly, this time.'

Between us, we got him to his feet and over to the Victorian sofa. We sat on either side of him and watched as he sniffled, took another sip of brandy and shuddered. He was so young.

'Don't you have a handkerchief?' Evangeline asked tartly.

'S-s-somewhere—' He began fumbling at the assortment of zippers decorating his outfit. There were three little zippers on each sleeve, several all over the body area and another collection up and down the legs. He explored them without success.

'Here—take this!' I thrust a slightly-used paper handkerchief at him quickly—before he unzipped the wrong compartment and embarrassed himself more than us.

'Thanks.' He grabbed it and blew his nose heartily, then dabbed at his eyes. 'Sorry,' he said. 'It—it's the shock.'

'You weren't the only one to be shocked.' Evangeline refilled his glass and, this time, added glasses for ourselves. 'Suppose you tell us all about it.'

This sent him back into a state of shock. His eyes glazed and he stared off into space.

'Come along,' Evangeline said sternly. 'Start at the beginning. Who is—was—this girl? Was she one of your flatmates?'

'No. Her name was Fiona—that's all I know. She was new. I—I don't even know what she was doing in our flat. I—I found her in Des's bed . . . like that. Dead. I couldn't leave her there.'

Evangeline nodded, but I disagreed. 'You should have called the police. Or, at least, a doctor.'

'Why? She was dead. A doctor couldn't do anything about that.'

'Then the police.'

'No! Never! Don't you see—?' He was coming to life, defending his position. 'A thing like that—it could ruin us at this stage of our careers. We'd never live it down. There'd be all the publicity— For the rest of our lives, we'd be known as those actors who were in that scandal about a dead girl. Whenever we achieved anything, it would all be dragged up again.'

'Yes, I do see how you might feel that way now,' Evangeline said, 'but I think you overestimate the interest of the public. Actually, they forget things pretty quickly.' She should know.

'Look—' I interrupted this little career advice session. 'You said that girl was in Des's bed. Where was Des?'

'He wasn't there. He went out before me this morning and hasn't come back yet. And *she* wasn't there this morning. I know because Des yelled to me to borrow some hair spray and I brought it in to him. That's why I found her. I went into his room to get it back—and there she was.'

'You say you hardly knew her—'

'She was practically a stranger. I don't know what she was even doing in our flat. I'm sure she didn't have a key.'

'You've been framed!' Evangeline delivered the line she had used to such effect in *Scars On Her Soul*.

'But why?' The idea seemed to bewilder him. 'Who would bother?'

'An enemy—?' Evangeline eyed him hopefully, but it was quite obvious that he was a bit too young to have made many enemies. He wasn't in her league. 'Well, perhaps an enemy of one of the others,' she conceded.

'I don't think any of us has any enemies. We've tried not to make any. We're just starting out.'

It was a cogent argument. The smart ones still went by the

old rule: Be nice to the people you meet on the way up; you'll meet them again on the way down.

'Are you sure about the others?' Evangeline was reluctant to give up her theory.

The front door slammed, making us all jump guiltily.

'Someone's home—' Mick tried to get to his feet, but didn't seem to be coordinating too well. 'I ought to go back upstairs and—'

'And what? You're in no condition to let anyone see you,' Evangeline pointed out. 'They'd start asking questions—and what would you tell them?'

'What have you had to eat today?' I had a sudden qualm of my own. 'Have you been drinking all that brandy on an empty stomach?'

'Er, yes,' he admitted. 'I'm afraid I have. That is, I had a piece of pizza about noon. It's all right,' he added, as I started towards the kitchen. 'I'm not hungry.'

'Perhaps not, but Trixie is right. You're going to have to eat something. You have a long night ahead of you.'

He finished his drink in one gulp, shuddered, and held out the glass for a refill.

'Have you . . .?' I hesitated, but there was no delicate way to phrase it. 'Have you decided what you're going to do with the body?'

Evangeline splashed more brandy into his glass.

'I've left it tied up in a plastic bin liner at the bottom of the garden. Later . . . when it's so late no one will be around . . . I'll get it and—' He paused to gulp at his drink again.

'I'll take it down and tip it into the Grand Union Canal,' he went on more firmly. 'The trickiest bit will be getting it across Prince Albert Road, but if I wait until two or three in the morning, it should be deserted. If there is any traffic, no one will be able to see much in this fog.'

'We'll help you,' Evangeline said promptly.

'We will not!' I was equally prompt. 'We're five decades too old for that sort of thing.' Not that we had ever indulged in running around before dawn hiding dead bodies—not unless we were following a script, that is.

'Please!' he said nervously. 'I can manage it by myself. I was going to, anyway, only you came home too early and—'

'And caught you.' Evangeline finished the sentence for him.

'The main thing is not to let anyone else catch you,' I said. 'Are you sure you'll be able to get to the canal unseen?'

'It isn't far and the fog is always worse near the water. It won't take a minute to slide her into the water. With any luck, she might float as far as Little Venice. Then no one would ever be able to trace her back here.'

'With real luck, she'll sink,' Evangeline said. 'I don't suppose you could put some rocks in the sack to make sure . . .?'

'Please!' He was shuddering again. 'I—I couldn't untie that sack and— It was hard enough putting her into it.' He was looking distinctly greenish.

'Perhaps the police won't connect her with this house.' I spoke quickly to distract him. 'But there may be other problems. What is Des going to say about his girlfriend disappearing?'

'Des?' Mick looked surprised. 'Oh, it's nothing to do with him. She wasn't *his* girlfriend—she was Jasper's.'

CHAPTER 8

'Jasper . . .' Evangeline said thoughtfully. 'That wouldn't surprise me. I haven't trusted a stockbroker since the Wall Street Crash.'

'All that thumping and banging around upstairs last night . . .' I was pretty thoughtful myself. 'And she was covered with bruises.'

'I suppose she was pregnant.' Evangeline got most of her

exercise these days by leaping to conclusions. 'It would have been deliberate, of course. She was trying to trap him into marriage.'

'I don't know. Mick said she hadn't been around very long. They hardly knew her.'

'Jasper could have known her a lot longer. In any case, time isn't relevant. All it takes is one—'

'Evangeline!'

'One *night*, I was going to say.' She looked at me coldly.

In the silence, the carriage clock on the mantel seemed to tick more loudly. In the distance, a church bell chimed three.

'This is ridiculous,' I said. 'Sitting up in the dark, waiting for Mick to come back. Why don't we put a lamp in the window? The scene lacks only that.'

'You can go to bed if you're tired.'

'I'm not. It's only early evening back home. My inner clock hasn't adjusted all that well yet.'

'Neither has mine.' She settled back in her chair. The glow from the dying fire was the only light in the room. I leaned forward and dropped a few more coals on the fire and then poked at it. I still felt a lot more comfortable with a poker in my hand.

'You don't really believe he's going to drop in and report to us on his way back?'

'It's quite possible. We're the only people he can confide in now. We're the only ones who know what's happened.' She glanced towards the ceiling. 'Except for the murderer, of course.'

'We don't know that it was murder—and we're not likely to know until the police find the body and conduct an autopsy.'

'She didn't get into Des's bed by herself.'

'You can't know that. Maybe she was friendlier with Des than anyone suspects. She might have got into his bed thinking she'd surprise him when he returned. Or maybe she

was just a congenital bed-hopper.' Heaven knew we'd seen
enough of those in our profession.

'Slipped into his bed—and bruised herself on the pillows?'

'Then who put her there?'

'Exactly! It was a dirty trick, planting the body on those
poor children. If they'd played it straight and called the
police, it could have ruined their lives.'

'It still could, if the police find out what Mick has done. It
wouldn't do our own reputations any good, either.'

'We had nothing to do with it.'

'I believe it's called being an accessory after the fact,' I
informed her. 'And the police take a dim view of it.'

'Nonsense!' The police view was a nothing compared to
Evangeline's. She rivalled Nelson at turning a blind eye to
any fact she didn't like.

'And I seem to remember something about compounding
a felony. And I'll bet they could cite half a dozen more
charges without pausing for breath. They'll throw the book
at us—and then they'll lock us up and throw away the key!'

'That boy has been gone too long—' Evangeline hadn't
been listening to me at all. 'He should have been back by
now. Something must have gone wrong. They've caught
him!'

'In that case,' I said, 'they've caught us all.'

The church bell had chimed four before we gave up our vigil
and went reluctantly to bed.

We slept late and awoke irritable and quarrelsome. Especially Evangeline. What else is new?'

First, the toast was too dark, then it was too light, then it
was charred. (Perhaps I shouldn't have re-inserted the too
light pieces and turned the control as high as it would go, but
she was getting on my nerves.)

Through it all, the radio burbled inanities. At half-hourly
intervals, the news was updated, with a fuller bulletin on the
hour. We called a truce to hostilities at these times in order to

listen avidly, but the news we were waiting to hear never materialized.

'No news is good news.' I tried to cheer us both after yet another recital of radioactive leaks at a nuclear power station, the progress of a domestic siege in the suburbs, the latest Common Market scandal and the assurance that frost and fog were to be our lot for the foreseeable future.

'That's just the sort of asinine remark I'd expect *you* to make!' She was so annoyed she bit into the charred toast and then had to pretend that she had intended to. 'I suppose he *did* come home safely after we'd gone to bed.'

'He might have been smarter and gone somewhere else. To someone who'd give him an alibi for the whole night, no matter what time he arrived.'

From overhead, there came a heavy thud.

'*He's* home, anyway,' Evangeline said bitterly. 'I wonder who he's murdering now.'

'I hope you're not going to go around making remarks like that. It's not only slander but, remember, we aren't supposed to know that the girl is dead.'

'I'm not a fool—' The telephone rang and we looked at each other hopefully.

'That may be him now.' Evangeline got there first and snatched up the receiver. 'Hello—?'

The line crackled briefly; she made a face at me. 'Oh, good morning, Beau.'

After that, the conversation got pretty one-sided. Evangeline spent most of it grimacing. Gradually, however, her expression changed and, when she replaced the receiver, she was almost in a good mood.

'That's more like it,' she said. 'Beau has arranged a Press Reception this afternoon. At the cinema, I'm afraid. He's out for all the publicity he can get. He'll parade us—and hope some of the glory rubs off on him.'

I looked at her suspiciously. It was most unlike her to use the word 'us' in connection with any publicity that might be going. And why should she? I was just along for the ride. It was her Retrospective.

'Hugh is going to collect us in an hour and a half . . .' Evangeline drifted back to her room. 'Shall I wear the pearl chiffon or . . .?' Her voice faded.

'You'd better wear something warm,' I called after her. 'He'll probably take us out on that damned roof again for the photographs.'

I began to enjoy the Press Conference when I caught on to the undercurrents. Evangeline and Beau were engaged in a silent head-on clash of wills.

Beau was determined to manœuvre Evangeline into juxtaposition with the *She put the Sin in Cinema* poster. Evangeline was doing some fancy footwork to keep away from it. All around the lobby, the photographers had their cameras poised.

'Come on, Beau—' I heard one of them cheer under his breath. 'Get her into frame.' They wanted the shot of the two Evangelines: the young gal she had been looming over the shoulder of the stately old galleon she had become. It would be sharp, poignant—and a potential award-winner. It would also be extremely cruel.

'Beau, darling—' Evangeline wasn't playing. She sidestepped him once again as he tried to box her in. 'I can't tell you how much it means to me to see your sweet face again—' Suiting action to words, she reached out to pat his face.

Several flashbulbs went off from various points around the room. It was better than nothing. The affectionate reunion of two old troupers.

'I'm only sorry dear Juanita can't be here,' Evangeline cooed. 'I've been so longing to see her again, face-to-face—'

Something peculiar was happening to Beau's face. It was slowly turning purple.

I caught a raised eyebrow from one cameraman and intercepted an exchange of knowing glances between two journalists. Something was happening here, but I did not possess enough information to decode the messages.

'Over here, 'Vangie—' Beau was reduced to grasping her elbow crudely and trying to drag her in front of the poster.

'Oh, Beau—' With a light laugh, Evangline whirled skittishly and drove her other elbow into his ribs.

Beau gave a muffled *'Whoomph!'* and lost his hold on her.

'Beau, dear, I know how sinfully proud you are of your glorious roof garden. We *must* have a few pictures out there —' She caught his hand and tugged him towards the terrace door.

It was all right for her, she had taken my advice and was wearing a lilac wool dress with several layers of thermal underwear beneath it and her blonde mink cape over it. Beau was dressed for his Something-in-the-City role in a dark blue pinstripe; his navy blue cashmere topcoat had been tossed carelessly across one of the chairs.

'Come, Beau—' Evangeline gave him no chance to reach for it; no time to think of it. 'Come, Beau—let's go out and *face* the music together.'

An icy gust of air swept through the lobby as they went out on the roof terrace. Most of the Press Corps dashed after them, jostling each other for the most advantageous positions. Hugh, tight-lipped, brought up the rear.

I stayed where I was. Somewhere along the line, the party had stopped being polite and was deteriorating rapidly. If one of them decided to push the other off the roof, I—unlike the Press Corps—did not wish to witness it.

'Oh, Twixie—'

I had been dimly aware of Gwenda circling in the background, awaiting her opportunity. I smiled, giving her the opportunity she craved.

'Twixie, may I intwoduce Waymond Wichards—he's a mad keen fan of yours.'

'How nice.' I shook the proffered paw. 'I didn't think anyone remembered me any more.'

'Oh, Twixie,' Gwenda said reproachfully, 'you should know better than that.'

'Yes, indeed, Miss Dolan,' her young man said eagerly. 'Why, *Kate of the Klondike* was screened at the NFT only a couple of seasons ago.'

'Please!' I winced. 'That was *not* one of my pleasantest memories.'

'It wasn't?' His face lit up. I was telling him something he hadn't known, confiding in him. 'Why not?'

'It was a lousy movie.'

'Oh, Twixie, how can you say that? It was wonderful. You were tewwific in it.' Gwenda sighed. 'I'd die happy if only I could do that *gwande finale* dance woutine the way you did—'

Humming the music under her breath, she shuffled her feet awkwardly, managing to get about one move in three right. I couldn't stand it.

'No, no, Gwenda. Not like that, like this—' I showed her.

'This?' She was a quick study, she got it almost right.

'Not quite. Take it slowly . . . follow me . . .' I led her through the steps.

'Oooooh!' She gave a squeal of delight as it began to come right.

'That's it, that's it,' I encouraged her. 'Now, twirl-and-kick, twirl-and-kick—'

'Oooooh!' She was getting it beautifully. In fact, she was getting beyond me. I twitched up my skirt to keep pace with her, vaguely aware that 'Waymond' had taken over on the humming as we grew breathless.

'*Now* . . . a really *high* kick. That's it . . . And again . . .' Her kick was nearly as high as mine. 'Great . . .'

I thought I'd overdone it when I began to see flashing lights. Then I heard the applause as we collapsed, giggling like schoolgirls, into each other's arms, while more lights flashed.

'Well!' The temperature in the room abruptly dropped several degrees and it wasn't just because the terrace door had opened. Evangeline stepped into the lobby, her icy disapproval freezing us all.

Even the photographers who had just been snapping me looked guilty. Then one, with great presence of mind, turned swiftly and snapped Evangeline. There was a brief storm of flashing lights as the others followed suit.

Evangeline smoothed her hair into place and advanced to the centre of the lobby, looking gratified. Behind her, Beau walked as warily as though he were tiptoeing through a minefield. The smile on his lips bore no relation to the look in his eyes. Neither had actually pushed the other off the roof, but it looked from here as though it had been a close thing.

'Trixie, dear—' Evangeline shot me a murderous look and I was suddenly glad that I wasn't standing at the edge of a roof myself. 'I was just telling Beau that we can't stay. Let's face it, we're not as young as we used to be. We must go home and get our beauty sleep before the opening tomorrow.'

Translation: *She* wanted to get away now and she wasn't going to leave me behind to get any publicity on my own.

'Oh, come now.' With the Press looking on, Beau paraded his gallantry. 'You don't look a day older—'

'Neither do you.' Evangeline reached up and patted his face while the flashbulbs exploded again. 'I don't know *how* you do it!'

Again, there was a subterranean tremor of amusement. I tried to pinpoint it, but couldn't. It seemed to come from several sources, yet everyone appeared occupied with their own business. Reporters were jotting down notes, cameramen took pictures. In a corner, Gwenda was earnestly imparting information to an interested young man. His pen made short strokes that might have meant he was using shorthand—or taking down a telephone number.

'My little Flower of the North!' Beau pulled her hand from his face and kissed it. This touching scene was duly recorded for posterity.

'Wicked Beau—if I took your statements at *face* value, I'd

be swept off my feet. And I'm sure Juanita wouldn't approve. But we must love you and leave you. Come, Trixie—' She swept across the lobby.

'Oh, Twixie—' My little friend caught up with me as I was about to follow Evangeline into the lift. 'Oh, Twixie, I was just getting it wight when all those wotten Pwess people intewwupted us. Do you think—?'

'Sure,' I said recklessly. 'Come down tomorrow morning —not too early—and we'll have a practice session. You have the makings of a hoofer—all you need is some practice and some of the tricks of the trade.'

'Oh, thank you, Twixie—' The lift doors slid past her radiant face. Well, it was true. The kid could probably be good—if she was willing to work at it. Why shouldn't I show her the ropes? Passing along the torch to the younger generation, that was what it was supposed to be about, wasn't it? Just my tough luck that my own daughter considered acting, singing, dancing and any form of the entertainment industry as a fate worse than death. Dear Martha was never going to put herself out to entertain anybody.

'If you *must*—' Evangeline gave a long-suffering sigh—'try not to wake me. Why don't you go up to her flat? You can make all the noise you like then. It won't matter if you disturb Jasper—if his conscience lets him sleep at all.'

'Evangeline—' I darted a warning glance towards Hugh, who was staring impassively at the blinking indicator lights marking our descent. It did not seem to come as any revelation to him that Jasper might be thought to have an uneasy conscience.

In fact, Hugh seemed to have something on his mind. He drove us silently and abstractedly back to the house in St John's Wood.

Nor did I feel like indulging in snappy dialogue. The closer we got to the house, the more I kept expecting to hear police sirens. I would not have been surprised to find the place surrounded by uniformed hordes. It suddenly seemed too much to hope for that the brilliant technicians of Scotland Yard would not have traced the girl's body back to the point and place at which it had become a body.

We turned the corner into a deserted street. No police lurked behind the gate pillars as we glided up the carriageway and pulled up in front of the dark and silent house.

It should have been reassuring, but it wasn't. Something awful was going to happen. I could feel it.

'I'll let you out,' Hugh said, 'and then I'll go and park outside so that I won't block the drive. I won't be long. Please leave the door open for me. I want to talk to you.'

'He knows!' I said as we watched him drive away.

'Knows what?' Evangeline was impatient. It was quite possible that she had forgotten all about last night. Or else had dismissed it from her mind as though it had been just a few more scenes from some long-forgotten film.

'He knows about you-know-what.' I followed her up the steps and into the front hall. Not being quite sure which door Hugh had meant us to leave open, I left them both ajar as we went into our flat.

'You're not making sense, Trixie. What am I supposed to know? What do you think Hugh can know?'

'*You* know.' I glanced around uneasily. Walls might not have ears, but the doors were ajar and the other occupants of the house were the type to take that as an invitation if they noticed. All we needed was to have a couple of the kids step into this.

'Oh, stop rolling your eyes like that!' Evangeline snapped 'And if you say, "We are not alone", I'll clout you!'

'Well, we may not be. Somebody could come in at any moment—besides Hugh, that is. And he already knows.'

'Really, Trixie, I can't face much more of this—'

'And that's another thing—' Her use of the word she had been emphasizing all afternoon reminded me. 'What is it with all this *face* business? You've been rubbing Beau's nose in it all day. What's the big idea?'

'You noticed, did you?' She was gratified. 'And you admit there's something *you* don't know?'

'Come on, what's it all about?' I followed her into her room while we both removed our coats and automatically checked our make-up in the extravagant mirror.

'Well . . .' Evangeline added another layer of lipstick and blotted it carefully.

'Evangeline—' I threatened her with the hairbrush.

'Well, the fact is that dear Juanita hasn't been seen for the past eight years. Beau's been telling everyone that she's gone into retirement and can't be dragged out of the country—'

'That's what he told us.'

'Yes, but the rumour is—and Cecile swears it's true—that Juanita is in hiding because she had a facelift that went wrong. Beau sent her to one of those El Cheapo Clinics and they made a mess of the operation. They were sued by some of their other clients, but of course Juanita didn't want to admit she'd been involved. Unlike dear Beau, pride meant more to her than money. The clinic was closed down—'

'I should think so!'

'But that didn't do *her* any good. *And*, to make matters worse, Beau went on to have a facelift of his own. But no cut-rate place for *him*. He wasn't saving money when it came to his *own* skin. He went to one of the best plastic surgeons in England. Juanita may never forgive him.'

'You can see her point.'

'They say she's so furious she won't even divorce him —just in case it might be what he wants. Still—' Evangeline placed her forefinger on a strategic spot just above one eye and pressed upwards—'you have to admit that it paid off for him. He looks ten years younger, maybe fifteen.' She studied the effect in the glass.

'Just remember,' I said wickedly, 'if you go home looking *too* much younger, you'll lose all those lovely *grande dame* parts that have been earning you so much money.'

'Hmmm . . .' She relaxed her finger and the bags fell back into their natural place beneath her eye.

'I suppose—' I half-closed my eyes to get the effect of a softened focus. 'I suppose it wouldn't do any harm if we got the surgeon's name—for future reference.'

'What's that?' Evangeline swung towards the door.

The sound of thundering feet shook the house. Several determined people seemed to be charging down the stairs at the same time.

'We'd better go see.' I led the way with some trepidation. My feeling of impending doom had returned, although I had always thought that the British police walked with a stately tread. You live and learn.

'We'll receive them in the drawing-room.' Evangeline pushed me forward as I was about to turn down the entry hall to the door. She was right, we needed all the props we could get.

They must have started from the top of the house. We had ample time to arrange ourselves in elegant postures before they arrived. Two eminently respectable elderly ladies about to be surprised by the arrival of the Law. We'd both played this scene before—give or take a few variations.

Mick burst into the room, wild-eyed, quiff quivering, as though all the hounds of hell were on his traces. 'I couldn't help it,' he gasped. 'I thought it was all right but—'

Des pounded into the room behind him, but seemed shorter of breath. He just stood there panting and looking at us expectantly.

Ursula slid in quietly, not a hair out of place, nor was she breathless. Her eyes were shining and avid as she looked at us, then turned to watch the door.

One last set of footsteps came down the hall with the tread of doom. My heart sank. Retribution was upon us.

'Mother!' Martha marched into the room and stared at me accusingly.

'She's been here for hours—' Mick had the steam-rollered

look I had learned to recognize on the faces of unwary males who had had a brief encounter with Martha. 'She talked us into letting her wait upstairs. Was it all right? She said—' He looked from her to me disbelievingly. 'She said you were her mother.'

'That's right,' I admitted grudgingly. 'She's my daughter. What are you doing here, Martha?'

'You never telephoned me back,' Martha accused. 'I was waiting by the phone. I was worried. Frightened. What was I to think?'

'You might have thought your mother was busy living her own life,' Evangeline said tartly. 'She's a grown woman.'

'I found her waiting on the steps,' Mick said. 'I didn't want to leave her out there, not knowing when you'd be back. I took her up to our place.' He sounded as though he had regretted it ever since. He probably had.

'Thank you, Mick,' I said comfortingly. 'That was very kind of you.'

'My suitcases are upstairs.' Martha looked at the two boys in annoyance. 'Didn't either of you bring them down?'

'We'll get them later.' Des obviously didn't wish to miss a moment of this touching reunion. 'Plenty of time.'

'Suitcases? It sounds as though you've come prepared to stay a while.' Evangeline rushed in where I dared not tread. 'What hotel are you staying at?'

'Hotel?' Martha regarded her with distaste. 'There's plenty of room here.'

'Oh no there isn't!' I was glad Evangeline was prepared to fight it out. Left to myself, I knew I'd have caved in and offered her my bed while I slept on the chaise-longue in Evangeline's room. 'You can see for yourself, your mother and I have a room each—and there's no extra space.'

'Nonsense,' Martha said. 'This is an enormous room —and that sofa looks quite adequate.'

My heart sank. This was Martha in her most mulish

mood; she was digging her heels in and there would be no budging her. Still, I had to try.

'I've noticed a nice little hotel not very far away. You'd be much more comfortable there and . . .' I had to pause and get my voice under control before continuing. 'And we can still see each other quite often.'

Evangeline snorted.

'I'm staying here,' Martha said flatly. 'Whether I am comfortable or not is beside the point.'

Before I could ask just *what* point she was talking about, Ursula sidled forward.

'I think I have the solution,' she said. 'I don't know whether you've noticed—' she glanced from Evangeline to me—'but you don't occupy the entire floor. The room opposite this one is a separate *pied-à-terre*—'

'Bed-sitter,' Des muttered loudly.

'It isn't rented at the moment and I'm sure—'

'Oh, we couldn't impose like that,' I said quickly, but that girl just wasn't able to take a hint.

'I'm sure,' she went on smoothly, 'that Jasper would be happy to let you rent it for as long as you like.'

'Jasper?' Evangeline raised an eyebrow at me.

'Jasper is our landlord.' That was one of the items of gossip I had almost forgotten in the press of other events. 'I understand he owns this house.'

'I could show it to you now,' Ursula volunteered. 'It's just a studio flat, but it's self-contained and very well equipped. I'm sure you'd like it.'

'I'm sure of that, too,' Martha said grimly. She'd sleep on the roof ridge if it meant she could keep tabs on me. 'Will he accept traveller's cheques? Or I can get to a bank first thing in the morning—'

'Oh, there won't be any problem,' Ursula assured her. 'Not with Miss Dolan to vouch for you.'

For a mad fleeting instant, I considered repudiating Martha entirely. 'That woman is an impostor! I've never

seen her before in my life!' But then I realized it was
far too late for that. I had already admitted she was my
daughter.

'Good.' Martha almost smiled at Ursula. 'Then perhaps
you'll have my bags brought down. I'll move in immediately.'

It was probably just as well that my hollow groan was lost
in the burst of activity.

Ursula gestured and both Mick and Des started for the
door. They narrowly avoided colliding with Hugh as he
entered. There was a brisk quadrille ending abruptly as they
all stopped short and waited suspiciously for someone to
make the next move.

'Is this Jasper?' Martha asked.

'Oh no, dear,' I said swiftly. 'Let me introduce you. This is
the kind man who's been looking after us so well: Hugh
Carpenter. Hugh, this is my daughter, Martha.'

'How do you do?' Hugh offered his hand.

'Hugh?' Martha whirled on him. 'Don't you dare "How
do you do" me, you—you monster!' She dealt him a back-
hand blow that sent him reeling across the room.

CHAPTER 9

'All I said was, "How do you do"—' Hugh backed away
from Martha's furious advance, nursing his cheek. 'What's
wrong with that?'

'Don't *speak* to me!' she snarled. 'Just have the decency to
get out of this house—if you know what decency *is*. And
never, never come near my mother again!'

'Oh no!' Suddenly I realized what this was all about.
Martha, never one to give me the benefit of a moment's
doubt, had believed every idiotic thing Evangeline had told
her. She thought Hugh was my gigolo and had rushed to

London to defend my honour—highly dubious though she had always found it.

'This—' I turned on Evangeline. 'This is all your fault. I hope you're satisfied!'

Evangeline inspected her fingernails, distancing herself as far as possible from the sordid scene. But she couldn't fool me; she was delighted with the results of her nasty little joke.

'Martha—stop that!' I rounded on my daughter. 'Leave that poor man alone! It's not your house, you can't order him out of it. Hugh, I apologize for my impossible child.'

'I don't understand—' Hugh bleated from the corner Martha had backed him into. 'What have I done? What did I say?'

'Never mind, I'll explain later.' I felt a wave of colour I had not attained in more than thirty years without the generous aid of Max Factor flood my face. 'Right now, I'd like to speak to Martha—privately.'

'Of course, of course. I understand—' Hugh side-stepped Martha and spurted for the door. 'I quite agree.'

He was the only one anxious to take his departure. Mick, Des and Ursula remained riveted in their places waiting to see what new development would take place. I had the feeling that they were compiling mental notes. Some day they might be faced with a script that called for them to abandon their English reserve and let rip—they would recall this evening and be prepared.

'"I pray you"—' This was all we needed. Evangeline rose to her feet and went into her routine. '"Stand not upon the order of your going"—'

'Oh no!' Ursula cried. 'You shouldn't have said that. It's the most awful bad luck. Everyone knows you should never quote from *Macbeth*!'

'You shouldn't even utter the name of *that play*—' Des had gone pale. 'It's bad luck upon bad luck. The most frightful things may happen now!'

I looked at Martha. If anything worse could happen, I

didn't want to know about it. Mick looked as though he might be about to faint—and that was another complication we could do without.

'Ursula—' I gave her my sweetest smile. 'Perhaps you'd like to show Martha her room. Mick, Des—I believe you offered to bring down Martha's suitcases—'

I got them all moving. Reluctantly, perhaps, but moving. The show was over, so far as they were concerned. The next few scenes were going to take place in private.

'Now—' I turned to Evangeline after the room had cleared. 'Now see what you've done.'

I woke in the morning with a feeling of impending doom. As usual. It seemed to have taken up permanent residence at the back of my mind.

I began some deep-breathing exercises, still lying there with my eyes closed, reluctant to get up and begin the day. In retrospect, the past few days seemed happy and peaceful, untroubled by any deeper worries—

'Mother! How could you?'

Martha stood foursquare in my bedroom doorway. Was I never to have any escape from those accusing eyes?

'How could you?' she asked again.

'How did you get in here?' I had a question of my own. Very mindful of my darling daughter just across the hall, I had made damned sure there weren't any doors left ajar last night. 'I *know* I locked the door.'

'Ursula gave me the spare key, of course. She knew I'd want to be in and out of the flat.'

'How thoughtful of her.'

'Don't change the subject, Mother.' Sarcasm had always been lost on Martha. 'I still want to know how you could do such an awful thing.'

'I've already explained—' I sighed and sat up, reaching for my new robe. There would be no more peace around here, I might as well get up and have breakfast. 'Evangeline was joking. It was a very poor joke but she has a warped sense of humour—and you'd have to know Hugh to realize how funny it really was.'

'Not that.' Martha brandished a newspaper at me impatiently. 'I mean—*this*!' She strode forward, unfurled the newspaper and waved it before my face. 'How *could* you?'

'Oh!' I looked at the picture in pleased surprise. 'Well, you know I've always kept limber. I found I could do it quite easily.' I removed the paper from her nerveless hand and inspected it more closely.

TRIXIE SHOWS HER TRICKS the headline shouted. And there I was, out-high-kicking a girl nearly one-third of my age. Not that Gwenda was any slouch. For someone untrained, she was keeping her end up quite creditably. I nodded approval and moved on to the caption beneath the picture—which took up almost half the page, I was happy to note.

Trixie Dolan, one of the greatest Hollywood Musical stars of her generation, proves that she still has what it takes —and plenty of it. Furthermore, she isn't shy about passing along her tricks to Gwenda Parsons, who proves an apt pupil. Here from Hollywood for a season at the Silver Screen in the Sky, Trixie shows that you can't keep a good hoofer down—and young Gwenda isn't far behind. Could this be the beginning of a promising new double act?

'I just can't understand—' Martha was close to tears —'how you can make an exhibition of yourself like that. And in a rag like that, too. Why, they have a nude on Page Three.'

'In that case, I'm quite respectable. In fact, I'm a fuddy-duddy by their standards.'

'It isn't funny, Mother!'

It never was with Martha. Poor girl, I had been a sore trial to her all her life. We always said the stork had dropped her down the wrong chimney: she should have gone to a Pillar-of-the-Community Churchwarden and his Social Worker wife.

'If it's such a rag,' I countered, 'what are *you* doing with it? I thought you'd go for a more respectable newspaper.'

'I didn't buy it!' Martha was shocked at the mere idea. 'I haven't even been out yet. I found it lying in the hall, just inside your door. I assumed it was yours—especially when I saw that picture.'

'No, I didn't order it. I didn't even know which paper the photographer worked for.' I had a pretty fair idea where the paper had come from—and she was right. I was delighted to see it, even if Martha wasn't.

'You don't care.' Martha followed me around the kitchen as I filled the kettle and set it on the hob, then loaded the toaster. 'You're enjoying this!'

'If you'd stayed at home where you belonged, you'd never have known about it. What the eye does not see, the heart does not grieve over. You'd have saved yourself a lot of grief.'

'So now it's all *my* fault!' Martha's voice soared hysterically. 'That's just like you, always twisting the truth—'

'*What* is going on here?' Evangeline came into the kitchen radiating disapproval. '*Must* you indulge in a family brawl the first thing in the morning? *Other* people are trying to sleep.'

'Good morning, Evangeline.' I set another place at the table. 'I trust you slept well—up to now.'

'Like a log—until the buzz-saw started.' Evangeline glared at Martha, but refused to speak to her directly. 'What's the matter with her now?' she asked me.

'Have you *seen* this?' Martha asked, unnecessarily, since it was quite obvious that Evangeline had just got up and couldn't possibly have seen a newspaper Martha had already commandeered. 'Just *look* at this!' She snatched up the tabloid from the table and waved it at Evangeline.

'Well, let go of it, woman!' They tussled briefly for possession of the newspaper. 'How can I see it, if you won't let go of it?'

'Don't tear it,' I said. 'I want it for my scrapbook.'

Holding the paper at arm's length—she would never admit she needed glasses—Evangeline frowned at the picture, then scanned the caption.

'They've got this all wrong,' Evangeline said indignantly. '*I'm* the one having the season at the Silver Screen, not you. They haven't mentioned me at all.'

Now there were two pairs of eyes looking at me accusingly.

'That's not my fault.' I caught the toast as it popped up, and took my cup of coffee. 'You can't kick as high as I can.'

I made a strategic retreat to my bedroom, closing the door firmly behind me. They could now hold their indignation meeting. For once, they had something in common.

I dressed in my leotard—I'd only brought it along to annoy Evangeline by wearing it while doing my exercises—and a trouser suit, then waited until the coast was clear before slipping upstairs. They'd never think of looking for me there.

'Oh, cwumbs! Was I supposed to be down there alweady? I'm so sowwy. I'll come wight along—'

'No, no, it's all right.' I slid past her into the room. 'I just had second thoughts. It occurred to me that it would be better to do our practice up here. Not so much furniture —and easier to roll the rugs back. If that's all right with you?'

'Oh yes, anything you say.' She was still in her warm woolly bathrobe. 'It's so kind of you—'

'Not at all.' I stepped over the cluster of coffee mugs in the middle of the floor. Were they the same mugs or had they been refilled several times since I had last seen them? 'I might as well do something useful while I'm here.'

'Would you like a cup of coffee?' Gwenda bent and swooped up the mugs. 'Some toast? Anything?'

'No, thank you, I've just had breakfast.' I caught a movement out of the corner of my eye and turned to catch a sleek dark head trying to dodge back out of sight.

'Come in,' I called.

'You know Ursula,' Gwenda said, 'but I don't think you've met Anni. She was out when you awwived.'

'Hello, Anni.' I nodded coldly to Ursula. Anyone who went around giving out keys to my flat was not going to lead my Popularity Parade. 'Hello, Des—' I waited, but no one else came through the doorway. 'What, no Mick?'

'He's sleeping,' Des said. 'At least, I hope he is. I heard him pacing the floor until all hours. He hasn't been sleeping well lately.'

I don't suppose he was. The memory of his grim task was not one he would be able to shrug off lightly.

'Oh, please—' Ursula stepped forward, clasping her hands in a parody of one of Gwenda's gestures. 'Miss Dolan, Gwenda told us you're going to give her a tap-dancing lesson. Please, please, may we watch?'

'It's your flat,' I said ungraciously. 'If Gwenda doesn't mind, I don't.'

'Oh, thank you—'

'We're going to need some space cleared—and those rugs rolled up.' I kicked at a corner of a runner intruding into the room.

'We'll do that.' Des bent and began rolling back the runner. Ursula effortlessly pushed a large armchair back against the wall. Anni smiled at me vaguely and let the other two do the work.

'What kind of music, Twixie?' Gwenda was back, offering a selection of tapes. 'I thought p'waps this one—' She held out a cassette titled *The 'Thirties Song and Dance*.

'That will do,' I agreed. Just about anything would do except rock and its later variations.

'Now!' I started Gwenda off with some basic steps as the music swung out. She was enthusiastic and eager to learn. As the lesson proceeded, it dawned upon me that she wasn't the only one.

Over on the sidelines, a fair amount of audience participation was going on. Anni and Ursula were attempting to copy the steps, even Des was furtively shuffling his feet, frowning with concentration. I might have known it.

'Oh, all right!' I gave up. 'Get over here into line—all of you. You can't see what you should be doing from over there.'

Gwenda was unperturbed as they dashed to line up on either side of her. She was right. They hadn't her aptitude, but knowing a good basic routine would never come amiss for any of them.

I put them through their paces until we were all limp and sweating. By the end of the session, I was aware of a growing uneasiness which finally crystallized into coherent thought:

Where was Mick? Why hadn't he given up his attempt to sleep and come out to join us? He couldn't still be sleeping through all this racket.

We were making enough noise to wake the dead.

'There have been three telephone calls this morning,' Evangeline said severely when I returned. '*All* for you.'

'How nice? Did they leave any messages?'

'Two were from newspapers who wanted interviews— with photos. The third said he'd ring back.' She gave me a tight smile and added casually, 'Martha told the newspapers that you wouldn't give interviews and were not available for photographs.'

'Oh, she did, did she?' I had been feeling tired after my unaccustomed workout, now the surge of adrenalin snapped me to attention, ready to fight the world. 'Where *is* Martha?'

'I sent her out sightseeing. She was getting on my nerves.'

'Just as well.' I did some deep breathing, trying to cool my temper. 'I might have killed her.'

'That would be too much to hope for. You should have dealt more firmly with that girl from the beginning. She has no right to rule your life the way she does.'

'She doesn't, really. Not when I'm around.'

'Precisely. And how many offers do you think she may have refused on your behalf when you weren't around to know what she was doing? It came as quite a revelation to me, I can tell you.'

It was a revelation to me, too, but I wasn't going to let her see that. But, once roused, the suspicion was hard to quell. Thinking back, I realized that my career had slowly begun to slip just about the time Martha graduated from college and came home to live with me.

There was that TV series I had been approached about and then heard no more—until it went on with someone else in the role. Could Martha have intercepted a vital telephone call and told them I'd lost interest? And how about that tantalizing whisper that there might be a lead in a Road Company revival of *Broadway Follies*? That, too, had come to nothing—at least, so far as I was concerned. Was it possible that I had not so much chosen retirement as had it forced upon me?

'Let's go out to lunch.' Evangeline glanced at her watch.

'I'm not hungry.' I had shared frozen pizzas and coffee with the kids after the lesson. It had taken me back more years than I cared to count to be sharing a scratch meal, laughs, dreams and theatre gossip with a group of young hopefuls.

And that was another grievance against Martha: if she had minded her own business instead of mine, got married and produced a few heirs, I'd have a gang of grandchildren to frolic with and teach now. The pizza was awful, of course, but a couple of antacid tablets would put me right.

'That's not the point,' Evangeline said. 'If we go out to lunch now, we can stay away until it's time to come back and get dressed for the Opening. We'll miss Martha altogether, if we can time it right.'

*

Some time during that day, the body was discovered. The Stop Press column of the early edition carried the item. An unidentified woman found in the Grand Union Canal. The later editions, or maybe the morning papers, might carry a fuller story. Or maybe they wouldn't. The clear implication was that suicide was suspected.

I pointed it out to Evangeline and gave her the newspaper, but we were in a taxi on our way home and could not discuss it. We exchanged glances and nods.

I couldn't say anything, but I knew we weren't nodding about the same things. Evangeline was nodding a cool professional appreciation of a job well done; the body disposed of without fuss and discovered far from where it could rebound on any of us.

I was just relieved that it had been found. I hadn't liked to think of that poor young thing floating in the cold water, shrouded by the damp heavy fog.

The fog was heavier than ever now and the taxi was just crawling along. We were going to be late. If only, I thought wistfully, the fog had been this bad yesterday, perhaps Martha's plane wouldn't have been able to land and would have been diverted to an airport on the Continent.

'Here we are. Don't bother driving up to the house,' Evangeline said to the bemused driver, who was not even aware that we had reached our destination, far less that there was a driveway concealed somewhere behind the fog. 'We'll get out here.'

'She got out and disappeared into the mists, leaving me to pay the driver. I knew what that meant: she had slipped into her most regal mood. Royalty doesn't carry cash. She was getting ready to Queen it at the Opening tonight.

Martha was still nursing her grievances when I got in, but I gave her short shrift.

One *prima donna* at a time was enough.

CHAPTER 10

All things considered, it was amazing how well *Revenge of the White Squaw* had stood up against the passage of time.

There had also been some magnificent restoration work done on it. Ursula had told me this morning, with justifiable pride, the bits to look out for; otherwise I would never have guessed that the archive restorers and not the scriptwriter or director had been responsible for some of the linking scenes. The big dramatic scenes had fortunately survived almost intact—and how much power they had, even today.

The audience was swept by emotion as the young Evangeline, carrying her baby son, fled from the pursuing party of Indians on the War Path. They groaned as she was caught, gasped at the audacity of the implied mass-rape, and handkerchiefs began to flutter as she became a slave to the squaws of the tribe and plaything of the braves. Then came the moment when she held her dead son in her arms and gave that famous silent scream.

There wasn't a dry eye in the house—mine included. We needed the cut to the Army headquarters as the news reached them of her capture and they mounted a rescue mission to pull ourselves together after such intensity of emotion and to brace ourselves for what was still to come: The Revenge.

The moon rose over the desert and a silhouette of a howling coyote filled the screen. The Indian camp was silent, shadowed, then something stirred. Evangeline, tethered to a stake beyond the dying campfire, slowly sat up and pulled the knife she had stolen earlier from beneath her concealing skirt. She cut the rawhide thong tethering her and crept into the tepee where the Chief slept.

He stirred. She froze. He turned over and was quiet again.

She waited, then moved forward, hatred blazing in her eyes, knife held high. He sensed another presence, he frowned in his sleep, his eyelids flickered and opened.

Too late. Evangeline struck. He died without making a sound. She stood looking down at him, then she withdrew the knife and leaned over the body. Working swiftly, she made the V-shaped incision where the scalplock sprang back from the forehead, then slashed along the sides of the scalplock. Hands slippery with blood, she grasped the forehead flap and tore with all her might.

The audience screamed. She straightened triumphantly, holding aloft the bleeding trophy. The White Squaw had taken her first scalp.

But not her last. As the moon faded, the coyote slunk away, the campfire went out, Evangeline slipped from tepee to tepee, her trail marked by the blood dripping from the scalps hanging from her waist.

'*Came the dawn* . . .' The titles resumed, no one had missed them. Another stock silhouette, this time of a crowing cock. The sky lightened, the Indian camp began stirring. The old squaws rose, yawning, and began to make up the campfire, to prepare breakfast for the braves. Then a squaw ran out from one tepee, screaming. The others gathered round her, listening with disbelief, then pushed her aside to enter the tepee.

They gazed down incredulously at the butchered brave, saw the drops of blood leading from the tepee and followed them. From tepee to tepee, with increasing despair and horror.

'*The Chief. Who will dare to tell the Chief?*'

Crowding together, arguing and frightened, they approach the Chief's tepee, but . . . what's this? Drops of blood are here, too. It can't be! It is!

A shout from a squaw who had stayed behind to build up the campfire. She gestures, holding up the rawhide thong where the captive had cut herself free from the stake. Now *they* are out for revenge. They begin the search for the White Squaw.

'*Meanwhile* . . .' The cavalry mounted at dawn and began the ride to the rescue. Grim-faced heroic soldiers ride across the barren landscape . . . Intercut with shots of the angry squaws coming closer to Evangeline's hiding place . . . Back to the cavalry . . . back to Evangeline, prepared to sell her life dearly as the squaws burst into her refuge . . . Back to the cavalry . . . will they be in time?

What else? Only a certain amount of grim reality was permitted in those days. The heroine had to survive to be rescued by the handsome hero. Still draped in scalps, Evangeline swooned into Beauregard Sylvester's manly arms.

Evangeline got a standing ovation, of course.

The house lights went up and Beau led her onstage, holding up his hand to try to quiet the hysterical audience.

'I think you'll all agree,' he said, 'that we've got the Evangeline Sinclair Season off to a rousing start.'

After another minor uproar, he was allowed to continue with his speech. He must have written it himself, the cinema began clearing while he was still speaking. Unfortunately, I had to remain to the end.

Most of the audience dispersed then and the crowd remaining had invitation cards to the Champagne Reception which followed. I cheered up considerably then and it wasn't just the champagne.

There were a lot of familiar faces around. Familiar from stage and screen, even though I hadn't met many of them personally. Quite a few had seen my photograph in the morning papers, however, and I soon had a circle surrounding me, smaller but more select than the crowd besieging Evangeline.

The usherettes were serving drinks and canapés and Gwenda took it upon herself to see that my group was kept well supplied. Naturally, some of them recognized her as the pupil in the photograph and, equally naturally, she was delighted. It all got very convivial and I found myself having the best time I had had since we landed.

The same couldn't be said for some of the others. Over in one corner, Hugh was morosely nursing his one measly glass of champagne since he was driving us back. Martha was mooching around by herself in another corner, sulking. The house had been sold out, not even standing room, and she had not been able to get in to the film. She had been given a ticket to the reception, but that wasn't good enough for Martha. I'd never hear the end of her complaints.

Gwenda refilled my glass and I stopped fretting. Let's face it, Martha would enjoy having a legitimate grievance more than she would have enjoyed the movie. Too bad about her.

The next time I noticed her, she had gravitated to Hugh's corner and they were both talking earnestly. From the expressions on their faces, they were both apologizing. Fine, that could keep them gainfully occupied for hours.

As I watched, a tray of drinks was carried past them and Hugh absently reached out and took another glass of champagne. Even better. He looked as though he could use some relaxation. It couldn't be an easy life, being a go-fer and I'd bet Beau ran him right down into the ground. We could always take a taxi home.

Someone raised a hand to me in farewell as he slipped out into the lift. I waved back automatically, then blinked as I realized who it had been. Earlier, I had seen Des's multi-coloured spikes bobbing about as he mingled with the crowd; now his hair was back to its normal shade, lying flat and rather damp. He was obviously on his way to work some-where.

I didn't see any of the other kids from the flat-share there. Of course, Ursula had worked on restoring the film, she would have seen enough of it. Anni was still an unknown quantity, neither her absence nor her presence would have been surprising.

It was Mick I was worried about. Even if he'd managed to sleep all day to compensate for his sleepless nights, he should have been stirring by now. But he wouldn't necessarily show up here. After his nightmare experience with the girl's body, he wouldn't want to be harrowed further. He didn't need to add grisly filmatic scenes to his memory bank; his real-life experiences were grisly enough.

Jasper was quite ostentatiously present, however. He appeared to be the sole escort for at least three beautiful girls. As I watched, another one came up and joined them. He obviously was not pining for the girlfriend who had disappeared; if, indeed, he had even noticed her absence.

Or if, as Evangeline believed, he had killed the girl himself, his conscience obviously wasn't troubling him in any way.

Or was it? Despite the fact that the night was still fairly young, he seemed to need the assistance of the girls on either side of him to keep him upright—which didn't stop him from commandeering a fresh tray of drinks as they went past. It was going to take a whole fleet of taxis to get us all back to the house tonight.

One of the cinema flunkies brought over someone he introduced to me as a Diary snoop just then. (He'd been helping himself rather lavishly to the drinks, too.)

All right, I'll admit it, I was knocking back my share. Otherwise, I might have been more discreet. I had had warnings about the English gossip writers and their headlines, but I was caught off-guard.

'How does it feel to be a piece of living history?' he asked. What kind of a question is that?

'You'd better ask Evangeline,' I said. 'She's a lot more historic than I am.'

His eyes lit up and, too late, I saw the trap I had fallen into. Fallen? I'd taken a head-first dive into it. And, come morning and the big black headline, Martha would be '*How could you*-ing' at me again. She was here—why wasn't she stopping me from making quotable catty remarks instead of brow-beating Hugh in corners?

'Excuse me,' I said icily, 'I must go and speak to my—to someone.'

When I looked back over my shoulder, I saw that he was heading straight for Evangeline. Just as I'd thought, he was determined to stir up trouble.

Martha and Hugh were not in the corner when I reached it, but they had been there only a moment ago. I had distinctly seen them both take fresh drinks and give every indication of settling down for the evening. Apparently, they weren't going to settle here.

Another survey of the lobby proved that Martha and Hugh were not in sight and that Evangeline was snorting fire at the gossip columnist. Her head reared back and her eyes flashed flames as she looked around the room. I knew who she was looking for.

Fortunately, the lift doors opened just then and disgorged a few late-comers to the party. I dodged behind them and into the lift. I'd go home by myself and make sure that I was asleep before anyone else got back. By tomorrow, Evangeline would have cooled off.

I don't like taking sleeping pills, but two of them seemed a strategic necessity that night. I left the bottle ostentatiously displayed on my night table and everyone must have taken the hint. I slept without disturbance until the morning.

I did not wake refreshed. Unremembered nightmares clung like cobwebs as I drifted up towards consciousness. In fact, I woke to a fresh nightmare. Someone was trying to strangle me.

I was fighting for breath. My nostrils were pinched together, my chin was forced down, holding my mouth open and someone was blocking my breathing and blowing into my throat. I hit out feebly.

'She's coming wound,' a voice shrilled. 'Keep going, Des. She's coming wound!'

Another blast of second-hand air was forced into my lungs.

'Stop that!' I flailed feebly at the head so uncomfortably close to mine. 'What do you think you're doing?'

'He's giving you the Kiss of Life. Oh, Twixie, why did you do it?'

'Kiss of—' That snapped me back to full wakefulness. I sat up and pushed Des away. 'Do what? What are you talking about?'

'There,' Des said. 'I told you it was an accident. She woke up in the middle of the night, forgot she'd taken any and took some more. It happens all the time.'

'Now see here—' It was beginning to make faint sense. 'This is ridiculous. You're over-reacting to a perfectly normal—' Automatically, I looked at the bedside table. The bottle of sleeping pills lay on its side.

It was empty.

'No,' I said. 'That isn't possible. I only took two. There was almost a full bottle left.'

'You see? You don't wemember.'

'There's nothing to remember! Look at me —' I leaped out of bed and stood before them. 'Do I look as though I'd taken an overdose?'

'Put your wobe on before you catch pneumonia.' Gwenda held it for me. 'You *do* seem all wight,' she admitted.

'Of course I am!' There was nothing like a surge of fury to get the adrenalin flowing and all the little grey cells ticking over. 'Someone emptied that pill bottle while I was asleep. Where's Martha?'

'We sent her into the kitchen to make coffee. She was too distwaught to be helpful in here.'

'I'll bet,' I said grimly. Martha knew what my mood would be when I awoke to find myself being worked over by a couple of enthusiastic would-be rescuers who had misread the situation because she had confiscated the remainder of my sleeping pills.

'And we've been twying to keep it quiet. Evangeline is still asleep and we don't want to distuwb her.'

'Pity.' I couldn't hold back a grin. 'You're sure she's having a nice natural sleep? Maybe she helped herself to the rest of my sleeping pills. You wouldn't like to go in and wake her up the way you woke me? Go on—make her day!'

'Oh, Twixie, I'm sowwy—'

'We thought we were doing the right thing,' Des defended. 'How were we to know? Martha came rushing upstairs, hysterical—'

'Martha got you down here?'

'She found you. She thought . . . She was tewwified. Who wouldn't be? But she didn't want any publicity, so she wushed to us for help, to see what we could do before she called a doctor.'

'I see.' That sounded like Martha, all right. Except that, in this instance, she was right. No one needs that kind of publicity. Even when it was discovered to be all a mistake, some of the mud would stick. People always like to believe the worst.

'Here's the coffee—' Ursula came into the room carrying a tray. 'Oh, good, she's better.'

'There was nothing wrong with me—'

'Mother!' Oh, fine, that was all I needed. Martha rushed into the room. 'Mother, why did you do it? Where have I failed you?'

'It's all wight—she didn't do it.'

'It was all a mistake—'

The voices rose in frantic babble. I sat down on the edge of the bed and reached for the coffee Ursula had set on the bedside table. The empty bottle had been pushed aside by the tray and one more little nudge would send it flying off the table. I looked at it thoughtfully, realizing I wasn't quite as awake as I thought I was. There was a nagging idea trying to come through—

'And *now* what is going on?' Evangeline's voice, trained to reach the farthest corner of the second balcony in the days before everybody pranced around wearing throat mikes, soared effortlessly over the others, silencing them abruptly.

'Sleep is impossible in this house!' she declaimed.

'You can say that again,' I muttered.

'Trixie.' Evangeline's icy look let me know that I had not been forgiven for last night's *faux pas*. 'Can you explain all this hubbub?'

'No,' I said. I took another sip of coffee. I wasn't even going to try. 'I don't know anything about it. I was sleeping —or trying to.'

'That was the twouble—' Gwenda leaped into the breach. 'We thought—'

'You mean Martha thought,' Ursula corrected. 'We didn't know anything about it until she came running upstairs to get us.'

Ah, yes . . .' Evangeline gave a long-suffering sigh. 'Martha. I might have known it would come down to Martha.'

'Martha,' I echoed thoughtfully. 'Martha, why don't you be a good girl and go and bring me back my sleeping pills?' Even as I spoke, the flaw in my reasoning became clear to me: if Martha had taken away the pills, the empty bottle would not have upset her.

'I haven't got them,' Martha said. 'Why do you always accuse me of everything?'

Because you're usually responsible. I bit back the answer and tried for a softer one.

'I was only asking. You didn't take them?'

'Certainly not! Why would I do a thing like that?'

'Then where are they? *I* didn't take them, either.'

'Are you sure?' Martha eyed me suspiciously. 'All we have is your word for that—' Her voice began rising. 'You might just be having a momentary rally before you collapse. I think you ought to have your stomach pumped!'

'Pull yourself together, Martha!' Evangeline's tone was a slap in the face. 'You're hysterical! Stupid and hysterical! I'd suggest you go and take a walk in the fresh air to clear your brain and regain control of yourself.'

'There isn't any fresh air.' Martha's voice was sulky. 'There's nothing but fog out there.'

'Whatever there is, it can only improve you.' Evangeline took her elbow and marched her firmly towards the back door. 'Walk to the end of the garden and back six times —taking a deep breath at every step. It will do you a world of good.'

It wouldn't do us any harm, either, to be rid of all that hysteria and pulsating emotion. Martha was one of the most exhausting people I knew.

We heard the back door slam, then Evangeline came back into the room and looked at me sternly. 'That woman is in a bad way,' she said. 'You should have sent her to a psychiatrist long ago.'

'I did,' I said, 'but she bit him.'

'I thought that was the dentist.'

'She bit him, too.'

Martha had only been gone a few moments when she suddenly began screaming.

CHAPTER 11

The screams were loud, insistent, bloodcurdling. We erupted from the house and charged down the garden path in a body. The fog was thick, damp and impenetrable. We could not see two feet in front of us.

Only the high-pitched, agonized shrieks kept us on course. She was at the very end of the path, hand covering her face, shutting out something that lay behind the fog.

'Martha—' I caught one arm and pulled her hand away. 'What is it? What's the matter?'

'Have a thought for the neighbours, woman!' Evangeline snapped. 'If you keep on like this, they'll call the police—and I won't blame them. You're disturbing the peace.'

'There—' Martha gasped. 'It's— He's—' She pointed into the fog with a shaking hand. 'On the garden bench!'

'I'll stay with Martha,' Ursula volunteered nobly, sounding a little sick. 'You go ahead.'

We approached the bench cautiously. As we drew nearer, we could see the dark motionless figure slumped there.

For an instant, I could have sworn my heart stopped. That was where Mick had left Fiona's body through that long night. But it couldn't be. She couldn't have come back. They had found her body in the canal. This was someone else. This was—I stepped forward for a closer look.

'Mick!' Gwenda identified the body a split-second ahead of me. 'It's Mick!'

He's dyed his hair red, I thought inconsequentially. *And he's flattened it down. How odd. I wonder why he did that.*

My mind refused to let me realize what I was looking at.

'Good God!' Evangeline was tougher. She faced the body unflinchingly and pronounced her verdict. 'The boy's been scalped!'

Whatever you do, don't ever ask Evangeline if she doesn't think the English police are wonderful.

By the same token, if you value your skin, you won't inquire of Detective-Superintendent Heyhoe if he asked Evangeline Sinclair for an autographed photograph as a souvenir.

It was hate at first sight.

He wasn't very fond of the rest of us, either.

It didn't help that we all got off on the wrong foot—or collective feet. That was Evangeline's fault. She had brought the kids into the drawing-room and dispensed generous libations against shock. None of us had had much in the way of breakfast, the kids weren't used to drinks of that strength and Evangeline kept the glasses topped up. By the time the police arrived, we were feeling no pain.

The pain was all Detective-Superintendent Heyhoe's.

'Not interrupting a party, are we?' He looked around disapprovingly.

Des had gone upstairs and brought down his clarinet. He hadn't been playing it, he was just clinging to it as to a liferaft, but Detective-Superintendent Heyhoe wasn't to know that.

Gwenda and Ursula were off in a corner dulling their reactions by trying to pretend that it was important that they master the dance steps I had taught them.

Martha was sprawled inelegantly on the sofa. Of us all, she was the most sober, but was projecting an image of utter abandon, if not depravity. She looked like the morning after the orgy. Her skirt was awry, disclosing far more of her thighs than she would ordinarily have allowed, but she was past caring. She lay motionless, eyes closed, mouth slightly open.

Detective-Superintendent Heyhoe strode over and stood looking down at her sombrely for a moment, then raised his head. 'When did you discover the body?' he asked.

Someone giggled from the corner.

'That isn't the corpse—' Again, I considered disowning her, but I knew it wouldn't work. 'That's my daughter, Martha. She discovered the body.

'Martha, sit up! The police are here.'

'About time, too.' Martha opened her eyes and glared at the Detective-Superintendent. 'What took you so long?' She tugged down her skirt with the clear implication that he had been taking advantage of the view.

A younger policeman was standing at a respectful distance, his carefully expressionless face betraying that he was enjoying his superior's discomfiture all too much.

'The body is at the bottom of the garden,' Evangeline said.

Detective-Superintendent Heyhoe looked at her suspiciously and I remembered what else was supposed to be at the bottom of the garden.

'It's true,' I told him. 'Shouldn't you go out there and inspect it?'

'All in good time, madam.' He glared at the three of us and then transferred his glare to the rest of the audience. 'Isn't anyone here English?' he demanded.

The kids crowded forward and I could see him regretting his question.

'We are.' Gwenda took the lead, her hair had shaken loose from half its bulldog clips while she danced. 'And we're so glad that you've come to help us in this time of tewwible, tewwible twagedy.'

Detective-Superintendent Heyhoe closed his eyes briefly and visibly stiffened his upper lip.

'We're ever so near the Zoo,' Ursula said helpfully. 'Have you checked to make sure that none of the wild animals have escaped? The way poor Mick was mutilated—' She could not continue and turned away.

'You knew the deceased?' Detective-Superintendent Heyhoe seized on the least emotive opening in her speech.

'We all did,' Des answered. 'We live in this house. Mick is—was—part of our flat-share.'

'See here, Heigh-Ho—' Evangeline poured more Scotch into Ursula's glass. 'Why don't you go and solve your case and stop harassing these poor children?'

'That's Heyhoe, madam.' He gazed at her with disfavour. 'And what might your name be?'

'I—' she drew herself up—'am Evangeline Sinclair.'

'Indeed.' He gave no sign of recognition. 'Would that be Miss or Mrs?'

'Mzzzzz,' Evangeline snarled.

The name may have meant nothing to Detective-Superintendent Heyhoe, but his sidekick quivered and went

on point like a bird dog flushing a covey of particularly fine
pheasants. His eyes lit up and he all but wagged his tail.

'Evangeline Sinclair,' he breathed. '*The* Evangeline Sinclair! Forgive me for not recognizing you at once, but I never
dreamed we'd meet under these circumstances. I'd read you
were in town.'

'Dear Boy—' Evangeline gave him her most gracious
smile. 'How nice to know that the Arts are not unappreciated
by *some* members of the constabulary. You are—?'

'Detective-Segeant Julian Singer.' He almost bowed and,
still bent, swivelled to include me. 'And *you*—' he breathed
—'must be Trixie Dolan.'

Say what you will, there is nothing like a nice obsequious
minion for restoring one's *amour propre*. I beamed at him as
fatuously as Evangeline. 'I'm very pleased to meet you,
Sergeant Singer. Do I gather you're a film buff?'

'Completely, utterly, hopelessly. This is a great moment in
my life. I never dared hope I'd have the honour—'

Detective-Superintendent Heyhoe cleared his throat
meaningfully and his sergeant fell silent abruptly.

'Quite finished, are we?' he asked nastily. 'I wouldn't like
to cut short a meeting of the fan club, but we *do* have a
murder to investigate.'

The statement was punctuated by the slamming of car
doors in the carriageway outside. There was something
businesslike and definitive about that series of small explosions; the rest of the technical crew had arrived, the investigation was about to begin.

I noticed that the doorbell didn't ring. That would mean
that they had left another policeman guarding the door to let
in his colleagues. We heard the heavy tramping of innumer-
able feet marching down the hallway to the back door. There
would be a doctor among them to certify the death, photographer to record it, various specialists to disperse themselves around the garden hunting for footprints, fingerprints,
bloodstains—there would be plenty of those . . .

I began to feel faint and sank and down on the sofa, just missing Martha's feet. She swung herself into an upright position and put a protective arm around my shoulders.

'We demand a lawyer,' Martha snapped at the senior officer. 'I believe we are allowed one. We refuse to say anything more until we have a lawyer present.'

'Certainly, madam.' Detective-Superintendent Heyhoe seemed to be trying not to grind his teeth. 'That is your right. You may telephone your legal representative now.'

'Oh—' The wind went out of Martha's sails. She had no more idea of who to call than any of us. 'Yes—' She looked around distractedly.

'Oh, cwumbs!' Gwenda said. 'We'd better start by calling Hugh.'

Hugh, Beauregard and Jasper arrived within minutes of each other, uttered a few meaningless noises at us and went to join the police in the garden. If there was a lawyer anywhere in attendance, I didn't see him.

I had half-expected the Press to be hot on their heels, but it appeared that we were to be spared that for a while longer. Evidently no one had yet connected the event that had happened with the visitors in the house. I wondered how much longer that kind of luck could last.

Not much longer. The young detective-sergeant popped his head round the door to goggle incredulously at Evangeline for a moment. It was clear that he had just come from viewing the body. What a pity that we'd had to get a film buff in the investigating squad. On the other hand, there were bound to be some reviews of last night's shindig in the morning papers, so someone would be putting two and two together and getting five any minute now.

'Did anyone get any newspapers this morning?' Evangeline seemed to be following my train of thought.

'Cwumbs, I forgot! I was so fwightened when I thought that Twixie had—'

'I think we'll forget all about that little episode, dear,' Evangeline said firmly. 'It doesn't add anything to the situation we have here now.'

'Oh, wight. I'll go and get the papers—' Gwenda started for the door.

'Perhaps it might be a good idea if Martha went,' Evangeline suggested. 'I'm sure she could do with a bit of air and a nice little walk to calm her down.'

'I am perfectly calm!' Martha snapped. 'You just want to get rid of me!'

'They probably wouldn't let any of us leave, anyway,' I said regretfully. 'Why don't we just telephone the shop and see if they'll deliver?'

'I'll do it.' Ursula rushed for the telephone, obviously delighted to have something to occupy her.

In fact, we could all do with something to occupy our minds and keep them from dwelling on the macabre figure slumped on the garden bench, blood oozing from his ripped scalp. It must be even worse for the kids; we had just met him, but he was a friend of theirs. They were putting up a brave front, but there were moments when tears glistened in their eyes. They had probably never experienced death before, far less a violent death with malicious disfigurement. They were so young, so vulnerable; my heart ached for them.

My heart ached for Mick, too. This was what he had tried to spare them. Now he was the reason that they were in the midst of a police investigation. Pretty soon, the police were going to come back and start asking why anyone should have wanted to murder him.

That meant that Evangeline and I had better think up some fairly snappy reasons for having helped Mick conceal that earlier death. I had the nasty feeling that the police weren't going to like any explanation we could give them. As I had pointed out to Evangeline at the time, we were several kinds of accessory after the fact and the police weren't going to be happy about it.

Where was that lawyer? My heart had stopped aching
abruptly and my head had begun. We were in big trouble.

Not that it seemed to bother Evangeline. It was quite
possible that she had forgotten the earlier incident, that it
had sunk to the bottom of her consciousness where it lay
among dozens of similar scenes she had played when the
cameras were turning. The fact that I had spent a good many
years as an actress myself never blinded me to the realization
that our grasp of reality was sometimes tenuous.

At the moment, she was more concerned with needling
Martha. And Martha, of course, kept allowing herself to be
needled. If she would only ignore it, Evangeline would soon
stop her silly little game. The sound of their bickering was
beginning to grate on my nerves.

So were the heads that popped round the door to survey us
and then withdrew quickly again. They were starting to
inspire a strong desire to hurl an ashtray at the next one to see
if I could still hit a moving target.

Finally, a familiar face dithered there—and the impulse to
hurl something intensified.

'Come in, Hugh,' Martha said. 'And, for heaven's sake,
tell us what's going on out there.'

'Yes, well . . .' Hugh sidled into the room and stood at the
back of the chair Martha now occupied, giving the strong
impression that he was hiding behind her skirts. 'Well, the
police have been very busy. Measuring, photographing, all
that sort of thing. I think they're just about finished now. I
mean, they're moving Mick— His body—'

I realized that Hugh was as shocked and stunned as the
kids. He had known Mick, too. The realization even seemed
to reach Martha, she twisted in her chair to look up at him
anxiously.

'Yes . . .' he said vaguely, as though someone had asked a
question. 'Well, they're talking to Jasper now. They want to
talk to everyone who lives in the house.'

'Do they?' Ursula looked around the room, her eyes bright

and sharp. 'They'll be lucky! Where's Anni?'

'Cwumbs! That's wight.' There was no sharpness in Gwenda's eyes, only anxiety, as she looked around. 'I haven't seen her since yesterday. Where is she?'

'Either she didn't come home last night—' Ursula spelled out the possibilities, just in case we had missed them. 'Or else she left early this morning—very early.'

'I don't think we should jump to any hasty conclusions.' Hugh immediately made matters worse. 'There's probably a very good explanation if we happened to know it.'

'Does she usually stay away all night?' I asked quickly.

'Er . . .' Des was trying not to shock the elderly ladies —bless him! 'Well, it wouldn't be the first time.'

So much for Anni.

'And . . .' Evangeline nodded, as though it had been no more than she had expected. 'And was she a *particular* friend of Mick's?'

'Er . . .' Des was looking very unhappy. 'They were rather good friends, yes. I think you could say that.'

'Oh, Des!' Ursula said impatiently. 'They were living in the same room and you know it.'

'Er . . . yes . . . but . . .' He wriggled uncomfortably.

'*And* they had a double bed in there,' Ursula persisted relentlessly. 'Don't be so mealy-mouthed.' She had a more realistic assessment of our shock quotient than he had.

'I think what Des is twying to say is that they haven't been getting along at all well lately. They've spent as much time fighting as—oh, cwumbs!' Gwenda clapped her hand over her mouth as the implication struck her.

'But she couldn't have,' Des protested. 'Not Anni.'

'Someone did,' Hugh said sombrely.

Not surprisingly, this remark threw everyone into a brooding silence.

Detective-Superintendent Heyhoe walked straight into this silence and stood in the centre of the room radiating deep suspicion of each and every one of us.

CHAPTER 12

It was too quiet. Outside, we could hear slow footsteps coming down the outer hallway, moving with the measured tread of men matching steps to carry something heavy. Even without Hugh's information, we would have known what they were doing. A ripple of distress passed through the room. Gwenda choked back a sob.

'Hrrmmph . . .' Detective-Superintendent Heyhoe cleared his throat too briskly and too loudly. He didn't succeed in kidding anybody, but I appreciated the attempt. 'It's going to be necessary to have a little chat with each of you. Do you think we could use this room?'

'Go right ahead, Superintendent,' Evangeline said. She settled herself into a corner of the sofa and smiled at him regally.

'I meant, in privacy, madam. One at a time.'

'Our lawyer isn't here yet,' Martha pointed out quickly.

'I think he's upstairs with Jasper,' Hugh said. 'Shall I go and get him?'

'If you would,' Martha said. 'Please.'

'Perhaps you wouldn't mind if I asked a few preliminary questions of someone other than your mother while we're waiting?'

'She's not my mother,' Martha said.

'Sorry. I meant, your grandmother,' he corrected.

'Martha is *my* daughter,' I said hastily, before Martha and Evangeline could both fly into a fury. 'And I don't mind answering any of your questions.'

Actually, I minded very much. I could think of several dozen questions I would rather not be asked. Especially without a lawyer present. Why did I have to open my big mouth?

'Yes,' Detective-Superintendent Heyhoe said unenthusiastically. 'We'll come to you later, thank you.'

Paradoxically, I was furious. I flounced over and perched on the arm of Martha's chair while Heyhoe turned to the kids.

'Do I understand that all of you share the flat at the top?'

'Maisonette, actually,' Ursula said.

'And you're all here now?' The question was pointed. I could not be the only one to remember that he had just been talking to Jasper.

'There's also Anni,' Des said reluctantly. 'But she didn't come home last night.'

'That we know of,' Ursula added quietly.

'And you were all living together upstairs?' Heyhoe made it sound like a twenty-four-hour-a-day orgy.

Out of the corner of my eye, I noticed that the Sergeant had quietly moved into a chair and was busy with pen and notebook. What a pity his shorthand couldn't possibly encompass the verbal nuances of his superior.

'Just for the record,' Heyhoe said with elaborate casualness, 'perhaps you wouldn't mind running over your movements last night. Say, perhaps, from about six p.m. to midnight.' He was speaking ostensibly to the kids, but his gaze slid towards Evangeline. I began to feel that I had even more reason to worry than I had feared. What was he getting at?

'That's easy,' Gwenda said. 'We were all at the cinema —the Silver Scween in the Sky—for the pwemiere of *The Wevenge of the White Squaw*, stawwing Evangeline Sinclair. And she was fabulous in it! That was followed by the weception. It was a totally fantastic evening. A weal twiumph for the gweat Evangeline Sinclair!'

'It *was* quite a pleasant occasion.' Evangeline barely refrained from smirking.

'So you were all at the cinema from six p.m. to midnight?'

'Er, actually,' Ursula said uneasily. 'I wasn't there at all. I—I had a prior engagement.'

'Anni was there for the showing,' Des said, 'but I don't know how long she stayed. I had to leave soon after the film to get to work.'

'I left early myself—' I spoke quickly to draw Heyhoe's fire from the kids. 'I wasn't feeling terribly well. So I came back here, took a couple of sleeping pills and went to bed. Well before midnight.'

'I was there the whole time,' Gwenda said. 'I'm one of the ushewettes at the Silver Scween in the Sky.'

'Thank you,' Heyhoe said. The Sergeant's pen was flying over the notebook pages. 'That's most helpful. Now, perhaps you could be even more helpful while we try to narrow down our timings.'

Martha had remained silent. I carefully avoided looking at her, lest my thoughts became apparent. She had not been able to get a seat for the screening, and both she and Hugh had disappeared from the reception before I left.

Also, I had not seen Anni there at all. That didn't necessarily mean that Des had lied, of course.

'This is just a preliminary inquiry,' Heyhoe said encouragingly. 'I'll be talking with each of you separately later.'

That took care of the encouragement. I didn't trust that sneaky smile of his for one instant. Neither did anyone else. The kids looked at each other and moved closer together.

'Now then . . .' The false heartiness of his voice was not reassuring, either. 'Perhaps you could give us details—' he turned to Ursula— 'of that prior engagement. Where you went, the names of the people you met, how long you were there—'

'No,' Ursula said firmly, 'I'm afraid I couldn't. It was extremely personal. Private, in fact.'

'I see.' Heyhoe's face darkened, but he was obviously trying to project an understanding persona. He glanced around at the rest of us and bared a few more teeth. 'Well, we'll come back to that question when we're alone.

'Meanwhile—' he fixed Des with a relentless gaze—
'perhaps you wouldn't mind telling us where you were
working last night and what time your gig broke up.'

'Actually—' Des swallowed, but could not be less brave
than Ursula—'I would. It was a private party. I couldn't say
anything more about it without the express permission of my
employers.'

'I see.' Heyhoe nodded as though he had expected nothing
better. 'We'll take that up in private, too. Meanwhile,
perhaps you'd get on to the telephone and get that permission from your employers.'

'It will take a while,' Des said. 'It was a farewell party.
They've flown back to Saudi Arabia. I don't have a telephone number for them—and I don't know when they'll be
back in England again.'

Heyhoe turned an interesting shade of purple. I couldn't
blame him. It was a good story, but Des was not a good liar.
He spoke too loudly, he met no eye, and a nervous tic had
begun twitching at the side of his mouth. He might even be
speaking the truth, but the way he spoke it he would never
get the benefit of any doubt.

'And you—' Heyhoe glared at Gwenda. 'You say you were
at the cinema—?'

'Evewy minute,' Gwenda assured him. 'We worked flat
out all evening, fwom showing people to their seats for the
pwemiere to handing wound canapés and dwinks at the
weception. And then Evangeline was kind enough to give me
a lift home in her taxi. We got back to the house about one
a.m. and I went stwaight to bed. I was exhausted.'

'Hmmm . . .' Heyhoe casually slipped a question in
Evangeline's direction. 'And I suppose you went to bed
exhausted, too, madam?'

'On the contrary,' Evangeline said. 'I was far too exhila-
rated. It had been a most stimulating occasion. I fixed myself
a nightcap and sat up and read for a while. I might add that I

heard several people come in and go upstairs.'

'I don't suppose you could identify any of them?'

'Certainly not! I was in my room. I didn't get up and go out into the hall to check on them. I'm not a night watchman.'

'And you had no curiosity at all about who might be coming in so late?'

'Why should I? It isn't my house.'

'You couldn't say which footsteps were male and which were female?'

'Even if I were paying that much attention—which I wasn't—I don't believe could differentiate.'

'You didn't hear any footsteps go out the back way—into the garden?'

'I wouldn't have noticed.' Evangeline shrugged. 'I had other things to think about.'

'Ah yes, the premiere.' Heyhoe spoke with obscure satisfaction, as though they had arrived at their destination after following a long and circuitous route. 'Quite a momentous occasion, I understand. One of your early pictures restored and just like new. It must have brought back a lot of memories. The film's outstanding feature, I understand—' he glanced at his cohort and got a faint nod of the head in reply—'was the melodramatic ending portraying a certain . . . disposition of the corpses—'

'See here, Hee-Haw—' Evangeline's eyes flashed dangerously. 'Are you trying to insinuate that I was so overcome by nostalgia that I went out and scalped that poor boy just for Old Time's Sake?'

'Don't let him trick you!' Martha cried. 'Don't say another word until the lawyer gets here!'

'I can do without the vote of confidence, thank you, Martha.'

'Shh, please, Martha,' I whispered. 'You're just making matters worse.' Now Heyhoe knew that Martha didn't trust Evangeline's mental stability.

'But you heard him,' Martha wailed. 'How much worse can they get?'

We found out.

'This is your daughter, madam?' Heyhoe zeroed in on me. 'A bit highly-strung, isn't she?'

'She's just not the trusting type,' I said. 'And she's had a terrible day—she discovered the body.'

'Ah yes,' Heyhoe said. 'I was going to ask about that. Went walking in the garden, didn't she? Strange thing to do in weather like this.' He waited expectantly.

The silence told him that he had struck a nerve. The trouble was, he didn't know which nerve.

'She just wanted a breath of air,' I said quickly. At any minute, he might decide it was time to start questioning us all separately. It was essential to establish a general line we could all stick to. As Evangeline had pointed out earlier, we didn't want publicity given to the erroneous idea that I might have taken an overdose of sleeping pills.

'Ah yes, madam.' Now I had drawn Heyhoe's fire. 'You were at the premiere, too, weren't you? That means everyone here has seen—or heard about—that film and the famous scalping scene.'

'Oh, don't!' Gwenda cracked abruptly. 'It's *Mick* who died like that. Mick! How can you talk about it like that? It's—it's *wotten* of you!' She burst into sobs.

'What's going on here?' Hugh returned with a stranger at his heels, presumably the lawyer. 'Are you harassing these youngsters?'

'Here, now, honey—' Beauregard Sylvester was right behind them. He crossed to Gwenda and put an arm around her shoulders. 'Don't take on so. It's going to be all right.'

'All wight?' Gwenda shook herself free. 'How can it be? Mick's dead—*dead*! Nothing will ever be all wight again!'

'Dear Beau,' Evangeline sighed. 'He always means so well—and he always says the wrong thing. There's only one

way to handle this.' She went over to Gwenda and dealt her a
brisk slap.

'Take a deep breath—' She caught her by the shoulders
and shook her lightly. 'Straighten up. That's it. Keep on
deep-breathing. Someone get her a glass of water—'

Martha leapt from her chair in response to the command
and nearly collided with Jasper in the doorway. Jasper was
looking pale and shaken. He made directly for the abandoned chair and sank down into it.

I looked at him thoughtfully, then got off my perch on the
arm of the chair and tried not to be too ostentatious about
putting some distance between us. I had not forgotten that it
was probably the death of his unmourned girlfriend that was
responsible for this train of events. Most probably. Only
Mick could have told for certain—and Mick was going to tell
no tales. Someone had seen to that.

Meanwhile, the police were working blind, without half
the vital information they ought to have. Evangeline would
have a fit if I tried to supply it. I wasn't too keen on the idea
myself. It would lead to an awful lot more questions, like why
had we concealed the death in the first place? I wasn't even
sure of the answer myself any more.

Perhaps I could send the police an anonymous letter . . .
very anonymous. There must be no possible way they could
connect it with either me or Evangeline. It would have to
very carefully worded . . .

Beau had drifted over to Ursula and was patting her
shoulder. She seemed to be appreciating his particular brand
of sweetness and light more than Gwenda had. Des was
gently stroking his clarinet, looking off into the distance and
shuddering occasionally.

Heyhoe had momentarily retreated from the whole scene
under guise of conferring with his sergeant, but those beady
little eyes weren't missing a trick. He had seen me move away
from Jasper, he noted that Evangeline was getting Gwenda
back under control, and the eyes narrowed as Martha re-

turned, carrying a glass of water.

His suspicions were infectious. For a split second, I looked at Martha through his eyes: past her first youth, thin-skinned and highly-strung—as neurotic, in fact, as it was possible to be and still remain uncertified. *Had* she strolled to the end of the garden and, finding Mick there, possibly dozing on the garden bench, impulsively scalped him?

Except—common sense reasserted itself—why should she be carrying a sharp knife on a stroll through the garden? And why on earth would Mick be asleep on the bench in a thick wet fog? No, someone had found Mick there—but it hadn't been Martha. Nor was it likely that Mick had been asleep. He had more probably already been dead. The inevitable autopsy would produce the reason.

It would also tell us whether he had still been alive when he had been scalped. I hoped not. Surely he couldn't have been. There would have been signs of a fearful struggle. He must have been dead—or dying and deeply unconscious —before such an atrocity could have been perpetrated.

Unconscious . . . or dying . . . or dead. Someone had entered my room after I had fallen asleep last night and taken away all my sleeping pills. Almost a full bottle—a fatal dose. Had they been dissolved in a drink of some sort and given to the unsuspecting Mick?

Abruptly, I needed to sit down. I tried to collapse gracefully into the corner seat of the sofa. Unfortunately, this meant I was now facing Jasper. I looked away.

This was a mistake. It put me in eye-to-eye contact with Heyhoe and he came over to me. I tried not to quail as he loomed above me, but had to remind myself that they didn't have the Third Degree in this country, that we were slightly too important for him to risk using it if they had—and besides there were too many witnesses.

Not that anyone seemed to be paying any attention. Even Martha had her back turned towards me as she urged more water on Gwenda.

'You and Miss Sinclair have known each other a long time, haven't you?' Heyhoe asked.

'Practically for ever.' That chummy air didn't fool me; he'd been talking to his film buff sergeant too long and too earnestly. I made a mental bet that I was about to be served up with another rehashed version of The Feud.

'Good friends all your lives, eh?'

'I wouldn't say that. Most friendships have their ups and downs—especially in Hollywood.'

'Really?' He looked disappointed. Obviously, he'd hoped to catch me in some sort of lie about 'never a cross word'.

'There were *years* when we didn't speak to each other,' I admitted honestly. 'But, after just so long, it gets to seem silly and so, when we ran into each other at a party, we got talking again and made a date for lunch the next day and diplomatic relations were restored.'

'And the friendship was restored, too?'

'Wasn't that what I just said?' I noticed that the sergeant had sneaked up behind us, notebook at the ready. 'Anyway, it was what I meant.'

'And no lingering hard feelings? No regrets? No grudge still being nursed?'

'None,' I said firmly. 'I've even forgotten what it was all about in the first place.' That had been my story for years and this was no time to start changing it. I didn't like the way these questions were going.

'And does Miss Sinclair remember?'

'I wouldn't know. We've never discussed it.' I tried to be unobtrusive about signalling over his shoulder for help. This was getting serious.

'How did you like the film last night?' He changed tack, alarming me even more. 'Had you seen it before?'

'I saw it the first time round. I was just a child, of course. I saw it at a Saturday matinee.'

'Children were allowed to see a film with all that horror

and violence?' Heyhoe's voice expressed open disbelief. 'Over here, it would have had an X Certificate.'

'Violence never bothered anybody when I was a kid. All they ever censored was sex. Today they don't seem to bother about that, either.'

'Seeing that film at an impressionable age—didn't it haunt you? Give you nightmares?'

'American kids are tougher than that.' I tried a careless laugh. 'It was just one of a bunch of scary movies. We had ways of dealing with them. When the action got too tense, somebody would throw a popcorn box at the screen. They did it for love scenes, too. Then boxes would fly at the screen from all directions. Empty boxes, of course, we rarely got so carried away that we wasted good popcorn. Everybody whooped and hollered and, by the time the ushers got us quieted down, the worst of the action was over and we settled back until things got too exciting again.'

Heyhoe winced. He did not seem to find my reminiscences of childhood filmgoing as lovable as I fondly remembered them. His sergeant, on the other hand, was busily scribbling in his notebook.

'So . . .' Heyhoe said consideringly, 'you were hardened to scenes of violence at an early age.'

'Now wait a minute,' I protested. 'I didn't say that. Just what are you driving at?' As if I didn't know. As if I couldn't see that he was considering the possibility that I had killed Mick, for whatever reason of my own, and then scalped him to throw the blame on Evangeline, thus getting revenge for whatever she had done to me in the past.

'Oh, nothing, nothing. Much too early to be driving at anything at this stage in inquiries. I'm only exploring possible avenues . . .'

'Well, you can forget that one—it's a dead end.' Too late, I realized my choice of expression might not have been the wisest. With relief, I saw that Des had caught my mute appeal and had drifted over to us.

I appreciated the gallant gesture and was sorry that it attracted unwelcome notice to him.

'Ah—' Heyhoe looked at him coldly. 'Remembered where they had the party last night, have you?'

'Somebody else was driving.' Des promptly produced more explanations. 'I wasn't paying any attention. I don't know where we went. I just know it was a big house with lots of people.'

'Ah yes, all those jet-setting Arabs. Undoubtedly, someone there will remember you—if we ever find any of them. Meanwhile, perhaps you'd be good enough to give me the name of that driver.'

'Er, Dave, I think. Yes, I'm pretty sure. Dave.'

'I don't suppose he has a surname?'

'I don't know it. It was all pretty informal. They're not my usual group. I met them in a pub and they needed one more for the gig. They invited me to sit in.'

'Ah yes, the proverbial meeting in the pub and the impromptu arrangements.' Heyhoe spoke wearily, he had heard it all before. He didn't believe it then and he didn't believe it now.

To be honest, neither did I. I began to wonder just what Des had really been doing last night that he was so anxious to conceal.

CHAPTER 13

'I don't trust them,' Martha said. 'I don't trust a single one of them. Let's get out of this awful house. Let's move to a hotel. Right now!'

'I'm glad you managed to restrain those sentiments until Hi-Ho left. You might as well keep calm and make the best of it. I'm sure the police wouldn't allow us to leave now.'

'They might be able to keep us in the country,' Martha

argued, 'but they can't force us to remain in this house. I'll start packing.'

'I don't want to move anywhere,' I said. 'On the contrary, I just want to lie down.' I also wanted to get rid of Martha. I had a few things to discuss with Evangeline, any one of which was guaranteed to send Martha into hysterics.

'So do I,' Evangeline quavered and suddenly looked very frail. 'This has all been most exhausting and a great shock. I do believe I have one of my frightful headaches coming on.'

'Neither of you will need to do a thing,' Martha began organizing. 'I'll call some hotels and get us a reservation, then I'll do all the packing.'

'Oh no you won't!' Evangeline rallied amazingly. 'I mean, I do think we should stay here. What's the point of leaving? The damage has been done. Nothing worse can happen.'

'What makes you think so?' Martha challenged. 'That boy is dead. Somebody killed him and then—then *scalped* him. And you know perfectly well that policeman thinks it was you!'

'All the more reason for not running away. It would be taken as an admission of guilt.' Evangeline lifted her head, straightened her back and stared soulfully upwards—the same pose she had used as *Joan of Arc* when the soldiers began to light the brushwood at her feet. 'I must stay and prove my innocence.'

'And how do you propose to do that?' Martha and I were rarely on the same side, but sheer irritation at Evangeline occasionally united us. If Evangeline had developed hare-brained notions of running around sleuthing, perhaps moving to some hotel as far away from the scene of the crime as possible was not a bad idea.

'Just remember—' Evangeline smiled smugly—'I always solved the crimes in *The Happy Couple* series.'

'Just remember you had a script.'

'I shall watch for signs of guilt. I shall observe everyone closely—'

There was no use talking to her, she was lost in her fantasy.

'Don't be silly,' Martha snapped. 'You're far too old!'

'Age does not wither the powers of observation.'

I observed that, if there had been a tomahawk handy, Martha's scalp would have been parted from her skull in two seconds flat. Why, after all my efforts, had Martha never learned a bit of tact?

'You go and rest, Mother—' The combination of an order and unwanted concern promptly alienated me again. 'I'll start telephoning.'

'I'm not moving to any hotel,' Evangeline said. 'But you can, if you want to,' she added hopefully.

'Yes,' I chimed in, without any real hope. 'You go ahead, but I think I ought to stay here with Evangeline.'

'I'm not going without you.' Martha reacted as I had feared. 'We all go together—or none of us will go!'

'Frankly, dear,' Evangeline sighed. 'I preferred the version of *The Three Musketeers* with Doug Fairbanks in it.'

'Why don't you both go and lie down and try to get some sleep? Have a little nap.' Martha switched to sweet reasonableness. 'After some rest, perhaps you'll come to your senses. Meanwhile, I'll check out some hotels.' She exited, still smiling sweetly.

'Martha—' Evangeline brooded—'is the sort of woman poor, dear John Barrymore was talking about when he said, "There's only one way to fight a woman—with your hat. Grab it and run!"'

'At least, we're alone now and can talk. Look, we've got to tell Heyhoe about that dead girlfriend of Jasper's. He's working in the dark if he doesn't know that. And we ought to tell him about all my missing sleeping pills, too.'

'Stuff and nonsense!' Evangeline snorted, reverting to her Ethel Barrymore best, presumably since she had just been thinking about dear John. 'We'll do nothing of the sort. He's the detective. Let him find out for himself—if he can.'

'How can he when he doesn't even know where he should

be looking? We're distorting the whole case by not giving him the information he needs.'

'Hmmph!' This thought was not going to disturb Evangeline unduly. Those had been the conditions that prevailed in every thriller she had ever made. But Heyhoe was a far cry from Jimmie Gleason and Bill Demarest.

'Look—' I tried again despairingly. 'These aren't comedy cops. We're up against the real thing—and we could be in real trouble.'

'Oh, you always exaggerate so, Trixie. They can't do anything to us—we're stars!'

'We *were* stars.' Now I was getting worried. Her grip on reality was slipping again. 'That was a long time ago. We don't have the Studios behind us any more. In fact, the Studios aren't there any more. We're on our own, six thousand miles from home—this is no time to play games.'

'Oh, Trixie, sometimes you get as boring as Martha! We are not without influence in this country, remember. Dear Beau is a person of some consequence here and we can rely on his protection.'

'Oh yeah? If Heyhoe pins this rap on either one of us, I'll give you odds that your precious Beau will disappear so fast you won't see him for dust.' I'd been in a few thrillers myself.

'So—' Evangeline's eyes narrowed as she fell into the familiar script—'you think we ought to rat on the boys?'

'I think we ought to sing like canaries.' I found I had not lost the knack (acquired for *Gold Diggers Behind Bars*) of talking without moving my lips. 'Mick's dead, nothing we say can harm him now.'

'What about the others?' Evangeline dropped the act abruptly. 'Mick was trying to protect them.'

'One of them doesn't deserve protection,' I reminded her darkly. 'The others will have to take their chances.' A momentary cynicism overcame me. 'Who knows how deep they're all in it, anyway?'

'I wonder—' Evangeline mused. 'I just wonder where that

boy, Des, got to last night? He's acting as though he's hiding the Guilty Secret of all time.'

'And, these days, guilt isn't what it used to be.' I didn't want to suspect Des, but Evangeline had a point there. 'Nowadays, people cheerfully admit to things they'd have paid blackmail to keep quiet in our time.'

'Flaunting it,' Evangeline said bitterly. 'When I think what you and I went through just to—'

'Maybe we'd better forget about that. There are too many people getting interested. Even Heyhoe was asking questions. He seems to think we might have buried the hatchet, but not the feud. He's pussy-footing towards the theory that I dug up the hatchet and used it on Mick to try to make it look as though you did it.'

'That's an improvement over his theory that I was overcome by nostalgia and decided to treat myself to one last scalp on my belt.'

'It's only an improvement so far as you're concerned. I'm not overjoyed about it myself.'

Evangeline didn't quite turn her snicker into a cough in time.

'I'm glad you think it's funny.' My own sense of humour had been in abeyance since I awoke this morning to find our little chums working me over. 'Perhaps they'll hang me —and then you can have a real laugh!'

'Don't be absurd, they abolished the death penalty here years ago.'

'They're bringing it back in the States. Who knows what will happen next? You may get lucky—'

A knock at the door brought us both to attention. We broke off our squabble and looked at each other.

'I'll go,' I said.

'We'll both go.' Evangeline closed ranks. We marched together to the door and opened it.

'Er, hello—' Des stood there, fidgeting nervously under our challenging stares. 'I—Uh, *we* . . . Uh, it's long past lunch-time and none of us has had anything to eat. I'm going down to the Chinese takeaway—' He waved a menu at us. 'What do you fancy?'

'Everything!' Suddenly, I realized I was starving. No wonder I had been self-pitying and snappish. I couldn't even remember when I had last sent anything reasonably solid down to my long-suffering stomach.

'Beef-and-green-peppers, fried rice, chicken subgum and noodles.' Evangeline ordered rapidly, not even glancing at the menu.

'Peking duck,' I decided, 'perhaps some plain boiled rice, king prawns, and Martha likes sweet-and-sour-pork—'

'Wait a minute,' Evangeline said. 'I'll get my purse.'

'No, please,' Des said. 'You're our guests—all of you.' He took a deep breath. 'If you don't mind eating with us. Gwenda and Ursula are brewing up tea and we'll mix everything together. That's what Chinese meals are all about, isn't it?'

'That sounds marvellous,' I said warmly. 'But you really must let us pay for our own—'

'No, honestly, we have plenty of money. You're our guests, please. It will be our pleasure . . .' He moved off to the sound of coins jingling in every pocket.

'Those poor, sweet lambs,' I said, 'they must have emptied their piggy banks. But I suppose we must allow them their pride.'

'We'll make it up to them later,' Evangeline said. 'Next time, we can claim it's our turn and take them out someplace really nice.'

'We'll do that before we leave—if they let us leave.' Then I remembered something else. 'I wonder what's happened to Anni?'

Martha grumbled, but followed us upstairs. She objected to dining with a group of suspects in a lurid murder, but the only alternative was to go out and find a restaurant on her own; then there would be the inevitable long wait for her order to arrive. She hadn't eaten in a long while, either, so hunger won out over prejudice.

I was not surprised to find that Beau had left—Chinese takeaways weren't exactly his style. Hugh was talking earnestly to Jasper in a corner; they rose to their feet as we entered.

'Weally!' Gwenda bustled about, settling Evangeline and myself into the best armchairs. Martha, she left to her own devices. 'The questions those policemen asked! It was disgwaceful! They see a mixed gwoup of young people in a flat—and they jump to one conclusion. They have absolutely filthy minds!'

'*And* you're theatrical people,' Evangeline commiserated. ''Twas ever thus. We're always suspect, you know. Thieves, vagabonds and rogues—the old feelings about us have never quite disappeared.'

'That's wight!' Gwenda brightened. Evangeline's liberal use of the plural had cheered her immoderately. '*We* do meet with a lot of jealousy and suspicion fwom non-theatwicals.' She preened slightly. 'People can be so silly. Do let me get you another cushion—'

'I'm quite comfortable, thank you.'

But Gwenda had darted of in search of a cushion. Hugh, I noticed with interest, had abandoned Jasper and was now deep in conversation with Martha. She seemed to be complaining—probably about us—nothing new about that. Hugh was nodding his head and making soothing noises.

Jasper had wandered over to the window and was looking down on the carriageway. I approached him casually and also looked down at the carriageway.

'Have the police all gone?' The carriageway was deserted, but someone might still be on guard in the garden.

'For the time being,' he said gloomily. 'They'll be back when they think of some more questions. Probably after the . . . the autopsy.'

'It *is* a disturbing thought.' I tried to sound sympathetic. This was the second of Jasper's friends to be autopsied. I wondered if he knew that. I also wondered how I could find out. I wasn't supposed to know anything about it. I couldn't just ask him if he'd noticed he was one girlfriend short lately.

'Has Anni come back yet?' Perhaps I could lead him towards a gradual realization that more than one girl was missing.

'Anni?' He looked vaguely startled and turned away from the window, scanning the room. 'I haven't seen her . . .'

'Strange that she should disappear last night, of all nights,' I mused. 'You don't suppose she had anything to do with it, do you?'

'No, she couldn't. Not Anni.' He shook his head dazedly. 'I'll grant you it's strange that she . . . disappeared, but no stranger than what happened to Mick.' He shook his head again. 'It's all a nightmare.'

'Maybe she saw something. Maybe the killer took her away.'

'You mean, she's dead, too?' I had him on the ropes. I only wished I knew what that *too* meant. How many bodies was he counting?

'I'm not sure what I mean,' I said honestly. 'I only know the whole situation makes me very uneasy. And poor Martha is a nervous wreck.'

'I can see that.' He looked across the room at Martha, who was acting more distraught by the minute. Hugh wasn't being the calming influence I had hoped.

'It must have been quite terrible for her . . . finding him like that.' There was something wrong about his tone. I looked up at him in surprise—and caught the expression on his face.

He suspected Martha! It was written in every lineament. He actually thought Martha had—for neurotic reasons best known to herself—killed Mick and then scalped him, and then pretended to discover the body. Or maybe he thought,

having done the foul deed, she had given way to an attack of
hysteria and pretended that it was because she had stumbled
over the body.

'Oh!' My gasp was inaudible. I was so startled I could not
speak. If he could think that, then it must mean that he
hadn't done it himself. He was innocent.

Either that, or he was the best actor of the lot and was
wasted in the stockbrokerage. That, too, was possible.

'Here we are—' Ursula bustled into the room juggling an
assortment of flat-surfaced items. 'I thought it would be
more convenient if we ate off trays. We don't have enough
room in the kitchen.'

So that's what they were supposed to be. She dealt out the
makeshift trays. I got one which looked as though it had just
been snatched off a dressing-table and hastily dusted of
hairpins and powder. Martha got a baking tray and Evangeline, being guest of honour, got the only *bona fide* tray in the
lot. It got worse as she reached those she obviously considered family. Jasper got an oven pan and Gwenda a cake
plate.

There was a thump at the door and Gwenda flew to open
it. Des stood there, laden down with bulging Chinese takeaway carrier bags. Delicious fragrances wafted from the bags
as he went through the living-room to the kitchen; he no
longer jingled when he walked. I realized just how hungry I
was.

So was everyone else. They wasted no time dishing out the
food into an assortment of crockery even more eccentric than
the trays and we got down to the serious business of eating. I
noted that the flatmates were eating directly from the takeaway cartons and wondered if it would hurt their pride if we
gave them a matched set of dinnerware as a parting gift.

'Isn't this fun, Twixie?' Gwenda brought her carton over
and sat on the floor at my feet. 'At least,' her face clouded, 'it
would be if it weren't for the circumstances. Oh, Twixie—'

'Never mind that right now,' I said hastily. 'You just get

some food into you. You'll feel better then.'

'I'll twy . . .' She sighed and rapidly began to demolish the savoury contents of her carton. She looked better after the first few mouthfuls

Ursula, having bagged the seat next to Evangeline, spent a great deal of time hopping up and refilling teacups and mugs. Otherwise, we ate rapidly and silently, too hungry to be social.

'My goodness, I needed that,' I said happily, as I finished the last bean sprout in my soup bowl. I was even feeling chirpy enough to try an old joke. 'I was so hungry my stomach thought my throat was cut.'

There was a ripple of nervous laughter, dying away as we slowly realized that it was a rather unfortunate pleasantry, given the circumstances. Of course, it hadn't been a throat that was cut . . . not yet.

'I don't like it,' Jasper said abruptly. He did not mean the feeble joke. He had been brooding silently throughout the meal. 'Anni should have been back by now—even if she stayed somewhere else last night. Hasn't she telephoned?'

'No, we've had no word at all.' Ursula looked frightened. 'You don't think—'

'I don't like it,' Jasper said again.

'We're not exactly cwazy about it ourselves.'

'Doesn't anyone have any idea where she might be?' Evangeline was growing impatient with the casual attitude of the flatmates. 'Why don't you start telephoning her friends and ask if they've seen her?'

'We could,' Ursula said, 'if we knew who they were. We only share a flat, you know, not an address book. We each have our own circle of friends and we've only ever met a few of each other's friends—and then it was at casual parties and we wouldn't have bothered with last names.'

'How awkward.' Evangeline gave an exaggerated sigh, but it had been the same in theatrical hostels in our early days. Only the public imagined that we were one great friendly amorphous mass. We were always aware that we were distinct personalities, with our own cliques, claques, friendships, loves—and hates. And, of course, if anyone had a particularly dishy male on the string, he was kept well away from the competition.

The telephone rang in the hallway.

'Anni!' Gwenda leaped to her feet, radiant with relief. 'It must be Anni! I'll get it.' She dashed out into the hallway.

We settled back limply, smiling weakly at each other. How silly we had been to worry. Everything was all right. Of course, it was all right.

An agonized howl suddenly reverberated through the room.

'If this continues—' Evangeline raised a nerveless hand to her forehead—'I shall have to buy some ear plugs.'

CHAPTER 14

'No-o-o . . .' Gwenda wailed in anguish. 'No! No! No!' She slammed down the receiver and burst into tears.

'Gwenda!' 'Gwenda!' We made a concerted dash for the hall. 'Was it Anni?' 'Gwenda, what's the matter?'

'Child, what did they say?' I found Gwenda had hurled herself at me and, head on my shoulder, was sobbing her heart out.

'I can't!' she choked. 'I won't! They can't make me do it!'

'There, there, of course, they can't.' I patted her comfortingly. 'Do what?'

'Who was it?' Ursula demanded. 'Was it Anni? What's the matter?'

'Oh, it's tewwible, tewwible.' Gwenda raised her head and looked at us tragically. 'The news is out. It's been on wadio. Television will have it in the next news pwogwamme. That was Mummy on the phone. She's insisting that I come home immediately. To stay. To Llandudno—in November!'

'Inhuman!' Ursula breathed.

'Tell her the police won't let you.' Des had more practical advice.

'You shouldn't have hung up on her,' Hugh fretted. 'She'll only ring back. When she does, let me speak to her. Perhaps I can calm her. You really can't leave London now, you know.'

That information did a lot towards calming Gwenda, whatever it might do for her mother.

'I'm all wight, weally.' She straightened and gave herself a little shake. 'It's just that it was so unexpected—'

The telephone rang again. Hugh started forward.

'No—let me.' Gwenda picked up the receiver and listened cautiously, then her face cleared. 'It's for you—' She held the receiver out to Des.

Never send to know for whom the bell tolls . . . Des paled, but took a deep breath and manfully grasped the receiver.

'Yes?' His shoulders slumped. It was just what he had expected. 'Hello, Mum, Dad. Yes, yes, I'm fine. We're all fine—well, almost all.'

The receiver crackled briefly. Des opened his mouth and made several croaking sounds, unsuccessfully trying to stem the flow. It was the same all over the world. I had momentarily lost sight of the fact that they were so very young. Of course, they had parents who were still vigorous, commanding—and influential.

'I don't think our MP can do anything about this, Dad—' At last Des got a word in edgewise. 'I mean, it's not his sort of territory, is it? Anyway, the police have been quite good, really. No, no, I can't. They won't let us leave. Quite customary. No—' His voice rose in anguish. 'No, don't do anything. You'll only make things worse. Yes, yes, I promise I'll get on to you immediately if there's anything you can do—'

After a few more assurances and protestations, Des replaced the receiver, looking as though he had just gone through the proverbial mill. The telephone rang again almost immediately.

Ursula backed away from it, an expression of dread in her eyes. It could only be for her . . . or Anni.

'Tchah!' With an impatient exclamation, Evangeline strode forward and snatched up the receiver. As she did so, her face changed, lengthened, her skin grew tauter, even her eyes seemed to slant slightly.

'Hong Fu Lo Chinese Takeaway,' she intoned in a sing-song chant. 'Today's Special: Foo Yung Dan . . .'

The other party slammed down their receiver in exasperation. Evangeline clicked the cradle, then set the receiver down on the table beside the telephone.

'Press,' she announced briskly. 'They'll keep getting a busy signal from now on, but that won't hold them for long. They'll be on their way now. Let's get out of here.'

'Cwumbs!' Gwenda glanced at her watch. 'It's time for me to get to the Silver Scween. I'll be late—' She dashed for her room.

'Why don't we all go to Cinema City?' Ursula suggested. 'They won't think of looking for us there.'

'We've seen the film, thank you,' Evangeline said drily.

'Ah, but you haven't seen the whole cinema complex,' Ursula said. 'The entire floor below the actual cinema holds the archives and the laboratory—that's where I work. Now that we've successfully restored *Revenge of the White Squaw*, and copied it on to acetate safety film, we've begun work on *Scars On Her Soul*. Come and see. I think you'll be pleased with what we're doing.'

There was a sudden commotion out in the carriageway below, a roar of several motors, voices shouting . . .

'Oh, God!' Hugh was the first to reach the window. He looked down on the scene with despair. 'It's the BBC and ITV OB vans!'

'Oh, do speak English,' Evangeline said crossly.

'The Television Outside Broadcast vans,' Hugh translated. 'Yes, and some radio cars, as well. Plus assorted journalists and photographers—' An engine gunned, brakes shrieked below. 'There are more of them arriving every minute. We're besieged!'

'We can go out the back way,' Jasper said. 'It isn't too bad—' He smiled encouragingly at Evangeline and me. 'There's a gate in the fence that leads into the next street. That's a cul-de-sac, so no one will think of our escaping that way. Not until it's too late, I hope. We can cut through and pick up a taxi at St John's Wood Roundabout. But we'll have to hurry before the Press think of posting a lookout at the back door.'

The front doorbell pealed sharply. After the briefest pause, it pealed again, then continued to ring incessantly.

'It's going to be a war of nerves,' Evangeline said. She had experienced these sieges before. We both had.

'I'll go and keep them occupied while you get away,' Hugh said nobly. 'So long as they have someone standing in front of them saying, "No comment", it will keep them occupied.'

'I'm weady.' Gwenda came back into the room. 'Are we leaving now?'

'This very minute,' Evangeline said firmly. 'Martha, fetch our coats and we'll be on our way.'

We leaned over the Moviola watching the miniature figures go through their paces. They seemed distant and remote, more like memories than an actual film. Of course, full-size, projected on to a proper screen, the film would come into its own again.

'I *love* this bit,' Ursula said earnestly. She looked at me approvingly. 'It's your death scene.'

'Thanks,' I said ironically, but I could not quite repress a shudder. Someone had just walked over my grave.

'I always loved that part myself,' Evangeline said. She had had the picture to herself after I was out of the way, the whole closing reel of it.

But this was the scene the critics had raved over. Stills from it featured in every book of cinema history. I had come close to an Academy Award for this one, my first nomination as Best Supporting Actress.

'Oooh, yes, it's tewwific—' Gwenda had slipped down to join us after the film had started upstairs. 'Oh, if I could only learn to act like that, I'd die happy!'

'Shh!' Ursula said sharply. 'It's starting now.'

We concentrated on the tiny figures reaching out to us from a world—a lifetime—away.

My Chorus-Girl-with-a-Heart-of-Gold and Evangeline, my childhood friend and now a big Broadway star, faced each other across the luxurious Art Deco drawing-room of the gangster's lair. She had taken him away from me. I didn't really want him, but I knew that he was poison for her. He would cost her her reputation, her career, perhaps even her life. We began to quarrel soundlessly—the Moviola was without sound reproduction equipment.

Enter the gangster, the law not far behind on his heels. He rushes to the desk to get hold of and destroy the incriminating evidence before the District Attorney's men arrive. He ignores both of us. We hurl ourselves at him, begging him to pay attention to us, to make a decision. He shakes us off impatiently. There's no time for women now.

There was no time for anything. Beauregard Sylvester, the Assistant District Attorney, burst through the doorway, chest heaving with what looked like emotion if you didn't know that the Director had made him run three times around the set in order to induce a state of breathlessness that would look like emotion.

Evangeline, who had once been engaged to him before she became infatuated with the villain, fell back, hand pressed to heart. I, too, stepped back out of the way to give hero and villain a clear view of each other for the big confrontation.

Beauregard was alone, anxious to save the reputation of his beloved, to get her out of here before the squad cars arrived—and the photographers. He snapped an order at her. She did not move. The villain sent her a craven smile and held out his hand, seeing her now as his only chance to escape.

Frozen with indecision, she could not move. In the distance, sirens were wailing as the police cars drew near. The villain hurriedly stuffed the last of the vital documents into his briefcase and started for the door.

Beau moved to block his way. They stared at each other across the intervening space, then the villain pulled a gun. He had nothing to lose, he would fry anyway if they caught him. His intention was clear to see. His finger tightened on the trigger. Beau was doomed—or was he?

Evangeline might be paralysed, but I was not. I rushed forward into the path of the speeding bullet. I would save her true love for her (also I was a bit sweet on him myself). The bullet struck me and I collapsed.

The villain dashed away and Beau gave chase. As I lay dying, Evangeline moved at last. She came forward and knelt beside me, cradling me in her arms, recognizing my sacrifice, realizing what a fool she had been.

Evangeline and I glanced at each other with wry smiles above the Moviola and the absorbed heads of our newest audience. In my mind, I could hear the violins that had played throughout the scene.

'I've seen this bit eight times already,' Ursula said, with a catch in her voice. 'And it still makes me cry.'

On the tiny screen, Evangeline and I stared silently into each other's eyes. Her hand supported my head, I clung to her other hand with both of mine. Slowly her eyes filled with tears. We were saying the long goodbye.

'It's tewwific,' Gwenda breathed. 'Simply tewwific. The way you look at each other. All that love, all that understanding . . .' She sniffled and groped for her handkerchief. 'It's heart-bweaking . . .'

Yes, the critics had reacted that way, too. They had

written lyrically of 'the silent struggle to express themselves in these final moments'.

No one knew what a genuine struggle it had been. Evangeline had been doing her best—or worst—to steal the close-up. Throughout that affecting scene, she had been wrestling with my head, trying to turn my face against her bosom so that the back of my head would be to the camera.

Naturally, I wasn't going to take that lying down. Out of camera range, I caught her little finger and slowly bent it backwards. That was when those big expressive eyes gradually filled with tears. Our silent battle raged while the cameras turned. Then, just short of a broken or dislocated finger, she gave up and stopped trying to turn my face away from the camera.

After that, I released her finger and died like a lady.

On the miniature screen, the tension snapped. The Chorus-Girl-with-a-Heart-of-Gold gave one last chipper little smile and sagged in Evangeline's arms. The camera dwelt lovingly on my closed eyes, then panned up to Evangeline's face as a tear slid down her cheek and her lips quivered.

Happily, the boom mike failed to pick up the word she murmured at me. Fade-out.

'Oh, that was so beautiful,' Gwenda sobbed.

'I told you I always cried,' Ursula sniffled.

Hugh, who had slipped in quietly while the scene was running, was blinking rapidly. I turned to take the handkerchief count of the rest of our audience. Des and Jasper seemed quite impressed, too.

'I suppose it's really quite a nice little period piece.' Trust Martha! She was unmoved. Of course she had seen it before, but so had Ursula—and Ursula always cried.

'Oh, what a pity!' Martha leaned forward and frowned at the Moviola critically. 'The rest of the print is ruined. What a shame.'

The next scene, a long shot of Beau chasing the villain, was running through the machine and we all stared glumly at the starbursts, scratches and pinpoints of light characteristic of a deteriorating film.

'No—it's not hopeless.' Ursula snapped off the machine. The tiny screen went dark. 'We just haven't got round to restoring that bit yet. We worked on the major scenes first.'

'Oh?' Martha was nonplussed. 'I thought you'd start at the beginning and work your way through chronologically.'

'Sometimes we do, but when the film is in a bad state, the priority is to save the key scenes. We can patch up the linking scenes later. We don't particularly like doing it that way, but sometimes it's necessary.'

'Apart from which,' Hugh said, 'it's dangerous to have too much of that old nitrate film lying around. The stuff is too volatile—flammable. Beau stores the film not actually being worked on in an outbuilding at his country place. And these rooms are all fireproofed, you may have noticed. Even so, the insurance situation might be tricky if anything should happen.'

I had noticed, as we entered, the reinforced steel door, like that of a bank vault. Presumably the floors and ceiling were similarly reinforced. It could be very nasty if a fire broke out here, with a crowded cinema directly above. *The Towering Inferno* wouldn't be in it. For the first time, I noticed the fire extinguishers clamped to the walls and the little boxes containing the fireproof blankets used to smother flames.

'It's really quite safe.' Hugh correctly interpreted my thoughtful stare. 'Ideally, of course, the laboratory and work rooms should be out in the country, too. Beau wanted it that way, but Juanita refused to countenance it. It was all he could do to persuade her to allow the old films to be stored on their property. Unfortunately, she seems to have taken against films these days—especially the ones in which she didn't appear herself.'

'I'm not surprised,' Evangeline said. 'Beau and I were a romantic team long before Juanita appeared on the scene. It always rankled with her.'

'It's iniquitous!' Ursula clenched her fists, the fire and passion of the true archivist coming to the fore. 'Archivists all over the world are in a race against time to save these cinematic masterpieces. We need all the help we can get. And to think that someone who was actually in the Industry can refuse to—'

'I'm afraid the old girl is actually rather a hindrance,' Hugh said apologetically. 'We've all taken a turn talking to her, but she just won't see reason.'

'She was always a jealous cat,' Evangeline said. 'I'll bet she cooperated all right when it came to her own films.'

'Oh yes.' A wan smile, reminiscent of battles lost and won flickered on Ursula's lips. 'She practically stood over me, trying to tell me how to do it. She seemed to think I could work miracles. I finally had to tell her that my work stopped with the print itself—I couldn't improve her performance.'

'Whe-ew!' Jasper whistled. 'So that was why she was in such a filthy mood last winter.'

'I shouldn't have said it.' Ursula was only partially repentent. 'But I lost my temper. After that, she went back to the country and locked herself away again. She tried to make Beau stop the whole restoration project. Thank heavens he didn't listen to her.'

'Why such urgency?' Martha was puzzled. 'What did you mean when you said you're in a race against time?'

'Because the original film stock was nitrate film and the nitric acid in the stock causes chemical decomposition with the passage of time. It's highly unstable in itself, as well as flammable. Unfortunately, almost all early 35mm films were shot on nitrate stock. The forecast is that most of the early films will have disintegrated beyond restoration by the year 2000. National archives and private archivists all over the world are fighting that deadline to save, restore and copy on to acetate stock as much film as we can.'

'I had no idea it was so complicated,' Martha said.

'Most people haven't. Even we are still discovering all the

complications.' Ursula grinned wryly. 'Once the films are on acetate, the forecast is that they'll be preserved for another one hundred years, or possibly, two. Provided, of course, that they're stored in optimum conditions. Archivists in tropical climates have already had a nasty shock; they've discovered even the triacetate stock is beginning to decompose in their hot and humid conditions. Experiments are going on now with polyester-based stock.

'So, you see, it's still a race against time. Perhaps the best we can hope for is to gain another century, so that future archivists can save our fragile heritage of film art permanently by recopying the work on to material that hasn't even been invented yet.'

Ursula was so intense—and so young. The way she tossed remarks about centuries around. It was beginning to give me a nasty suspicion about her definitions.

'Just how early,' I inquired cautiously, 'are those early films? When did they stop using nitrate stock?'

'They were using it up until 1951.'

'That recently?' Evangeline was as aghast as I. It seemed like only yesterday.

'And I suppose different copies of the film deteriorate at a different rate,' Martha said thoughtfully. 'Evangeline's copy, for instance, is in a lot better state of preservation than the one you seem to be working from.'

'The California climate is probably better for it,' Evangeline said. 'I should imagine the humidity in England—'

She broke off, becoming aware that everyone in the room was staring at her.

'You—' Ursula took a half-step forward. 'You have a copy of *Scars On Her Soul*? A complete copy?'

'Well, it wouldn't be much good if it were partial, would it? Of course I have. I have copies of most of my films. A few companies were too cheap to give me one, but most—'

'Most!' Ursula whispered. 'Do you . . . do you have *When Angels Fall*?'

'No,' Evangeline said grimly. 'I'd fondly imagined we'd destroyed every copy of that.'

'But *Flower of the North*? *Destiny of Darkness*? You have those?'

'Those,' Evangeline said complacently, 'and *Disposing of Larry, Never Since Eve, The Happy Couple, Beast of the Barbary Coast* . . . Really, dear, it would be simpler for me to tell you the titles I *don't* have.'

'Aaah . . .' Ursula's gasp of satisfaction was echoed from the far corner of the room. Jasper met Ursula's eyes and they nodded at each other.

'Beau was right,' Jasper said. 'She still has the first film she ever made.'

And Beau still had the first dollar, but I didn't say it. Evangeline met my eyes and conveyed her own opinion in her Ethel Barrymore voice.

'I believe we have just discovered the real reason why we were so generously invited over here. Retrospective, indeed!'

CHAPTER 15

'I don't know whether I'm feeling my age, or whether some sort of reaction has set in.' I kicked off my shoes and collapsed on the sofa, profoundly grateful to be back in our temporary home.

'Probably a bit of both. I'm quite exhausted myself,' Evangeline admitted. 'Thank heavens Hugh has taken Martha off somewhere.'

'Yes . . . Evangeline, do you think there's something brewing there? I mean, do you think it might come to anything? Hugh actually seems to be seeking Martha out. I wouldn't have thought she was his type at all.'

'Nonsense, they were made for each other.' Evangeline was at the brandy decanter again; we'd have to replenish it in the morning. 'He's a masochist, if I ever saw one.'

'But Martha's not a sadist,' I protested.

'Perhaps not, but she'll keep him apologizing for the rest of his life. He'll have a wonderful time—so will she.' Evangeline brought me my glass and raised her own. 'Here's to them! You may get that girl off your hands, after all!'

'You're sinking an awful lot of brandy these days.' If she could hit below the belt, so could I. 'You'd better be careful. That Ethel Barrymore impersonation is all very well—but you don't want people going around saying they could trot a mouse on *your* breath.'

'I do *not*—' Evangeline quivered with fury—'impersonate Ethel Barrymore!'

'Since when?'

'Mother! Mother!' Martha began her yodeling out in the front hall and continued all the way into the flat.

'I knew it was too good to be true,' Evangeline sighed. 'He's dumped her already.'

'Mother—' Martha burst into the drawing-room and hurled herself at me. 'Mother—' She clung to me.

'What's the matter?' It took a lot to alarm me where Martha was concerned, but I could feel her trembling. 'What's happened?'

'Mother—there's someone sleeping in my bed!'

'Oh no!' I cried. 'Not again!'

'If you're telling your mother the Story of the Three Bears—' Evangeline covered my slip quickly. 'Then you've got that line wrong. It should go, "Someone's *been* sleeping in my bed"—'

'No,' Martha said. 'She's still there.'

Evangeline and I exchanged uneasy glances. It wasn't possible, of course, but on a night like this, it would be very easy to believe in ghosts.

'What did you mean, Mother?' Martha pushed herself away from me and stared at me. 'You said *Not again?*'

'Never mind that now.' Evangeline took the words right

out of my mouth. 'If this isn't your idea of a joke, you'd better show us what you're talking about. Who is it? Do you know?'

'I never saw her before. I—I couldn't look at her too closely—' Martha shuddered. 'She looked hideous—grotesque.'

'Was she—?' My mouth had gone dry. I swallowed a few times and tried again. 'Had she been scalped, too?'

Martha gave a wail of horror and began to cry.

'Oh, come on.' Evangeline pushed us aside and started across the hall. 'We might as well know the worst.'

The form was huddled and still on Martha's bed, but at least she was breathing—in fact, snoring.

'Don't tell me this is Anni?' Even as I spoke, I saw that the hair spread across the pillow was black, so it couldn't be the missing Anni.

'Wake up, you!' With reinforcement behind her, Martha was bolder. She stepped forward and shook the sleeping woman. 'Who are you? How did you get in here?'

'Oooh . . .' The figure on the bed moaned, groaned, stretched and rolled over. 'Wha—?' Then she sat up, but her face didn't.

'Juanita!' Evangeline was a split second ahead of me in identifying her. 'What are *you* doing here?'

'Evangeline—?' Faintly slanted eyes peered up at us from St Bernard pouches. The tip of her nose seemed twisted and one jowl drooped lower than the other. 'How did you get in here?'

'How did you?' Martha snapped. 'That's the question. This is *my* room.'

'I beg your pardon.' Juanita shook herself like a dog coming in out of the rain and her features fell back into place . . . a little. 'This is my *pied-à-terre*. It always has been.'

'*Dear* Juanita.' Evangeline braced herself, then stooped and kissed one lumpy cheek. 'You're looking very . . .' Not even she could finish that sentence.

'I know how I look,' Juanita said harshly. 'I've been trying to spare the world the sight. However, that is no longer possible. I caught the news on television, but they didn't report fully. I had to come to find out for myself. What has been going on here?'

'I wish we knew,' Martha said. 'We're as much in the dark as anybody else.'

Juanita dismissed Martha's plaint with a nod. It did not escape her attention that Evangeline and I had remained silent.

'And what have you two to say for yourselves?' she demanded.

'I might say, "How do you do", if anyone bothered to introduce me,' I said.

'You must be Trixie Dolan,' Juanita said dismissively. 'Beau told me you were accompanying Evangeline. But—' she glared at Martha—'who is this?'

'Martha, my daughter. She, er, joined us later.'

'Indeed?' Juanita inspected Martha closely, then turned back to us. 'I see.'

'That's more than I do,' Evangeline said. 'I understood you chose to remain in the country these days. If you've changed your mind, why come to this house?'

'Where else should I go, when I am needed here?'

'Who needs you?' I realized belatedly that that sounded ruder than I had intended, but I knew that she would not have rushed to Evangeline's side in any hour of need. They had barely been on speaking terms since the days when Beau was courting Juanita while co-starring with Evangeline.

'I mean,' I tried again, 'who—?'

'My grandson!' Juanita stood and drew herself up to her full height. The effect was impressive, so long as you didn't look at the face. 'He is in trouble. Horrible things have happened under his roof. How could you think I would not come to him—at whatever cost to myself?'

'Jasper!' It had come clear to Evangeline, at least. 'I knew there was something familiar about those beady little—I mean, now that I think of it, he *does* remind me of you. And Beau, of course.'

'He takes after his father's side of the family,' Juanita said contemptuously. 'Even to all this stockbroker nonsense.'

'It must be a severe trial to you, I'm sure.' Evangeline was not as sympathetic as she might be. It was obvious that she felt that the world was not missing out on any great talent if the Sylvester line retreated from the stage.

'I'm tired,' Martha complained. (Sometimes, I worried about that girl's stamina.) 'This day has gone on for ever. I want to go to bed and she's—"

'*She*—' Juanita turned a menacing gaze on her. '*She* is occupying her rightful place in a family home. *You* are trespassing!'

'Oh no I'm not,' Martha countered. 'I'm paying for this accommodation. I was told it was all right—'

'Obviously,' Evangeline said quickly, 'since you haven't been coming up to town for such a long while, Jasper thought you wouldn't mind if he let someone else use the place. I take it you've arrived unexpectedly?'

'I telephoned,' Juanita said sulkily, 'but there was no answer. Naturally, I came straight to my own quarters—I was not to know I had been dispossessed.'

'Where am I going to sleep tonight?' Martha's voice began rising. 'That's what I want to know.'

Never volunteer. That chaise-longue was probably lumpier than Juanita's face. I kept my mouth shut.

'Jasper must be home now,' Evangeline said. 'Why don't you go up and talk to him, Juanita? If he has the whole flat upstairs, there must be room for you there.'

'I have always tried never to invade his privacy,' Juanita said. 'That is why I have my own quarters. He is young, hot-blooded, he does not want his grandmother playing duenna—'

'Nevertheless—' Evangeline took her arm firmly and steered her towards the door. 'I'm afraid he's going to have to put up with it for tonight. Martha is right, it's been a long day and she needs her sleep. We all do. Let's go and throw ourselves on Jasper's mercy.'

It was a close thing, but I did not wind up on the chaise-longue in Evangeline's room. I continued to occupy my own room and Martha kept the studio flat across the hall. We found that Jasper, despite his hot blood, was not entertaining female company that night and was gratifyingly glad to see his granny. He happily settled her in his guest room and we all got a good night's sleep.

In the morning, I decided I had had enough—more than enough—of the lot of them. I dressed quickly and quietly, didn't stop for breakfast, just scribbled a note telling them I'd declared a holiday and they could expect me when they saw me, and silently left the house.

Oh, the glorious freedom! I treated myself to Harrod's, a pub lunch, and a matinee of the latest comedy. Then, pausing only for more refreshment, I went on to an evening performance of another show. It left me purring. This was the sort of thing I had come to London to enjoy. Two theatres in one day—this was more like it.

I was so pleased with myself by the end of the evening that I decided to be an absolute daredevil and take the Underground home. After all, millions of people did it every day, it couldn't be all that hard. And I could always ask directions if I got lost—I was in an English-speaking country.

I went into Leicester Square Station and the man didn't seem at all surprised when I asked for a ticket to St John's Wood, so I figured I was doing all right. An idiot could have read the colour-coded map of the Underground on the wall. Signs were plentiful and those helpful colours kept you heading in the right direction for the line you wanted.

According to the wall map, my best bet was to go to Charing Cross and then change to the Jubilee Line which would take me straight to St John's Wood Station. It couldn't be simpler.

Except that I must have taken the wrong turning somewhere. I found myself trudging miles of passageways with rounded walls and roof (I could see why it was also called the Tube). I began to think that I was going to walk all the way to St John's Wood.

I turned yet another corner and went down a deserted passageway. Ahead, I could hear a faint melodic echo which gradually grew louder as I moved nearer, giving the promise of life and human company somewhere deep in these echoing caverns. I hurried my steps, anxious to find the Pied Piper at the end of the corridor.

The music lilted and soared, lifting my heart and tempting my feet to dance. The unknown musician was good—very good. There was something of Benny Goodman about him, not an imitation, just a faint shadowing.

Of course. I turned the final corner and nearly stumbled over him—it was the instrument: the clarinet.

Unexpectedly, the musician blew a sour note and missed the next note altogether. And he had been doing so well.

'Trixie!' It was my fault. He lowered the instrument and stared at me in horror.

'Des!' He had recognized me before I recognized him, but I knew him now. 'What are you doing here?'

It would be difficult to say which of us blushed harder then, because it was all too clear what he was doing. Coins gleamed on a square of sacking at his feet. As we stared at each other, mutually aghast, hurrying footsteps sounded behind us and someone pitched a fivepence piece at the sacking. It missed, hit the floor, bounced and rolled.

Automatically, I put my foot on it before it could get away. Then we both blushed again. This was ridiculous! I stooped, picked up the coin and tossed it on the sacking.

'You earned it,' I said. 'Never be ashamed of money honestly earned. You're a damned good musician. I've worked with a lot and I know. I'm delighted to have had a chance to hear you play.'

'Thank you.' He seemed overcome. 'This is just temporary, you know, until I get a proper job again—'

'Do you think I don't know? Believe me, I've done my share of "resting" in my time. Only nothing so civilized as busking—not where I came from. I was stuck with slinging hash and pearl diving. Doing waitress work—' I spelled it out for him, as he looked confused. 'And washing dishes. The hours were rotten, the tips were lousy, and it was a toss-up which was going to cave in first, your feet or your back. But it was honest work and I earned an honest dollar. I'm not ashamed of it and neither should you be.'

'I'm not, really,' he said. 'It's just that, it may be honest, but it isn't quite legal. They have laws about busking in the Underground. There are heavy fines if we get caught.'

'Don't worry, I'm not going to go around telling anybody.' It was now clear why Des had refused to tell Heyhoe where he was working the other night. The rigmarole about Arab parties *was* better than admitting to illegal busking in the Tube. If Heyhoe knew that Des was breaking one law, he would assume that Des would break any and all laws.

'No,' Des said. 'You wouldn't, would you? You're not that sort.'

'Play something else for me.' I wasn't fool enough to insult him by opening my purse. 'I'd love to hear some more. You just about had me dancing down the corridor.'

'Right you are!' He raised the clarinet to his lips, winked at me and swung into *I'm Looking for a Man with a Heart of Gold*, the *Gold Diggers'* theme song.

Well, I know a cue when I hear one. I hiked up my skirt and went into the old routine.

Suddenly, we had an audience. I had been dimly aware of a roaring sound in the distance. It seemed that a train had come into the station and disgorged its passengers. Some of them hurried past, but a lot of them stopped to watch.

'Hey—look at the old girl go!' It could have been better phrased, I thought, but it didn't stop me. I was caught up in the music and the dance.

'Jeez!' a tourist voice said. 'They make their grandmothers work with them in this country?'

I could still do it. I high-kicked his silly hat off.

There was a burst of laughter and applause. A shower of coins rained on the sacking. The incautious one retrieved his hat and came up grinning—he tossed a pound coin into the kitty.

'Let me through, please—' Someone on the edge of the crowd began pushing to the front.

'Oh-oh, watch it!' someone warned.

'Transport police!' Des broke off abruptly. 'Let's get out of here!'

'The money—' I bent to gather up our takings, as Des pulled at me. I got most of it gathered up in the sack before he won the tug-of-war.

'Come on!' He gripped me, I held tight to the sack and we ran, jingling, towards another roaring sound in the distance. Behind us, pounding footsteps pursued.

Again, we were caught up in endless corridors, the footsteps drew nearer. My legs were weakening, there was a stitch in my side, I could not catch my breath properly.

'I can't—' I gasped. 'I can't run any more. You go ahead—let him catch me. I don't care.'

'Right.' Des did not slacken his pace nor let go of my arm. 'You want me to tell Martha to come down and bail you out at the Magistrates' Court in the morning?'

He'd said the magic words. Suddenly, my second wind came through. Now I was ahead of him, racing down the flight of stairs.

Ahead of us, the doors of the waiting train began to slide shut. We put on one final burst of speed, Des wedged his shoulder against one door and held it while I slipped through.

Des let the doors slam shut, the train began to move, and we collapsed into seats as the baleful face of the transport policeman receded.

'We made it!' I crowed. 'And I've still got all the money. Look!' I jingled the sack at him.

'Hey—great!' He threw his arms around me and we hugged and giggled wildly.

'You were terrific!' he said.

'So were you!'

We began to notice that we were getting some very peculiar sidelong glances from our fellow passengers, but that just made us giggle harder. Des tootled his clarinet at them, but we were laughing too much and he couldn't play it properly.

'We change here.' The train slid to a stop at the next station and we got out, doubtless to the great relief of the other passengers.

After that, it was clear sailing until we got to St John's Wood.

CHAPTER 16

'And where have you been all this time?' Evangeline demanded.

'Mother, we've been worried sick. You might have let us know—'

'I left a note,' I pointed out indignantly. 'What more did you want—hourly bulletins?'

'They wouldn't have come amiss,' Evangeline said. 'And it might have kept you in touch with what was going on here. While you've been kicking up your heels all over London—'

I kept my face blank. She couldn't possibly know how close to the mark she'd come.

'—we've had quite a day. The police were back.'

'They wanted to know where you were,' Martha said ominously. 'And we couldn't tell them.'

'Good.' It had obviously been the right day to disappear. In retrospect, I'd had an even better day than I'd thought.

'Well,' Martha said, 'where *were* you?'

'Oh, here, there and everywhere.' With my most innocent expression, I pulled out the programmes for the matinee and evening shows and tossed them on the table. 'I've been catching up with some West End productions.'

'Not a bad alibi,' Evangeline said judiciously. 'I suppose you also have the ticket stubs, and you were undoubtedly chatty enough with the box-office people and the programme sellers so that they'd remember you?'

'Undoubtedly.' I used my innocent smile this time. It cut no ice. 'So you've had a busy day with the police, have you?'

'Indeed, and furthermore—' Perhaps Evangeline had taken my earlier comments to heart, she no longer sounded like Ethel Barrymore in the last stages of despair.

'Furthermore—' She was now using a straight documentary Voice of Doom. 'We have had Juanita flinging a fandango all over the place all day.'

'Well, it's her house,' I said. 'Or her grandson's.'

'That's part of the problem,' Martha said. 'The police took Jasper away as soon as he got home from the office. They said they wanted him to help with inquiries—but he hasn't come back yet.'

'Oh!' That was serious. 'But I thought they'd cleared him of any involvement with Mick's death.'

'It wasn't Mick they were inquiring about this time.' Evangeline carefully avoided my eyes. 'Anni is still missing . . . and it seems that they've pulled a body out of the canal recently . . .'

'Oh!' That was even worse.

'Yes. And, since Jasper owns the house and is older than the others, they took him to look at the body and see if he could identify it as Anni's.'

'Oh!' No wonder he wasn't back yet. He'd be lucky if he was out by New Year. No matter which way that cat decided to jump, he was for it. If he told the truth and identified the body as Fiona's, he'd opened a whole new can of beans and they'd be questioning him for days yet. If he decided to lie and claimed that it was Anni's body, he was still going to have a lot of explaining to do.

'Exactly,' Evangeline said grimly.

'Oh! Oh dear . . .'

'For heaven's sake, stop saying *"Oh!"* Mother! Can't you see how appalling this situation is?'

'Oh yes,' I said. If Martha could see half of what I was seeing, she'd be on the next plane back to Los Angeles —police permission or not.

'I thought I heard the front door—' Juanita came into the drawing-room and looked around eagerly. She saw me and her face fell—more than usual, that is. 'Oh, it's you.'

'Sorry—' I apologized.

'Pah!' she spat and turned on her heel.

Evangeline rolled her eyes at me, obviously close to the end of her tether.

'I warn you—' Juanita spun on her heel and faced us again. 'If anything happens to my grandson, I shall wreak such vengeance as the world has never known!'

'*Dear* Juanita, that always was one of your best lines. Why don't you save it until morning and give Superintendent Hi-de-Ho the benefit of it?'

'Pah!' She exited, leaving silence behind her as we waited uneasily to see if she was going to take an encore.

'Sometimes,' Evangeline said at last, 'one wonders whether one has underestimated dear Beau's patience—or his stupidity.'

Across the hallway, a door slammed.

'I can't stand much more of this,' Martha said tear-fully. 'Mother, can't we go home?' She was quivering with nerves.

'Why don't you go to bed?' I suggested. 'Things will look better in the morning.'

'I can't!' Martha wailed. 'That awful woman has taken my room again!'

'Then go upstairs and take hers!' I snapped.

'Oh no, I couldn't do that. Jasper might come back.'

'So what? Even if he does, you don't think he's going to try to climb into bed with his grandmother, do you?'

'Mother!' She couldn't even take a joke.

How had it happened? Despite her age, Martha and the Permissive Society had missed all contact. She was a throwback to a Victorian generation. Or was it some basic insecurity? Was it because she had never had a father around during the vital years? It wasn't really my fault. I had divorced twice and been widowed once. Not a bad record, as Hollywood records go. Still, with Evangeline's censorious gaze on me, I felt guilty.

'Oh, all right,' I said. 'You can take *my* room and *I'll* go upstairs.'

'Mother, you can't!' But Martha cheered up immediately.

'Why not? If Jasper isn't back by now, it's highly unlikely he'll be back tonight . . .'

I was less brave as I entered the *terra incognita* of Jasper's flat. It was not until the doorknob turned under my hand and I was able to walk in that it occurred to me that possibly the flat should have been locked.

On the other hand, Juanita had been flouncing in and out of the flat all day, so perhaps it wasn't surprising. She was great at slamming doors; I doubted that she was so good at locking them.

Half-expecting to be challenged, I moved through the shadowed flat. The lights seemed dimmer than the lights downstairs. The layout was different, somehow, more old-fashioned, despite the more modern furniture. It occurred to me that this was probably the way our flat had looked before the extensive renovations.

This was a good adequate flat, but no one would ever mistake it for a love-nest.

That expression again—why did it keep teasing at the corner of my mind?

I opened the wrong door on a masculine room in terminal disarray which looked even worse because of the unmade bed. I snapped off the light and shut the door again quickly.

The next door obviously opened into the right room. I could smell Juanita's perfume and did not appreciate it. Opening the window would take care of that.

The light revealed a room nearly as slovenly as Jasper's —he came by it honestly, it seemed. This bed, too, was unmade. Evidently, the landlord didn't get his own flat serviced—which seemed a bit odd.

Of more concern to me at the moment was the sudden distaste I felt about slipping between those rumpled sheets.

I opened the window and let the room begin to air while I thought it over. I would feel silly about retreating downstairs again—anyway, it wouldn't do any good, there was no bed for me and Martha would just have something more to complain about.

The day was catching up with me and I was so tired I could have slept on a picket fence. I would have preferred a clean picket fence, but life is a series of compromises, anyway.

The room smelled fresher now, if damper. Most of the lingering traces of the cloying scent clung to the pillows. I stripped off the pillowcases and the bottom sheet and dropped them in an untidy (it was catching) heap just outside the bedroom door. Then I tucked the top sheet down firmly and let the blanket serve as the second sheet.

It was only marginally more satisfactory than that picket fence, but I was too tired to be choosy. I closed the window and fell into bed. I was asleep almost as soon as my head touched the pillow.

*

At first I thought I was having another nightmare. Then I thought vaguely that it was an action replay of my awakening the other morning—but that wasn't quite right, either. At least I had been getting second-hand air then; none at all was reaching me now. Something soft and smothering was being pressed down over my face . . . Finally, my groggy brain snapped to alertness—almost too late.

Someone was trying to kill me!

I pushed at the pillow covering my face, but the person bending over me, holding it down firmly, was prepared for that feeble struggle.

I began to fight back furiously in the only way I could, taking my attacker by surprise. Thank heaven for my dancer's muscles! I drew my legs up and lashed out with them, catching someone in the stomach.

The pressure on the pillow disappeared and I hurled it away from me. Now I could hear someone scrabbling across the floor towards the door, panting for breath.

Or was that me? I was drawing in great lungfuls of air, not silently at all. I fumbled for the lamp switch, but the door opened and closed before I found it. When the light went on, my assailant was gone. I decided to quit while I was ahead —I wasn't going to chase him.

I staggered over to the window and opened it wide, leaning out into a night that had unexpectedly become clear and crisp. A bright moon illuminated the garden beneath.

A full moon—was that the answer? Why else would anyone want to kill me? It must have been a lunatic. A homicidal lunatic, triggered off by the night of the full moon.

It had happened like that in *Moon Without Mercy*. For a moment it seemed quite possible, reasonable, even.

Then the oxygen began clearing my brain and a more logical explanation sprang into it: everyone had known Juanita was using this room, someone was trying to kill *her*.

They'd have had a good chance of succeeding, too. You could tell just by looking at her that she hadn't kept herself in shape. She'd let her muscles go flabby and put on too much fat—she would never have been able to fight off the attacker the way I had.

It must have been a nasty shock for someone when I kicked them across the room. Almost as nasty as the shock I had had when I came back to consciousness to find that pillow over my face.

Suddenly I was shivering, and it wasn't just from the cold night air. I wanted—I needed—human warmth and companionship. And I didn't care if I damned well *did* disturb everyone in the house. Someone wasn't sleeping anyway.

'Don't be absurd, Trixie,' Evangeline said coldly. 'You've had a nightmare, that's all.'

It was infuriating. I had no proof that I had been attacked —not even a bruise to display. If the killer had succeeded and removed the pillow before anyone found me in the morning, there was every good chance that it would have been written off as a natural death.

As for Juanita—in the shape she was in, there would have been no doubt at all.

'Oh, Mother—' I had tried to be quiet, but Evangeline had begun making such a fuss that she had wakened Martha. 'Mother, you might have been killed!'

'That's right,' Evangeline said. 'I *told* you to let Martha have that room.'

Martha and I both looked at her suspiciously.

'Just as well I didn't—' Against my better judgement, I gave her the benefit of the doubt. 'Martha's muscles aren't in much better state than Juanita's.'

Evangeline flicked up her eyebrows in that way that meant 'Precisely'; fortunately, Martha missed that.

'Really, Mother, I'm younger and stronger than you—'

'But you haven't her rat-like cunning. If any of us had to be in that room, your mother was the best possible choice. However—' Evangeline abruptly remembered her earlier, more comforting stance. 'However, I don't believe a word of it. I think she just had a very realistic nightmare. Night terrors, I believe they're called.'

Someday I might have another serious go at trying to kill her. I wondered suddenly if the feeling was mutual. Was it remotely possible that it had been Evangeline who had sneaked up the stairs and into my room and held that pillow over my face?

No. Sanity reasserted itself. If it had been Evangeline I had sent flying, she would never have recovered so fast. Nor was she strong enough physically to have borne down on the pillow with that relentless pressure that had almost finished me.

'Listen!' I held up my hand for silence and we could hear stealthy sounds in the hall outside.

'He's trying to get away!' With reinforcements, I was ready to give chase. 'Let's go get him!'

Martha trailed behind us, whimpering protests as we rushed silently to the hall door and flung it open.

'Stay where you are!' Evangeline roared. 'I have a gun!'

'Don't shoot!' a terrified voiced pleaded. 'It's all right. It's only me.'

'Martha, get the lights!' I ordered.

For once, she did as she was told without protest. There was a click and the hall flooded with light. Hugh Carpenter stood frozen at the foot of the stairs.

'Please, put the gun away,' he begged. He'd believe anything of Evangeline. 'Why—' He blinked in the light as the truth registered. 'Why, you haven't got a gun at all.'

'Oh,' Evangeline said flatly. 'It's *you*. I might have known it.'

'What—?' The door opposite opened and Juanita filled the doorway, looking like the Phantom of the Opera after a bad night. 'What is going on here? Why have we a crowd scene in the front hall in the middle of the night?'

'Please, let's all keep calm,' Hugh said desperately. 'I'm

sorry I roused the house, we were trying not to disturb anyone. I've just driven Jasper home from the police station; they've just released him.'

'A likely story!' Evangeline snorted. 'Where is he? Produce him!'

'Here I am.' Jasper appeared at the top of the stairs. He had obviously entered silently earlier. It had been Hugh who had stumbled and given the game away.

'My baby!' Juanita possessed a good turn of speed for her age and condition. She raced up the stairs and entwined herself around the embarrassed Jasper. 'My *pobrecito!* Are you all right? Did they hurt you? We will sue them for false arrest!'

'I wasn't arrested,' Jasper said. 'I was just helping with inquiries.'

'*Pah!* That is what they always announce officially—just before they slam the cell door! They are liars and—'

Jasper swayed against his grandmother, going paler than ever.

'Take it easy, old man.' Hugh bounded up the stairs to take the weight from Juanita. 'Look—' he appealed to us, 'this lad's been through enough tonight. Let him get to bed now. You can continue this in the morning.'

'But what happened?' Juanita clung to Jasper as Hugh tried to detach her. 'You must tell me. That girl—it was Anni, yes? That is why you are so shocked. You identified the body?'

'Yes—' Jasper said—'but it wasn't Anni.' He gave his grandmother a guilty secretive look. 'It was Fiona.'

There was a strange silence.

'Who's Fiona?' Evangeline remembered that we weren't supposed to know.

Everyone ignored the question. Hugh caught Jasper around the shoulders and bundled him into his room.

Juanita descended the stairs slowly with an air of preoccupied satisfaction. A secret smile twisted her uneven lips.

I had the sudden conviction that she knew about Fiona
—and she knew a lot more than we did.

CHAPTER 17

'It should be obvious to the meanest intelligence,' Evangeline said. 'It was Jasper who tried to kill you last night, under
the impression that you were his grandmother.'

'If anyone caught you saying that, Jasper could sue you for
everything up to and including your back teeth. Jasper is
practically the only person in the house with an alibi—he
was at the police station all night.'

'Was he? Just remember, he appeared at the *top* of the
stairs. Who knows how long he'd been up there.'

'But Hugh had just brought him home.'

'So he says, but you know how long it takes Hugh to park
his car. There could well have been ample time for Jasper to
slip upstairs and try to kill you before Hugh came blundering
in and roused the house.'

'I hate to say it, Mother—' Martha poured more coffee all
around. 'But she might be right. There's another point:
Juanita was still in that room when Jasper left for the police
station, he wouldn't have known we'd all changed rooms
again while he was gone.'

'I'm sure it couldn't have taken Hugh that long to park at
that hour of the night—morning.' But there was another
pertinent fact I wasn't going to encourage them by mention-
ing. Those pillowcases and that sheet heaped just outside the
bedroom door and reeking of Juanita's scent would have led
anyone to believe that she was still there. In the darkness, the
heap of laundry would not have been distinguishable as
such, but the spoor from it would have convinced anyone
that they had come to the right room.

'Hugh isn't that clumsy,' Martha went off on a tangent

suddenly. 'He's just so abrupt sometimes that he seems awkward.'

'Hmmph!' Evangeline was always ready for a sparring match. 'That man could have more legs than a centipede and he'd still wind up with every foot crammed into his mouth!'

'That's unfair! Just because you don't like him, you—'

I tiptoed away and left them to it. Interesting though I found Martha's defence of Hugh, it would probably come to nothing. There had been other lame ducks over the years, but she had always elected to remain with the one she considered lamest of all—me. How did I get so lucky?

It was too much to hope for to be able to sneak away again today, but I decided to give it the old college try. I dressed rapidly and got as far as the front door. Then I made a major mistake: I opened it.

Detective-Superintendent Heyhoe stood there, his finger poised to ring the doorbell.

'Good morning, madam,' he said nastily. 'Going somewhere, were we?'

'I was just absconding to Honolulu with the Widows' and Orphans' Fund,' I said. 'How about you?'

Detective-Sergeant Singer snickered, earning black looks from both of us.

'We thought we'd make a few more inquiries,' Heyhoe said. 'Now that we have a bit more to inquire about.'

'Have you?' I asked innocently. 'You do start early in the morning, don't you?'

'You never can tell what the early bird will catch. May we come in?'

When it comes from a policeman, how do you say no to a request like that? I stepped back and they moved into the hallway.

'You want the upstairs flat, I suppose.' I tried to plant the suggestion in their minds.

'Now why should you suppose that? As long as we're downstairs, we might as well start here. The others are up, I trust?'

'In the kitchen, finishing breakfast. Would you like some coffee?'

'Coffee?' The door opposite opened and Juanita stepped out. 'Good! I could use some.' She paused to bestow an automatic smirk on the two male strangers, then lost no time heading for the kitchen.

'Who was that?' Heyhoe was reeling visibly. Juanita was no sight for anyone of a sensitive disposition first thing in the morning.

I toyed with saying, 'I never saw her before in my life—I thought she was with you,' but he was in no mood for games.

'That's Jasper's grandmother,' I said. 'She's rushed up to Town to defend what seems to be the only cub in the litter.'

'You mean—' Now Detective-Sergeant Singer was reeling. 'You mean *that's* Juanita Morez? Beauregard Sylvester's wife?'

'Come along, Singer,' Heyhoe said impatiently, having been the first to recover. He led the way down the hall, gave a perfunctory tap and threw open the kitchen door.

'Oh, it's you, Hoo-Hay,' Evangeline said wearily. '*Now* what?'

'That's Heyhoe, madam.'

'*What's in a name?*'

'Quite so, madam. Perhaps you wouldn't mind a few more questions?'

'Haven't we answered enough already?'

'In the light of information received, we find it necessary to reopen inquiries.'

'Who *is* this man?' Juanita demanded.

'This is the policeman—' Evangeline had no compunction about unleashing her on him—'who kept dear Jasper at the police station all night.'

'*You* did that?' Juanita advanced on him dangerously, every wattle quivering with fury. '*Pah!* I spit on you—and your questions!'

'As you wish, madam.' Buster Keaton couldn't have kept

a deader pan. 'Nevertheless, inquiries must be pursued.'

Detective-Sergeant Singer unlimbered his notepad and stood waiting.

'Martha,' I said, 'please pour the gentlemen some coffee.' They did not object and, for a wonder, Martha obeyed without argument.

'*Dear* Trixie—' Evangeline swept me with a glance that took in my hat, coat—and intentions. 'You were on your way out. You mustn't let us keep you.'

She wanted to get rid of me. She didn't trust what I might reveal—and she was right. I had no objections to getting out of the way myself.

'That's right.' I began sidling towards the door. 'I'll be getting along—'

'Just a moment, madam.' Heyhoe barred my way. 'We'd like a few words before you go.'

I didn't need Evangeline's warning glance to tell me that I had to be very careful.

'Fiona Jones,' Heyhoe said abruptly. 'What do you know about her.'

'Nothing,' I answered, adding with perfect truth, 'I never met her. Who is she?'

'Was she someone we met at the Press Reception or Premiere?' Evangeline asked helpfully. 'One meets so many people at these parties—the names and faces all blur together.'

'I don't think you'd have met her there, madam. She hasn't been to many parties recently.'

Juanita had gone very quiet. No longer projecting righteous fury, she had retreated to the farthest chair and blanked out all personality. She could have been a disembodied spririt, just barely visible, as she sat there sipping her coffee. If Heyhoe had been more astute, he would have realized immediately that he was questioning the wrong people.

As it was, it took him several more questions before he

began to notice something odd about the atmosphere. He paused in mid-question and lifted his head, sniffing almost audibly, like an old hound catching the scent.

Which was just what had happened. Juanita had shifted position suddenly, sending a shock wave of scent across the table. Her scent had more presence than she had—and it wasn't going to take the greatest brain in the Universe to wonder why.

Evangeline had been casting sidelong glances in Juanita's direction for the past few minutes.

Juanita raised her coffee cup and tried to hide behind it as she realized that every eye was upon her. For once, she did not appreciate being in the limelight.

'Mrs Sylvester—' Heyhoe spoke with deceptive gentleness, perhaps remembering that she and Beauregard had paid a great deal in taxes over the years. 'Mrs Sylvester, what do you know about your grandson's liaison with Fiona Jones?'

'It is not true!' Juanita flared. 'He had nothing to do with that girl!'

'Really? His friends seem to think otherwise. Perhaps he kept it a secret from you, knowing that you would not approve.'

'There are no secrets between us!'

It was as unlikely a story as any I had ever heard and, obviously, Heyhoe felt the same.

'Quite so, madam,' he said flatly. 'Nevertheless, the consensus of opinion appears to be—'

'*That* for your consensus!' Juanita hurled the contents of her coffee cup into his face and charged from the room while we all stood frozen.

The trouble with real life is that there is no Director to shout, 'Cut', and tidy up the action between shots. Heyhoe stood there, with coffee dripping from his jowls; Singer lowered his notebook and stared at him aghast. Martha sprang for a tea-towel and began mopping down Heyhoe—a gesture he did not appreciate. He snatched the towel from her and dabbed furiously at his face. Whatever else, Juanita had just forfeited her status as a respected taxpayer and joined the rest of us felons.

'I have a fearful headache,' Evangeline announced firmly. 'I'm going back to bed.'

'I'm afraid I still have a few more questions, madam.'

'You can speak to me later.' Evangeline continued her stately progress towards the door. 'I'm far too ill right now.'

'I can either ask them here, madam, or I shall be obliged to require you to accompany me to the station and answer them there.'

'You wouldn't dare!'

Anyone else would have known better than to speak to a senior police official like that. Anyone but Evangeline.

In *The Happy Couple* series, everyone from the local patrolman to the Commissioner of Police had caved in when she faced them with flashing eyes and imperious manner. Heyhoe just seemed to grow two feet taller; his eyes and voice turned to steel.

'Sergeant, have the car brought round,' he ordered.

'No, please—' Martha tried to intercede. 'You can't do that. She's old—she doesn't understand. She doesn't know what she's saying. She doesn't mean it.'

'Are you suggesting I'm mentally incompetent?' Evangeline snapped. 'I can assure you I mean every word I've ever uttered—especially to Hay-Hee here.'

'I never doubted that you did, madam.' Heyhoe's face was grim. 'That's why we're going to continue this little session at the station.'

'You ought to be ashamed of yourself!' Martha railed. 'Haven't you got anything better to do than run around harassing old ladies?'

'Just come along now, madam.' He ignored Martha.

'If you persist in this ridiculous· course of action—' Evangeline threatened. 'I won't solve your case for you.'

'I wasn't aware that I was relying on you to do so, madam.' Now she'd done it; he was livid with rage.

'Look—' I tried to distract him. 'This *is* ridiculous. Martha is right—you should have better things to do. Why aren't you out looking for Anni? She and Mick were lovers —everybody knows that makes her the most likely suspect. Now she's disappeared. She must have run away because she killed him.'

'Possibly, madam. But why should she have killed him?'

'Because he knew she'd killed Fiona! Maybe he was even the cause of it. I'll bet he made a pass at Fiona—or vice versa—and Anni caught them at it. In Jasper's flat. Then there was that struggle—heaven knows there was enough noise. Of course,' I admitted, 'it's possible Fiona's death was an accident. She may have hit her head when she fell and it was more fatal than it would have been for someone else —she seemed to bruise easily. But Mick got rid of the body—because he was doing it for Anni—'

'Trixie, shut up!' But not even Ethel Barrymore at her most thunderous could stop me now.

'After that, Anni decided she had to kill him, too, because he knew what she'd done and he was basically too honest not to tell someone eventually. She thought he was the only one who knew Fiona was dead. She didn't know we knew—'

'Indeed, madam? Neither did I.'

'Mother, what are you saying?'

'I told you to shut up, Trixie!'

'Ladies, ladies—' Heyhoe was almost genial, now that things were going his way. 'Be calm, ladies. We're *all* going to go down to the station now and sort this out.'

'Not Martha,' I said quickly. 'She doesn't know a thing about it. She didn't arrive until it was all over.'

'Ah?' Heyhoe was less than devastated at the news that Martha's presence was unnecessary. 'Perhaps not Martha, then. We can always speak to her later.' He began herding us towards the front door.

'Don't say anything more until I get there with a lawyer, Mother!' Martha followed us, shrieking instructions. 'I'll call Hugh—'

'Oh, fine,' Evangeline muttered. 'That will be a great help!'

CHAPTER 18

If I should live for another thousand years, I never want to have another day like that one.

Oh, the police were perfectly polite, charming, even. They poured tea into us until it was squirting out of our ears. They were patient, courteous—and relentless. By the time I had answered the same questions sixteen times, I couldn't have lied, even if I'd wanted to. Which I didn't.

Evangeline could get as mad as she liked, but it was high time Heyhoe knew the truth. Not that I knew whether she was still mad, or not. They had separated us almost as soon as we arrived at the police station and put us into different rooms. After all, it had become pretty much of a blur as various policemen took turns questioning me.

By the time they let us go, I felt like the victim in a science-fiction movie. One of those losers who'd been strung up by their heels on a meat hook and systematically drained of blood and desinewed to provide sustenance for some vampiric monster from Outer Space.

Evangeline and I slumped in opposite corners of the back seat of the police car and didn't even speak to each other. With luck, she might never speak to me again—but I knew I couldn't count on that kind of luck.

Nor, probably, could I could on Martha's having been locked up permanently. At one point I had heard her shrieking and Hugh bleating outside my interrogation room. Their voices had risen to an uncomfortable pitch of arrogance and demand—then, unaccountably, fallen silent. After a few minutes, it had become clear that, whatever else had happened, the rescue bid had failed.

The police car swerved into the carriageway and drew up at the foot of the steps. Detective-Sergeant Singer leaped merrily out of the front seat and came round to open the door for us. Ah, youth! He was as fresh as he had been first thing this morning. He held the door open as two bedraggled wrecks crept past him.

'I'll see you later,' he said to Evangeline, who surprised me.

Instead of snapping, 'Not if I see you first,' she nodded.

'Come for after-dinner drinks, dear boy,' she invited. 'We can discuss our little project then.'

'Very good.' He gave her an intimate look and patted his notebook pocket. Was he concealing evidence for her?

She was scheming again and it was more than I could bear. I went up the steps and left them to it. I was feeling too exhausted—too old—to try to cope with her. I could feel myself slowing down, each step seemed too high to mount . . .

'Twixie!' The front door flew open. 'Oh, thank goodness! We've been wowwied sick!' Gwenda rushed down the steps to hug me, nearly knocking me over. Then, arm around my waist, she half-carried me up the remaining steps.

When I turned at the top, Evangeline was still lollygagging with Detective-Sergeant Singer. She had obviously not been put through as much of a wringer as I had—and the thought annoyed me. However, with Gwenda babbling happily beside me, it was hard not to look on the bright side.

'Has Martha come back yet?'

'No, she went out wight after you did and I haven't seen her since. Hugh was going to meet her at the police station and I haven't seen him, either.'

'Oh well, they'll be along eventually.' I could guarantee it. Nothing was going to keep Martha away for very long. No matter how much she had annoyed the police, there was a limit to what they could do about it. I thought wistfully of a nice Court case where a Judge could sentence someone to a term in prison for Contempt of Court. No doubt the police had been equally wistful.

'Do you think we should wing the police station and find out what's happened?'

'I'd rather not know.' I followed her into the front hall. Evangeline was now climbing the steps behind us, leaning heavily on the wrought-iron railing.

Juanita's door remained closed, for which I was profoundly grateful. I had had enough for one day.

'Come upstairs,' Gwenda urged. 'I'll make tea—high tea. You must be wavenous.'

'Not tca.' I shuddered. 'I couldn't face another cup. Come to think of it, I can't face any more stairs, either. Why don't we all go out to dinner?' That would also postpone the evil moment when I would have to face Martha.

'Oh!' Her face lit up. 'That would be—'

'Nonsense!' Evangeline had come up behind us. 'I'm far too tired to go trailing out again to some restaurant. We'll telephone one of those catering services and have meals brought to us. It will be quicker and easier. Of course you'll join us, my dear,' she added to Gwenda. 'Perhaps you could recommend the best caterer.'

'Oh yes,' Gwenda said. 'Don't wowwy about a thing. I'll take care of it for you. Do you want Italian, Indian, English —or Chinese again?'

'English,' we chorused firmly.

Juanita's door opened and my heart sank. We should have known better than to stand discussing food in the entrance hall. It was the one sure way to smoke her out.

'Oh!' Ursula stood in the doorway, clutching an armload of towels and bed linen. 'I didn't realize anyone was out here. I was just—' She broke off in confusion.

'Just what?' Evangeline demanded.

'Well . . . servicing the flats,' Ursula admitted. 'It's Anni's job, really, but since she isn't around, we can't leave our guests with unmade beds and dirty towels.'

'Anni's job . . .' Evangeline was thoughtful. 'Does Haw-Hee know that?'

'I don't think so.' Ursula shrugged. 'I don't see why our domestic arrangements need concern him.'

'Quite right,' Evangeline approved; she loved the idea that she might know something Heyhoe didn't. 'And it's very kind of you to concern yourself with our comfort. We're just sending out for dinner, you must join us.'

'Why, thank you,' Ursula said hesitantly, 'I'd like that. I must just put this in the laundry basket first.' She turned and started up the stairs, stopped half way and turned back. 'You're sure—?'

'Quite sure,' Evangeline said. 'We'll be delighted to have you.'

Ursula gave her a shy half-smile, turned and vanished up the stairs. Gwenda was perhaps less delighted to have a rival for our attention, but followed us into the flat with good grace and began telephoning our orders while we went to our rooms to freshen up.

The rooms were neat and tidy, beds made and all surfaces sparkling—as they had been all along, both pre- and post-Anni. Remembering the state of Jasper's flat, I realized that Ursula was only extending her courtesy services to us and not to her landlord. Presumably, she drew the line at taking over Anni's chores completely. It was neighbourly enough of her to take care of us—after all, she'd been working hard all day.

Evangeline repaired her make-up, humming under her breath, and I remembered something else.

'Just what,' I asked suspiciously, 'have you got going with Sergeant Singer? I should think you'd never want to see him again after today. Why have you invited him round this evening?'

'He's a dear boy, really,' Evangeline said absently. 'He may have to earn a living in the police force, but his heart is in the right place—the cinema.'

'How nice.' Maybe I'd feel better after some food, but I was in a nasty mood right now. 'What a pity the parade's gone by. He'd better stick with the police, there's more of a future in it.'

'Oh, I don't know . . .' Evangeline was being maddening again. 'There are still opportunities—if one knows where to look.'

'I hope he isn't thinking of looking to Beau. You told me he was on the verge of bankruptcy.'

'That was several days ago,' Evangeline said complacently. 'I gather the situation is improving by the hour. Several more floors of Cinema City have been rented since all the publicity began.'

'You can't mean it! After all *that* publicity?'

'Trixie, you know perfectly well that there's no such thing as bad publicity—so long as they spell your name right.' Evangeline leaned into the mirror and applied fresh lipstick. 'In *our* business, at least. I'm not so sure Jasper's stockbrokerage is entirely happy about developments. But—' she blotted the lipstick—'that's *his* problem.'

'I'm beginning to feel sorry for poor Jasper. His family must be a sore trial to him—and now his friends aren't proving much better.'

'If you ask me—' Evangeline wore her Hanging Judge's face again.

'I didn't—and don't you dare accuse that poor boy of being a murderer again!'

Dinner was delicious. The girls were charming company and, perhaps best of all, Martha and Hugh continued to be absent. The party spirit only began to fade when the doorbell rang and Sergeant Singer joined us.

Evangeline poured brandy with a lavish hand. 'Trot, trot,

trot,' I murmured under my breath as she handed me my snifter.

'Dear Trixie has already looked too enthusiastically upon the grape,' she told the puzzled Singer, casting a poisonous look in my direction.

'Surely not,' he said gallantly, raising his own snifter to me.

Evangeline sniffed.

'Well . . .' Like a sleek cat scenting trouble, Ursula rose and prepared to escape. 'I can't thank you enough for such a lovely evening and delicious meal, but I'm afraid I still have some work to do. It's been *so* nice to meet you socially—' She smiled upon the bemused Singer.

'My pleasure entirely.' He sprang to his feet and hurried to open the door for her. 'Miss Sinclair has told me about your restoration work. Perhaps some day you'd allow me to—'

'Of course. Just ring me—you *do* have all our telephone numbers.' Ursula had claws, after all.

She made as neat an exit as any she had ever edited. Singer returned to his chair and Evangeline had the nerve to look expectantly at Gwenda. That was too much—Gwenda was *my* guest.'

'I can't tell you,' I said, as Gwenda looked to me uncertainly, 'how nice it is to be at home with my friends around me.' Sergeant Singer could interpret that any way he chose.

'Is Des still at work? We should ask him down to join us.

'Yes—' I was feeling more expansive by the moment. 'Yes —and Juanita, too. Let's have a party. Why not?'

'Why not, indeed?' Evangeline's eyes narrowed, but she wasn't as annoyed as I'd hoped she'd be. Was I playing into her hands?

'It's past midnight—' Gwenda glanced at her watch. 'Des should be coming home any minute now. But do you think we should disturb Mrs Sylvester this late?'

'As I recall her habits—' Evangeline wrinkled her nose in distaste—'the lateness of the hour would only add to the occasion for her. I'm surprised she hasn't tried to gatecrash us already. It's most unlike her to stay away when food and drink are circulating.'

'It is, isn't it?' Gwenda was vaguely uneasy. 'Do you think she's all wight?'

'Perhaps we ought to check.' Sergeant Singer was suddenly alert and half way out of his chair.

'Oh no, I forgot—' Gwenda relaxed. 'Ursula wouldn't have been servicing her flat if she was there. And I didn't hear her come in later, did you? She must be out.'

'The only reasonable explanation.' Evangeline still frowned. 'But . . . out where? She refuses to be seen in public. And I don't have the feeling that she and Beau are so close these days that she'd be spending a domestic evening with him . . .'

'No—' Gwenda giggled abruptly. 'He's not the domestic type.' She glanced around the flat. 'Not unless he's playing house.'

'Is that so?' Singer was almost as interested as Evangeline. I had already surmised something of the sort, of course. This flat was too much of a stage set.

'Oh yes,' Gwenda babbled artlessly—or was it? There was a familiar echo in her performance—I might have been watching myself when young. 'It's vewy useful, having a house in your gwandson's name. There's usually been a mystewious lady tucked away down here. That's why we were so wiveted to get inside and see the place—especially since it was wefurbished a few weeks ago. It was a gweat joke with us. We talked about taking bets on the next inhabitant. Anni said, at the wate of turnover, one of us was due to be offered it soon.'

'Really, my dear?' This time it was Evangeline who poured more drink into Gwenda's glass. Sergeant Singer had settled back and his hand was creeping towards his notebook. 'But surely, *you* wouldn't be interested?'

'Cwumbs, no! But I wasn't too sure about Anni sometimes. She's been having a bad time wecently, that's why she cleaned the flats instead of paying went. If she got an offer, I couldn't swear she'd wefuse. Especially as things hadn't been going well with her and Mick. And there's a persistent wumour that Beau may twy for a no-fault divorce. If he did that, Anni said, he'd be up for gwabs.'

'Would he?' Evangeline continued questioning, obviously having picked up some points this afternoon. Sergeant Singer was unobtrusively taking notes. 'But was Anni going to do the grabbing? Or Fiona?'

'Cwumbs! I never thought of that!' Head to one side, Gwenda considered it for a moment. 'You know, it could be. Jasper was never as affectionate with Fiona as with his other girls. P'waps that was because she wasn't weally his girl, at all.'

'I think we're getting somewhere,' Evangeline said with satisfaction. 'Juanita must have known all this—or suspected a good part of it. She always kept a closer eye on Beau than he realized. Even in Hollywood, she supported a couple of private eyes who spent all their time keeping tabs on Beau. I can remember the time . . .'

'Don't stop,' Sergeant Singer said eagerly. 'What do you remember?'

'That—' Evangeline had a reminiscent smile—'is hardly pertinent to this investigation.'

'Ah . . .' With a disappointed sigh, Singer tried another tack. 'Did Beau know he was under constant surveillance?'

'Sometimes he did, sometimes he didn't. Whenever he caught one of them following him, he had an almighty row with Juanita and she always swore she'd fire the agency and never do it again. Of course what really happened was that they'd just put a different agent on the job.'

'And you think that was going on in this country, too?' Singer underlined his last notation.

'Does the leopard change its spots?' Evangeline glanced restively towards the door. 'I don't believe she's out at all—she's just lying low because she knows we're catching up with her. Let's go and beard her in her den!'

Sergeant Singer was right behind her as she charged for the door. Gwenda and I sat where we were and stared at each other.

'Cwumbs! Does she go on like this all the time?'

'More often than not,' I sighed. 'This time there's a bit more substance to it but, basically, she's still playing the lead in *The Happy Couple*.'

'Better than than the lead in *The Wevenge of the White Squaw*—Oh, cwumbs!' Gwenda clapped her hand over her mouth. 'I didn't mean that. Not the way it sounded.'

'Maybe not, but you could be right,' I said thoughtfully. 'Someone deliberately scalped Mick to throw suspicion on Evangeline—and Juanita always hated her. Maybe—' I heaved myself out of my chair. 'Maybe we'd better get across the hall and find out what's going on.'

CHAPTER 19

Sergeant Singer was still hammering on the door when we caught up with them.

'Break it down!' Evangeline urged ghoulishly. 'She must be in there. She's hiding!'

'We can't—yet.' Singer hammered again and reinforced this with a couple of kicks. He was looking increasingly worried. 'Open up—' He gave voice, accompanied by another volley of knocks and kicks. 'Open up—it's the police!'

The information did nothing towards getting the door opened.

'I told you we'll have to break it down,' Evangeline said. 'Back off—' She began issuing directions. 'Run at it and slam it with your shoulder for all you're worth.'

'I don't believe I have enough grounds for that, madam.' For an instant, Singer sounded just like his superior. There was something of Heyhoe, too, in the carefully controlled look he shot at Evangeline. 'This isn't America, you know.'

'If you'll wait a minute,' Gwenda said reasonably, 'I'll go upstairs and get the key from Ursula.'

'If you'd be so kind.' Singer stepped away from the door gratefully. 'That would be the best solution.'

Gwenda was up the stairs and back in a flash with the key and a slightly puzzled expression. 'Ursula isn't there,' she reported, 'but the key was hanging on the hook with the others.'

'Thank you.' Singer relieved her of it deftly and opened the door. We all crowded into the studio flat behind him. One quick look was enough to show us that it was empty.

'P'waps she's gone back to Jasper's flat,' Gwenda suggested. 'After all, Martha weally belongs in this woom.'

'It would be most unlike her to be so cooperative,' Evangeline said, 'but I suppose it *is* remotely possible.' She led the way upstairs.

'I'll get Jasper's key.' Gwenda darted ahead of us.

'Keys seem to be freely available in this house.' Singer made another note.

'They certainly are,' I said bitterly, remembering the way Martha had burst in on me. 'And the flatmates aren't shy about handing them out.'

'Here you are.' Gwenda returned with the key and watched expectantly as Singer twisted it in the lock. He beat her into the flat by a short head, then had to pause.

'Which room is hers?'

'That one.' I pointed, surprised that he needed to ask. The heavy scent still hung in the air, marking the spot like an X. Perhaps she *had* returned to her grandson's flat. Then I noticed a torn sheet kicked into the corner—that was the source of the scent. It also answered the question I had been pondering: no one had serviced Jasper's flat. The sheet had been lying around since I had tossed it out of the room—only it hadn't been torn then.

'Empty—' Evangeline's voice floated out of the room and I moved forward to the doorway.

The room looked much as it had when I fled it so precipitately. If anything, it was even untidier. Pieces of crumpled paper scattered around never help. Singer bent and picked up one of them, smoothing it out.

'What does it say?' Evangeline tried to read it over his shoulder. When he blocked her view, she swooped and captured one of her own. Gwenda and I did the same.

'"I'm sowwy"—' Gwenda read out. 'That's all mine say.'

'"Forgive me"—' Evangeline had had better luck. '"My Latin blood overwhelmed me and I have brought disgrace upon my family. I am taking the only honourable way out"—'

'Cwumbs! They're suicide notes! How can we tell Jasper?'

'There must be a fuller one—' Evangeline bent and whisked the last piece of paper out from under Singer's fingers. 'One with a confession. She must be admitting to the murders—otherwise, why should she kill herself? She'd never do anything to please Beau.'

'"He wanted Fiona—"' Singer gave up and read out his fragment of the jigsaw puzzle. '"So she had to die. Thus perish all who try to steal what is mine."'

'Cwumbs! She'd have her work cut out for her if she twied to kill all Beau's mistwesses!'

'But it doesn't make sense,' I protested. 'Why all these scrappy notes? Why not just one?'

'She was probably working out her thoughts,' Singer said. 'Some suicides do that. They think they'll make an outline, then combine their entire rationale into one long dignified letter, only their problems overwhelm them before they finish and they rush out and do what they were intending to do all along.'

' "I always wanted to play *Anna Karenina"*—' I contributed.

'We are not interested in your unrealistic aspirations at this late stage, Trixie.' Evangeline was severe.

'No, no! That's what my note says.' I waved it at them. 'That's all it says.'

'Ridiculous!' Evangeline snorted. 'That would be even worse casting than putting *you* in the part.'

'But why bwing up *Anna Kawenina* at all? What has that do do with committing murder—or suicide?'

'Suicide—that's it!' Singer looked to us for confirmation. 'Didn't *Anna Karenina* step in front of a train engine at the end of the film? Hell! There are so many main line stations in London—which one would she choose?' His expression became dazed at the multiplicity of choices. 'Paddington? Euston? King's Cross? Victoria? Waterloo? I'll have to put out an all-points alarm and have them all watched.'

'There's something awfully wrong here—' That torn sheet still bothered me. 'I don't believe a word of this.'

'Actually, neither do I.' Evangeline scrutinized her note again. 'Juanita Morez was a semi-literate with Spanish as her first language. She had to learn to speak more or less properly when the Talkies came in, but it was as much as she could do write her name on a contract. All these words are spelled perfectly—and English spelling, at that.'

'And she never got nearer playing *Anna Karenina*—' I was following my own train of thought—'than the time she was tied to the railroad tracks in *Rails Going Westward*—' Suddenly, the torn sheet began to make sense. People were always tearing up sheets to use as bandages—or bonds—in the early films.

'Are there railroad tracks near here?' I demanded of Singer. 'Is there a place where the rails run over open land, easily accessible? Never mind the big stations—that's where we should start looking for her. If we're not too late . . . if the trains don't run too frequently . . .'

'The Magic Wailway!' Gwenda cried. 'It wuns over land of that descwiption wight by Pwimwose Hill!'

'What!' Evangeline glared at her suspiciously.

'The North London Wailway,' Gwenda clarified. 'People call it the Magic Wailway because it gets you fwom one part of London to another as if by magic. Also there's a twain when you least expect it. Oh, huwwy!'

'The car!' Singer dived for the stairs, we tumbled after him. He tried to outdistance us, but Gwenda slowed him down at the front door so that we could catch up. He yanked open the door and we hurtled past a couple of dark shapes at the top of the steps, nearly knocking them over.

'Mother! Where are you going?'

'I don't know—but don't get in my way!' We pushed into Sergeant Singer's car and roared off. Looking back, I could see Martha and Hugh hurrying down the steps and into Hugh's car to follow us.

'Why don't you radio for help?' Evangeline demanded.

'There's no radio, this is my own car,' Singer said. 'I thought I was off duty tonight.'

We careered through the night, taking corners on two wheels. It was too bad the car didn't have a siren, either, we could have used one. The old movie trick of being chased by indignant patrol cars for that kind of driving also didn't work. There's never a policeman around when you need one.

'Here—' Singer thrust a powerful flashlight at Gwenda. 'Shine the torch along the tracks. See if you can pick up anything.' He slowed the car as we ran parallel with some railway lines crossing level land.

'No, nothing. Twy the next—No, wait a minute—'

We saw it then. A large shapeless black blob lying across the tracks. The car slewed to an abrupt stop and Singer leaped out.

'It's twue! Oh, what a wotten thing to do to some poor twain dwiver!'

'Speaking of which,' Evangeline said practically. 'When *is* the next train due?'

'Oh, howwors! And we sit here talking!' Gwenda flung open her door and dashed after Singer.

'Come along, Trixie—' Evangeline opened her own door and stepped out. 'We might be able to help.'

'Not if we break a leg.' We lurched over the uneven land towards the pool of light by the tracks. I was dimly aware of the squeal of brakes as another car pulled up behind Singer's. Then we scrunched across the gravel bed and we were at the rails.

'Gwenda—' Singer was working frantically. 'Give one of them the light to hold and untie her hands.'

'Well!' Evangeline took the flashlight as I stepped across the tracks to help Gwenda. 'I never thought I'd play this scene again. I'd have sworn it went out with D. W. Griffith.'

'It may be corny, Evangeline, but it can still be deadly,' I reminded her. 'All it takes is for a train to come along.'

Gwenda and Singer redoubled their efforts. I stared anxiously both ways along the track.

'If you hear anything coming,' Singer said, 'start swinging that light and try to flag them down.' He clawed desperately at the knots.

'Don't you have a knife?' Evangeline asked disapprovingly.

'Not even the police carry concealed weapons,' Singer said. 'And just as well, or I might be tempted to get very nasty when I get my hands on the one who did this. He soaked the knots when he tied them to pull them tighter and made sure she couldn't free herself.'

The familiar scent drifted up from the sheeting, but there was something wrong. Evangeline directed the light alternately between the knots at the hands and feet while the others worked, but no one was paying attention to what was in between. Otherwise, they might have noticed that it was about eighty pounds lighter and considerably narrower than Juanita.

I crouched by the head and began to unwind the sheeting swathed around it. Had the head been covered because she was already dead? Or because she was alive and someone did not want to face the accusing eyes if she recovered consciousness? She was lying awfully still.

'What are you doing there, Trixie?' Evangeline swung the light on me just as I loosed the last strip and pulled it away. Blonde hair gleamed in the light.

'It's Anni!' Gwenda gasped.

'In that case,' Evangeline said, 'where's Juanita?'

I tugged at the gag and freed Anni's mouth. She wasn't dead, but she didn't look well. I tried to remember Des's technique with the Kiss of Life. We could have used him now.

'Mother . . . Mother . . .' The banshee wail was carried on the wind as Martha and Hugh stumbled towards us. For once, I was glad to see her. We needed every extra hand.

'Over here!' I called. 'Hurry!' I checked the track both ways again. There was still no train in sight, but we didn't want to push our luck.

'Good Lord!' Hugh looked down at Anni and her would-be rescuers. 'What's going on here?'

The question was rhetorical. Even as he spoke, he pulled out a Swiss Army knife, selected the largest blade, stooped and began sawing at the stubborn cloth. Threads began parting.

'Good man!' Evangeline approved of him for the first time. 'Now get her hands. Martha, rub her ankles and get the circulation going.'

'She's in a bad way, I'm afraid.' Hugh's assessment looked accurate. I'd be happier if she moaned—or moved at all.

'Mother, what are you doing here? How did you know about this?'

'We were looking for Juanita,' I said. 'She left a suicide note—several of them—that seemed to indicate the railway. Only she didn't write them—and she isn't here.'

'Juanita?' Hugh looked up sharply. 'Then where is she?'

'She has probably run away,' Evangeline said. 'Leaving this—' she gestured to the prostrate Anni—'behind her.'

'You think Juanita could have done this?' Hugh almost laughed. 'Don't be absurd.'

'The only absurdity,' Evangeline said coldly, 'is Juanita. Her head is so full of the old movies she made that this seemed the best way to dispose of a rival.'

'Impossible,' Hugh said flatly. The last strands parted and he began chafing Anni's wrists. 'I'm not arguing,' he said, as Evangeline begant to speak, 'that Juanita might not have *thought* of doing this. What I disbelieve is her physical capacity to implement the plan. She would have had to carry this girl across the wasteland to the track, then tie these knots so tightly we had to cut them. She couldn't possibly have done it. Could you?'

'Then she had an accomplice!' Evangeline avoided the distasteful question.

Unwillingly, I thought of Des. First Mick, and then Des, disposing of the bodies for an evil crazed old lady. The strong healthy boys, lending their strength to protect her from the consequences of her madness. And look at what had happened to Mick.

In the distance, a train whistle sent its melancholy two-toned whoop into the night.

'Get her off the track!' Singer ordered. He and Hugh lifted Anni clear of the rails and set her down parallel with the track. Martha covered her with her coat.

We stood there, feeling a sense of anti-climax, listening to the approaching train.

'Is that on the uptrack or the downtrack?' Hugh asked uneasily.

'Of course!' Evangeline was galvanized into action. 'There are *two* sets of tracks!' She moved forward, swinging the flashlight to provide the widest arc of light.

'The train—' I stumbled in her wake before the men could move. Perhaps because I had known her for so long, I could follow the way her mind worked. Gwenda followed me.

'Down there!' At the farthest edge of the ray of light, we could just discern another dark shapeless mass on the other track. 'We've found her!'

The men came running in response to Evangeline's call, leaving Martha to look after Anni. The train whistle sounded again—much closer.

This time there was no doubt that it was Juanita. Her black eyes flashed fury and relief above the gag covering her mouth.

These knots slipped easily. They had her free and clear of the track just as the train approached.

'In the nick of time . . .' Singer said shakily.

'Just like the old movies,' Hugh agreed grimly.

Then some fool took the gag off Juanita's mouth and the night turned blue with her comments—in two languages.

CHAPTER 20

We left Anni and Juanita at the hospital; Anni in intensive care. It seemed that she had been unconscious over several days and there was a build-up of sleeping pills in her system. *My* sleeping pills. Juanita, although bruised and bearing multiple abrasions from having been dragged along the gravel bed, was in better shape but was being kept in for Observation at, I suspected, Heyhoe's instigation. After taking her statement, he had plainly had enough of her to last him the rest of his life.

It was Gwenda who worried me. She was badly shaken and still incredulous. They were her flatmates and friends, she had never seriously suspected any of them.

Once more the police car drew up at the foot of the steps. We were immediately behind it in Hugh's car. Beside me, Gwenda shuddered.

'And now,' Evangeline announced with relish, 'for the final scene.'

Gwenda broke abruptly. She took a deep breath, turned towards Evangeline and shot off a volley of English and Welsh words full of lilting l's and rolling r's. The language was obscure, but the meaning was clear.

'There now!' Evangeline said triumphantly. 'I knew she could speak as well as anybody else if she put her mind to it!'

Gwenda ll'd and r'd her some more and leaped out of the car.

'Was the lisp bothering you?' Hugh asked in surprise. 'It's just an affectation a lot of the kids have these days. It's supposed to be an Edwardian accent. Gwenda does it because it keeps her from lapsing into a Welsh accent. Don't worry, it's nothing permanent. If she got an offer from the Royal Shakespeare Company, she'd forget it tomorrow.'

'So I can see,' Evangeline said drily.

The police were already at the top of the steps. Gwenda opened the door for them and followed them in. Hugh didn't wait for us, he rushed up the steps, leaving Martha, tight-lipped, to open her own door and then ours.

'I suppose he telephoned Beau from the hospital,' Evangeline said, 'like a proper little go-fer and toady.'

'What are you talking about?' Martha snapped. 'Hugh Carpenter is one of London's most successful producers. He has three shows running in the West End right now. Where did you get the idea he was working for Beauregard Sylvester? I can assure you, the shoe is on the other foot!'

'Well—' Evangeline had been corrected, but not daunted. 'He certainly gives the impression of being a go-fer.'

'He's been trying to help Sylvester clear up his financial problems to free him to work in a new play. *You* ought to know—' Martha was scathing—'how much *some* actors need people dancing constant attendance on them!'

At a less fraught moment I might have cheered them on,

but I decided to save my breath for the stairs. It was a long haul up to the top flat.

'Des!' I greeted him with relief as we entered. 'You're all right! I was getting worried about you.'

'Just working late.' He jingled his pockets and winked at me. 'It was a good night.'

'You must have been the only person who had one,' Gwenda said. '*Our* night has been terrible!'

And it wasn't over yet. The police were searching the flat. Hugh went downstairs and brought back Jasper, in pyjamas and half awake.

'What's going on?' Jasper demanded. 'What's happened now?'

'Nothing—' A policeman came out of the kitchen and shook his head at Heyhoe.

'All her things are still in there.' Singer came out of the bedroom. 'She's either flown the coop in just what she was wearing, or—' He shrugged.

'That's Ursula's room!' Des stepped forward. 'What were you doing in there? Where is she?'

'Just what we'd like to know,' Heyhoe said. 'Anyone got any ideas?'

'Ursula?' Jasper seemed dazed. He looked to Gwenda, huddled in a corner of the sofa. 'Has Ursula disappeared, too?'

'Ursula,' Evangeline informed him crisply, 'had good reason to disappear. She killed two people and has just tried to kill two more—one of whom was your grandmother.'

'My grandmother?' Jasper turned to Heyhoe. 'Is she serious? What's happened to my grandmother? Where is she?'

'In hospital,' Heyhoe said. 'She'll be all right. No thanks to your friend, Ursula, who tied her to the railway tracks.'

'But very lightly,' Evangeline pointed out. 'Unlike Anni, who was tied very tightly. Obviously, Ursula intended to return after the train had gone by and remove Juanita's bonds. Then it would look as though *she* had tied Anni to the tracks and been caught by a train coming the other way as she left Anni. As a fail-safe, there was the reference to *Anna Karenina* so that you could take your choice between suicide or a fatal accident. Very clever, our Ursula.'

'Quite so,' Heyhoe said. 'Especially the way she used the old movie methods of killing off people—or seemed to. I must admit—' he bowed towards Evangeline—'my first suspicions were directed to you.'

'By a very expert hand.' Evangeline granted pardon. 'Eventually, I'm sure you would have realized your mistake. A woman who spent her days restoring old films has her head filled with the early cinematic visions more surely than the elderly actresses who played the original roles. After all, we have moved on in time, done other things, and are looking to the future. We can hardly remember most of the roles we played. But they were all fresh in her mind.'

'And *she* thought she'd have a twy for Beau. That's why she killed Fiona and twied to kill Anni.'

'Why she killed Fiona perhaps—' Evangeline said—'and put her in Des's bed until she had a chance to dispose of the body. Only Mick came along and found Fiona there and saved her the trouble.'

'*My* bed?' Des squeaked; he was miles behind us.

'Except that she then had to dispose of Mick before he began questioning the situation,' Heyhoe supplied. 'She had free access to deadly chemicals always available in a photographic lab. We've had the autopsy report; he was poisoned and, as a finishing touch, she scalped him, since Miss Sinclair was living on the premises and the film premiere was still fresh in everyone's mind.'

'I can't believe she'd be so wotten! I mean, Ursula! I thought we knew her, we were fwiends—'

'She tried to kill me,' I said. 'Of course, she thought I was Juanita. I suppose she had no real faith that Beau *would* go through with that divorce and she thought she'd short-circuit the process.'

'Dear Beau,' Evangeline said. 'Even though he moved away from a place with Community Property Laws, a divorce would still be an expensive proposition for him. That would bother him more than keeping the marriage going.'

'Obviously, you knew him well.' Heyhoe could not resist the crack. Singer looked up hopefully.

'Evewyone knew that,' Gwenda said. '*And* he's been in financial twouble wecently. He'd never choose *this* time for a divorce—no matter what he told Fiona or Ursula.'

'Fiona may have believed him, but Ursula would have known better.' Jasper had a wry smile for his grandfather's naughtiness.

'She also had a pretty shrewd idea that the next woman who married him would be left a rich widow,' Evangeline said. 'Even with a goodly portion going to Jasper, Cinema City is an inheritance not to be sneezed at.'

'She did love old films so,' Gwenda said sadly.

'You have to give her that,' Evangeline agreed. 'But she got too immersed in them. There's a point beyond which affection becomes obsession. I doubt if she'd have been so interested in Beau if he hadn't represented so many past glories. Once she'd lived with him for a while, she'd have opted for an earlier widowhood than she'd planned. He's had a lucky escape—but I don't suppose it will persuade him to change his ways.'

There were footsteps on the stairs and one of the policemen who had been searching the garden came in and went straight up to Heyhoe. He spoke softly, but I caught the words, 'bin liner'.

I drifted over to the window and saw lights at the bottom of the garden, by the bench where Mick had rested. They were gathered around a black plastic sack and men were busy with it, but unhurriedly. There was no rush about it.

Poor Ursula, poor obsessed child. Another Hollywood victim, later and in a different way from the usual run, but Hollywood had claimed her, none the less. I hoped she had seen some splendid visions as she pulled the darkness of the sack around her and drifted away.

'Mother—Mother—' Martha was plucking at my elbow. 'Mother, Hugh has something to ask you—and I want you to consider it very carefully.'

'Don't tell me he's about to ask your mother for your hand,' Evangeline sneered.

'I hardly think that's necessary,' Hugh said coldly. 'And, if it were, I wouldn't know which of you to ask.'

'Don't look so stricken, Mother,' Martha said. 'I think I've always known.'

'I don't know what you're talking about,' Evangeline said coldly. 'You can't be egocentric enough to imagine *I* could have whelped you!'

My hands were around her throat before I realized I had moved. For the second time in our lives, we were deep in a knock-down drag-out fight—and I was going to murder her if I could. I was gripped by the same deadly fury that had gripped me on the far-off day when she had coolly informed me that she was going to have a baby by my husband but, since it would be embarrassing professionally for her to produce a change-of-life baby, she would graciously allow me to bring it up.

'Mother—let go! Mother—!' Which one of us was Martha appealing to?

'All right, that's enough!' Hugh's arms enveloped me, pulling me away. Singer had seized Evangeline and was leading her to the far side of the room.

Heyhoe beamed upon us both impartially. If he applauded, I'd try to kill him, too.

'That settles it,' Hugh said. 'I want you both for a revival of *Arsenic and Old Lace*—and I won't take no for an answer. You can do a limited run, if you like, and you won't have to do matinees—but I must have you.'

'Oh!' I shook myself free and tidied my hair. 'Well, I'll have to think it over.'

'Please, Mother,' Martha said. 'I'd like to stay in London for a while. And I think it would be marvellous for you to do stage work again.' It must be serious with Hugh.

'Well . . .' Evangeline said consideringly. 'It might work out rather well. Detective-Sergeant Singer wants to write my biography. Collaboration would be so much easier if we were in the same country.'

'Just one thing—' I said. 'Isn't there a nice little ingenue part in that? If you'll let Gwenda—'

'Yes,' Hugh smiled. 'I think that can be arranged.'

'Cwumbs!' Gwenda said. 'That's tewwific. And the day after we open, *I'm* taking *Twixie* to lunch!'